Seeing Sarah Bernhardt

WOMEN AND FILM HISTORY INTERNATIONAL

Series Editors
Kay Armatage, Jane M. Gaines, and Christine Gledhill

A new generation of motion picture historians is rediscovering the vital and diverse contributions of women to world film history whether as producers, actors, or spectators. Taking advantage of new print material and moving picture archival discoveries as well as the benefits of digital access and storage, this series investigates the significance of gender in the cinema.

A list of books in the series appears at the end of this book.

Seeing Sarah Bernhardt

Performance and Silent Film

VICTORIA DUCKETT

University of Illinois Press
URBANA, CHICAGO, AND SPRINGFIELD

1 2 3 4 5 C P 5 4 3 2 1
∞ This book is printed on acid-free paper.

Library of Congress Cataloging-in-Publication Data
Duckett, Victoria.
Seeing Sarah Bernhardt : performance and silent film /
Victoria Duckett.
pages cm. — (Women and film history international)
Includes bibliographical references and index.
ISBN 978-0-252-03966-9 (cloth : alk. paper)
ISBN 978-0-252-08116-3 (pbk. : alk. paper)
ISBN 978-0-252-09775-1 (ebook)
1. Bernhardt, Sarah, 1844-1923—Career in motion
pictures. 2. Motion picture industry—France—History.
3. Silent films—France—History and criticism.
I. Title.
PN2638.B5D83 2015
792.02'8092—dc23 2015012975

For Helen and David

Contents

Acknowledgments

I thank Carlo Ginzburg for his encouragement when I began developing this book. He is an astute critic and a constructive mentor. His integrity and passionate commitment to his role as educator provides me with a compass that still directs my professional life today.

Three scholars—Peter Wollen, the late Teshome Gabriel, and Vivian Sobchack—gave me crucial encouragement and invaluable advice. I thank, in particular, Vivian Sobchack for her early advocacy of my project and for remaining such a cheerful source of inspiration and guidance today.

This book has greatly benefited from my peripatetic career. In Manchester University my colleagues—Helen Day-Mayer, David Mayer, Marcia Pointin, and George Taylor, in particular—were instrumental in making me appreciate the interdisciplinary nature of film history. Stella Halkyard, of the John Rylands Library, was an immeasurably supportive colleague and friend. At the Universita' Cattolica, Milan, I must thank my Chair of Department, Francesco Casetti, as well as my colleagues Massimo Locatelli and Elena Mosconi, for developing my appreciation of film history in the context of continental Europe. Mosconi and Locatelli still collaborate with me today and are instrumental in my thinking about film and art nouveau. Elizabeth Presa, Head of the Centre for Ideas at the Victorian College of the Arts, University of Melbourne, was an inspiring and helpful mentor. More immediately, I am grateful to my peers at Deakin University, Melbourne. I extend particular thanks to Elizabeth Braithwaite for indexing this book in a professional and thorough manner and to Deb Verhoeven for providing such continual wisdom.

Silent film boasts a community that is both tightly knit and broadly international. In forums such as Pordenone's *Le Giornate del Cinema Muto*, Bologna's *Cinema Ritrovato*, and the biennial *Women and the Silent Screen* conference, I have developed a network of colleagues and friends. I would like to thank Janet Bergstrom, Giorgio Bertellini, Ansje van Beusekom, Ivo Blom, Vicki Callahan, Bryony Dixon, Annette Förster, Karola Gramann, Tom Gunning, Frank Kessler, Sabine Lenk, Giuliana Muscio, Charlie Musser, Susan Potter, Heide Schlüpmann, and Matthew Solomon for sustaining and supporting my research. Particular thanks are due to Richard Abel. The direct impact that some of these scholars have had on my critical thinking is acknowledged in my opening chapters. From this community, I also thank David Robinson for allowing me to publish a copy of his *Phono-Cinéma-Théâtre* programme in this book, Laurent Mannoni of the Cinémathèque Française for giving me permission to reproduce the *Phono-Cinéma-Théâtre* poster, as well as Kevin Brownlow and Haden Guest (in his previous capacity as the director of the Warner Brothers Archive at the University of Southern California) for sending me copies of their respective holdings on Bernhardt.

As a film historian, I cannot conduct research without the generosity of film archives and archivists. Early viewings of Bernhardt's films were arranged through the Cinémathèque Française and MoMA. Luke McKernan, in his former role at the British Film Institute, was also an invaluable resource. More recently, I thank Guy Borlée and Gianluca Farinelli from the Cineteca del Comune di Bologna, for ensuring that Bernhardt's existing films were brought together in my "Performing Passions: Sarah Bernhardt and the Silent Screen" program at *Cinema Ritrovato* in 2006. I thank Gian Piero Brunetta for providing me with a copy of *Queen Elizabeth*. Nikolaus Wostr of Filmarchiv Austria deserves a special mention for ensuring that I received a much needed copy of *Sarah Bernhardt at Home*. His colleague, Peter Spiegel, was generous in permitting me to reproduce images from this film in this book. Éléonore Winkler of Lobster Films provided me with a copy of *Mothers of France* and was similarly forthcoming in arranging my publication of stills. Agnès Bertola of Gaumont Pathé archives generously provided a photogram of Bernhardt in *Hamlet* from the *Phono-Cinéma-Théâtre*. I thank Thomas Christensen, Mariann Lewinsky, and Eric Le Roy for enabling and ensuring such smooth archival access. Finally, I am indebted to the indefatigable Ian Christie for prompting me to view the NFSA's holding of *Camille*: I thought I had seen all copies of the film but discovered, to my excitement, that this is the most complete extant version of the film.

On a more practical note, my research was enabled by the MA and PhD tuition scholarships I was granted by the School of Theatre, Film & Television,

UCLA. I also thank the UCLA Centre for the Study of Women for granting me a Travel Award. I am further grateful for being awarded their George Eliot Dissertation Award. Other awards—the UCLA Regents Fellowship, the Leonard Howard Fellowship, four School of Theatre, Film & Television Conference and Travel Awards, as well as the Charles Boyer Award for research in Paris—ensured the development of this project. The Charles Boyer Award, in particular, afforded me two years of research in Paris. I consequently began dialogue with scholars such as Claire Dupré la Tour, Anne Goliot-Lété, Michèle Lagny, Alison Matthews, Sarah Riggs, Geneviève Sellier, and Emmanuelle Toulet. The generosity and friendship these individuals extended to me buffered the many solitary hours I spent perusing holdings in the Bibliothèque Nationale, the Bibliothèque du Film, and the Inathèque. A Prudhoe Award and a Research Support Fund Award from the University of Manchester, as well as a visiting Fellowship to the Australian National University, have similarly given me the opportunity to present and develop my research. I thank, in particular, Jill Matthews for inviting me to the "History, Cinema, and Digital Archive" conference at the Australian National University in July 2014. The author gratefully acknowledges the Publication Subsidy she was awarded by the Australian Academy of the Humanities.

This book would not have been possible without the commitment and support of Kay Armitage, Jane M. Gaines, and Christine Gledhill. I thank them for including my work within their Women and Film History International Series. Christine Gledhill, in particular, shaped my thinking around cinematized theater. My anonymous readers provided much appreciated suggestions and comments. My editors, Daniel Nassett, Jennifer Clark, and Marika Christofides, as well as my copyeditor Nancy Albright, have provided careful guidance and attention at every stage of preparation.

Some of the information in this book has been presented at conferences and published in articles. I thank Wayne State University Press for allowing me to reproduce sections of my earlier article, "Investigating an Interval: Sarah Bernhardt, *Hamlet*, and the Paris Exposition of 1900," in *Reclaiming the Archive: Feminist Film History*, ed. Vicki Callahan (Michigan: Wayne State University Press, 2010), 193–212.

I must express my gratitude to Daniela Adamuccio, Lisa Bennett, Annalisa Caffa, Kate Cordukes, Nancy Everingham, Rita Gamberini, Dee Gill, Kristen Hatch, Sanna Liimatainen, Aimee Lind, Monica Margarido, Mehmet Mehmet, Paolo Monopoli, Jerry Mosher, Francesca Navarro, Karen Rose, Leesa Rowley, as well as the late George Custen and Lisa Kernan, who each individually sustained and maintained me. My parents, Tony and Frances, are unwavering in their support of me. I thank them for their unequivocal love. My sister, Louisa, is a companion I cherish and admire. And my boys, Umberto and Massimo, who today lament that I am "sooooo nineteenth century," keep my feet firmly planted in the real world. This book is dedicated to Helen Day-Mayer and David Mayer. Two scholars whose magisterial knowledge of the theater has deeply enriched my own work, they are also two generous and supportive friends. As most academics know, serendipity changes not only the content and direction of our research, but our very place in the world.

Introduction

> By digging into the texts, against the intentions of whoever produced them, uncontrolled voices can be made to emerge. . . . Fiction, fed by history, becomes material for historical reflection or else for fiction, and so on.
>
> —Carlo Ginzburg, "Introduction," *Threads and Traces: True, False, Fictive*

Sarah Bernhardt, the greatest theatrical star of the nineteenth century, was also the first major international film star. Appearing cross-dressed in a short *Hamlet* film before international audiences at the Paris Exposition of 1900, this 56-year-old French actress most famously went on to make *Camille* (*La Dame aux Camélias*, André Calmettes and Henri Pouctal, 1911) and *Queen Elizabeth* (*Les Amours de la Reine Élisabeth*, Henri Desfontaines and Louis Mercanton, 1912). This is a study of her crossover (from theater) into film and an analysis of what her films can reveal to us today. Rather than focus on the mechanics of the transition between two identifiable and separate practices—the late-nineteenth-century legitimate theater in France on the one hand, and early-twentieth-century film, driven largely by popular entrepreneurship, on the other—I address her films as historical texts that allow me to uncover what Carlo Ginzburg, following Marc Bloch, calls "uncontrolled voices."[1] Although historians have long discussed these voices in terms of marginalized people and in terms of lost customs, often reaching back centuries to explore past literature in order to extract from this evidence of a world we no longer know, I instead uncover unaccounted practices in early film. In the context of Bernhardt's early films, these practices emerge through written texts (contemporary film and theater reviews, biographies, publicity for her films) as well as through visual materials (films, paintings, sculptures, posters, costumes). I explore film as historians have explored earlier written texts, using this method to explain and contextualize aspects of the cinema that appear unusual to us today. The excessive theatricality of Bernhardt's films are not, I argue, evidence of her incommensurability with film but an unaccounted theatrical practice that reveals a different way of thinking about and relating to the cinema. Her gestural acting was not anachronistic on film but a means of asserting the theater's ongoing relevance at the opening of the twentieth century. What Bernhardt today tells us about the cinema—the details, facts, and influences embedded in her films—were not necessarily at the forefront of the minds of those who made, watched, or performed in films at the opening of the twentieth century.

My work is driven by the practical need to contextualize and explain Bernhardt's popular success on film even (or particularly) given the fact that no film or theater theorist, historian, or critic has ever applauded this work. I ask why audiences in the early twentieth century celebrated an actress on film who they might never have seen on the live stage. I am less interested in the simple fact of Bernhardt being recorded on film than I am in what Bernhardt's films tell me about the cinema. What roles were filmed? How did Bernhardt act? What, in other words, do we see, and perhaps hear? For too long, Bernhardt's theatrical origins have blinded us to the possibility of exploring her films in any depth. I argue that Bernhardt's films do not offer proof of her theatrical stage action. Even when we celebrate her capacity to remain publicly visible over a lifetime—film gave her an expanded audience from 1900 onward—we still need to ask what she achieved with film.

Most historians agree that Bernhardt mouthed her lines on film. There is the presumption that this indicates her inability to act in a fittingly naturalistic way for film. Furthermore, there is the related presumption that Bernhardt's famous "golden voice" is brutally denied in a media that gives us the spectacle of an actress mouthing lines that we cannot hear. In Chapter 1, "*Nullius in Verba*: Acting on Silent Film," I counter these ideas with the argument that Bernhardt's films record her gestural fame on the live stage. As important as her voice, this fame was associated with her use of the spiral as a structuring device for action. The spiral informed her movement; she brought a swiveling turn to most scenes, creating a swirl of costume around her thin body. Often, this swirl of costume marked the point at which physical action came to a conclusion, enabling spectators to contemplate Bernhardt's acting as a physical incarnation of art nouveau. Indeed, I argue that Bernhardt embodied art nouveau, bringing physical gesture and action to an artistic style that is usually associated with decoration and design. Her thin arms and turning form accentuated art nouveau's structuring spiral, creating tendriled lines that flowed into a serpentine S. Rather than present her in silence, I argue that her films allowed an embodied form of art nouveau to reach—for the first time—a global audience. Indeed, as an industrial product, film joined her tendriled art nouveau acting to a media that promoted visual craftsmanship and mass production.

However, the reviews we have of Bernhardt's films also speak to the emotional legibility of her work. This understanding means that Bernhardt was not merely recording an art nouveau aesthetic but that she engaged audiences with a visual language, one that was internationally legible. In my view, this development has its antecedent in the visual literature that developed around gesture in the Enlightenment period. Audiences at the opening of the twentieth century interpret film in much the same way as they earlier identified the passions in pictorial images or understood gesture on the live stage. As I explain, Bernhardt also physically recalled and enacted particular sculptures and paintings, reinforcing in a more specific and personal way the visual legibility of her body. The music that accompanied her films served the same purpose as it did on the live stage—to develop and expand the emotional resonance of her performance. Therefore, the question, "Why would an actress who was famous for her voice act on silent film?" unearths a series of overlooked practices—art nouveau acting, changes in visual literature, the ongoing use of musical accompaniment—all of which allow us to reinterpret Bernhardt's relationship to the silent screen.

In my subsequent chapters I interrogate the wealth of influences—art forms, practices, and people—that contributed to Bernhardt's work. Giving each chapter a single film as its focus, I move chronologically from Bernhardt's short 50-second film, *Hamlet* (made in 1900 and first projected at the Paris Exposition) through to *Mothers of France* (*Mères Françaises*, Louis Mercanton and René Hervil, 1917) and the effort to get America involved in World War I. I revisit films that many already purportedly know (*Camille* and *Queen Elizabeth*) and introduce some films that have all but disappeared from discussions of early film. This collection includes the celebrity home movie made on Bernhardt's holiday retreat at Belle Isle, Brittany (*Bernhardt à Belle Isle* (*Sarah Bernhardt at Home)* Louis Mercanton, Hecla, 1915), as well as the propaganda film mentioned earlier, *Mothers of France*. What interests me here are the changes we see as we move chronologically from film to film, as well as the way each work brings forth unaccounted practices that we can today identify and discuss. In *Hamlet*, for example, we can identify the new popularity of fencing in Paris as a sport for women, while in *Camille* we can associate Bernhardt's spiraling body with the appeal that the East (especially Japan and the Kabuki theater) held for Parisian audiences. Within each film I also identify the re-creation of famous paintings. In *Queen Elizabeth*, I discuss how Bernhardt restages paintings that are associated with Elizabeth I: there is a scene that visually recalls *Elizabeth in Procession* (c.1600, attributed to Robert Peake), another that stages *Queen Elizabeth Viewing the Performance of The Merry Wives of Windsor at the Globe Theatre* (David Scott, 1840), and the final scene that refers to Paul Delaroche's *The Death of Elizabeth I, Queen Elizabeth* (1828). In *Sarah Bernhardt at Home*, the home becomes an inclusive and expansive site that joins domestic culture to a global audience. In this film we see Pierre-Auguste Renoir's *Luncheon of the Boating Party* (1881) and Paul Gauguin's *Breton Girls Dancing* (1888) visually re-created while we watch Bernhardt write articles and send telegrams to audiences abroad.

I end my discussion with *Mothers of France* and the First World War, because the war brought closure to this fertile period of cultural and artistic exchange, a period that so prominently marked the art nouveau era in France. The playful ambiguity of the tendril, the interdependency of the arts and crafts, and the dialogue between cultures and countries now gave way to national alliances and somber uncertainty. In *Mothers of France* Bernhardt appears at her most "cinematic" in contemporary terms, because film allowed her, literally, to move after the amputation of her leg. This mobility gave her a spatial freedom she could not, in reality, enjoy. In this film, however, Bernhardt is also at her most serious. She is no longer a middle-aged woman incarnating lithe youth, experimenting with a new art and industry, and exploring the perceptual realities of film. She is instead an amputee commissioned by the French Government to engage the American public in war.

Mothers of France is the last complete Bernhardt film in existence; it also marks a more general closure for the purposes of my study. By 1917, art nouveau had been replaced by new tastes and concerns, and France had lost its hold on global film production. My focus on the period leading up to this point brings into relief the experiments, tastes, and achievements that Bernhardt brought to film culture in the two decades dominated by the French film industry. At the time of her death in 1923, American films had established a global domination in the industry, and film was a very different undertaking. At this point, René Clair was a young 25-year-old director who debuted with his Dadaist film *Paris Qui Dort*, and the film editor for the journal *Le Théâtre et Comœdia Illustré*. Writing Bernhardt's obituary for this journal, Clair illustrates the way in which Bernhardt's films had been retrospectively repositioned—in just under a decade—as examples of failed theater and not as experiments in cinematized theater that brought Bernhardt to a greatly expanded international audience. He states: "That the theatre is one thing and the cinema another, this is what is today beginning to be admitted. . . . Without doubt Sarah Bernhardt only knew the cinema in its primitive form. Legend goes that she [Bernhardt] fainted seeing herself on the screen in *La Dame aux Camélias*, performed *as on the stage*. Such an artist could not but feel there was something monstrous in this mutilation of the theatre, simply caught by the photographic lens."[2]

I have some sympathy for Clair's incapacity (or, rather, unwillingness) to empathize or engage with Bernhardt's films. They were of the epoch immediately preceding his own, referenced a different understanding of the cinema, and were stylistically very different from the experimental films then emerging in France. What is interesting about Clair's dismissal of *Camille*, however, is his belief that the theater was monstrously mutilated by film. Clearly, it was Bernhardt's silence, where she was "simply caught by the photographic lens," which unsettled and upset him. Later, in 1950, Clair develops this idea, stating that "poor Mounet-Sully and Sarah Bernhardt were seen yawning tragically on a white screen impervious to alexandrines."[3] This criticism of Bernhardt's films plays itself out in the very silence surrounding her films. My point is that even in 1923, when Clair wrote Bernhardt's otherwise generous obituary, her films were anecdotally framed as failed theater. There has since been no study of Bernhardt's films that explains her popular success or her relevance and legibility to a global filmgoing public. How did she reach audiences through film? If the screen was "impervious to alexandrines," what did it capture? My study explores these questions, arguing that Bernhardt's films challenge and change received ideas about what is and is not "cinematic."

Writing History Today

My study emerges today, in the material conditions that make it possible to return to the margins of film history. Bernhardt and her films can be explored afresh because we now have the tools that allow us to revisit them. In this sense, my task as a historian is materially easier than it ever has been. When I began research for this project in the mid-1990s, I had to travel from Los Angeles to Paris, London, and New York to access paper files and microfilm. There were no fast-track search functions: it took two years of scrolling through materials in the Bibliothèque Nationale to find advertisements, articles, and files about Bernhardt's films. To view the films was equally difficult: unless I dealt with the better known films (*Camille* and *Queen Elizabeth*, which were available through bootleg video copies of television transmissions), I had to watch Bernhardt's films in archives and on flatbeds. Sessions at the CNC were short and viewing appointments expensive. I could not afford to return and check my findings and could not, therefore, confirm visual details when I was completing my chapters. Today, I am able to conduct my research from Australia. Although I am geographically further from continental Europe than I have ever been, I have access to a previously unimaginable range of resources. Importantly, I can watch DVD copies of all of Bernhardt's extant films. Although only three of these have been commercially released (*Camille*, *Queen Elizabeth*, and *Mothers of France*), I work from copies of films screened in the Cinema Ritrovato "Performing Passions" program, which I curated in Bologna in 2006. In this sense, I am enormously privileged. I have access to the films I am writing about. I can choose a historical method (microhistory—I discuss this later) that has not been available to any other generation of film historian. My capacity to focus on the visual detail of Bernhardt's films, to explore moments that overlap and correspond to other arts (painting, the theater, and so on) is an aspect of my study that I have found challenging and something that separates it from any other study of Bernhardt or early "theatrical" film.

Selecting Films

I do not address all of Bernhardt's films. Most notably, I do not discuss *Jeanne Doré* (Louis Mercanton, 1915), Bernhardt's extant film about a mother's suffering over her son's addiction to gambling. I chose not to explore this film because I want to discuss Bernhardt's different approaches to making films and *Jeanne Doré* is a film that is modeled—like *Queen Elizabeth* and *Camille*—on her role in a stage play. *Jeanne Doré* is also available only in archives and so difficult to access; I thought it would be more productive if the theater-to-film examples I explore are generally familiar to readers. I want to underscore not simply the literal gaps in film history (the films that have been overlooked), but the gaps and oversights we have in our perception of film and film history itself. I can best demonstrate this through an analysis of theatrical roles and films we already presume to know.

My aim, therefore, is not to uncover lost films or to show what we might find when we reconstruct films but to uncover lost ways of looking at and thinking about Bernhardt's available works. While I would welcome any effort to reconstruct Bernhardt's lost films from this period (*La Tosca* [André Calmettes, 1908] and *Adrienne Lecouvreur* [Louis Mercanton and Henri Desfontaines, 1913]), I want to keep sight of the films we have at hand. I work closely and concretely with the moving image. My aim here is not to provide a comprehensive study of Bernhardt's films, but to offer an example of how microhistory can be brought to film. I want to demonstrate how a historical method that has long been discussed in terms of reading between the lines of a text can today be discussed in terms of reading into the moving image. I also work within a 17-year time frame, restricting discussion to the period in film history when France held world dominance. Above all, I want to ask whether France's foremost actress contributed—alongside a long list of French inventors, directors, and so on—to the early success of a national film industry.

Rethinking National Cinemas

Bernhardt's films emerge in a period of great ideological change and at a time when popular art forms and entertainments began to develop a global audience that joined previously distinct social groups around the one common object. However, with the exception of *Queen Elizabeth*, which was a French/U.K. coproduction, they also emerge in France. Does early film therefore articulate not just historic difference (a different way of looking at the world, a different visual style), but geographic and social difference as well? Might the monolith of "early film" be broken into different cultural spaces, so that our model for popular culture is not necessarily focused and centralized on America? Might margins be acknowledged on the international level and, in their turn, contested? Among the scholars who have returned to explore the development of film in the crucial teen years, Richard Abel was the first to clearly tie the question of how we might return to film history after the turn of the century to the question of nation and nationhood. In his work on early French cinema, particularly in *The Ciné Goes to Town: French Cinema 1896–1914*, Abel directed me to consider Bernhardt's changing relationship to geographic place and, consequently, her shifting relationship to mass culture.[4]

In this seminal work Abel argues that French cinema is distinct from American cinema in the prewar period and is not necessarily developing the same narrative models. The reasons for this are varied; they relate to the historic, cultural, and legal realities of the French Third Republic. Speaking about the close alignment between theater and film, for example, Abel notes how

> the French cinema can be situated historically according to its definition under French law, for the courts consistently classed the cinema as a *spectacle de curiosité*, subjecting it to the control and censorship of local officials. In 1906, a state decision to end all censorship restrictions against the theatre provoked efforts by the industry to upgrade the cinema's status. The consequences of this move to align the cinema with the theatre were profound—the theatre analogy, at the level of both commercial enterprise and critical discourse, became more deeply engrained in France than anywhere else.[5]

Abel goes on to note that the transition from André Gaudreault and Tom Gunning's cinema of attractions in the 1896–1904 period to the classical American cinema with its continuity editing system in the 1910s was enabled and even given "crucial impetus" by the French cinema. What he demonstrates is how we must be wary of contemporary models of cultural hegemony.

Debora Silverman's book, *Art Nouveau in Fin-de-Siècle France*, argues a similar point from the perspective of the French art nouveau movement:

French institutions and art practices at the turn of the twentieth century had their own cultural specificity and cannot be confused with the Arts and Crafts movement in America nor with the English Arts and Crafts movement led by figures such as William Morris and Edward Burne-Jones.[6] This argument might also be brought to a consideration of the slightly later Italian diva films: like Bernhardt epitomizing the cultural specificity of the French art nouveau movement and its particular relationship to film, Italian actresses such as Lyda Borelli, Francesca Bertini, and Pina Menichelli in the midteens welded a similar yet distinct relationship between theatrical acting, the Italian Liberty style, and silent film.[7] My work demonstrates these arguments in microcosm. It uses Bernhardt's films as a series of case studies that reveal the contribution France made to the development of early narrative cinema and the implication of film in the French art nouveau movement. Bernhardt's films need to be recognized and understood within the context of these two related points, even if this differs from received histories of film and art nouveau.

A Cinema of Art Nouveau

With Bernhardt as a protagonist, we see film as a fluid and transformative art form. Like the butterfly dances in vogue at the opening of the twentieth century, or like any number of Alphonse Mucha prints that emphasized Bernhardt's curving tendriled forms, Bernhardt's films show her in a state of constant transformation and change. Moving between an array of different images, roles, and emotions, Bernhardt is in a constant state of becoming. She is a youthful Danish Prince in *Hamlet* (1900), a 16-year-old French courtesan in *Camille*, the Queen of England in *Queen Elizabeth*, a patriotic French mother in *Mothers of France*, and a protagonist in her own home movie, *Sarah Bernhardt at Home*. Expressing herself in a media that was establishing itself as an international industry at the same time that it was asserting itself as the "seventh art," Bernhardt made film commensurable with, for example, the tendriled iron signs Hector Guimard fashioned for the Paris Métro.

Bernhardt's association with art nouveau relates to her acting style—and beyond that to her lifestyle and to her very life itself. Her spiraling gestures on screen and the clever way she makes her dress wrap itself around her body attests to the fact that art nouveau was a visual art movement that included and implicated theatrical performance. I argue that Bernhardt's films are, however, representative of art nouveau as a visual style and lifestyle choice more broadly, that it is not gesture alone that transmits this. In *Sarah Bernhardt at Home*, I therefore explain that Bernhardt's home, with its curved furniture, flowers, and union of art and industry represents the fashion and ubiquity of art nouveau in the early twentieth century. Infiltrating all aspects of modern life, art nouveau is not just a whiplash line but a lifestyle choice, a way of dressing, moving, and communicating in the world. Precisely because of its union of art and industry, it was exported through reproductive technologies and brought to international audiences: it circulated in physical objects but also through prints, photographs, and, finally, films. Indeed, Bernhardt brought a style that was first given its name in Paris by Siegfried Bing's Maison de l'Art Nouveau (opened in 1895) to her own home and made this her signature style, exporting it internationally through world tours and new technologies. In this context, Bernhardt is an originator of the art nouveau style, promoting its global consumption. Indeed, she was among the first to be identifiably modern in this new way, giving Alphonse Mucha his first public commission in the late nineteenth century, employing René Lalique to make jewelry for stage productions, and drawing young audiences to her performances in the 1870s precisely because of her unusual modulation of her voice and the way she made the spiral a common motif in her physical action. But Bernhardt was not only an art nouveau protagonist, she was also its consumer. She stamped her tendriled *SB* on her own household objects: on her standing mirror, on cutlery, plates, furniture, oriental fans, gloves, and letter-writing paper.[8] She made her home the locus of a design culture that reached out into the world. She made her films part of this culture, embracing a style that was—like these objects—portable and designed for interior display.[9] Today I explain her engagement in film as "cinematizing theater" and argue that this process is the culmination of the art nouveau movement, perhaps even its greatest achievement in terms of its global, cross-class, and intergenerational exposure. But this is a contemporary regard, one that Bernhardt could not possibly articulate. As I explain later, our temporal and cultural distance from these films allows us to enjoy them in new ways.

Polyphony and Performance

In an age in which handheld screens and digital platforms are changing the ways we think about and theorize the moving image, it is important to remember this nascent malleability of the cinema. André Gaudreault makes this point in his introduction to *A Companion to Early Cinema*. Here, he speaks of the "polyphony of early cinema," arguing that the cinema emerged between 1908 and 1912 from a seemingly ungoverned world, namely the "cultural and institutional hodgepodge of early kinematography."[10] In Gaudreault's opinion, we are seeing in digital media today a return to what he calls the "cultural series" of animation. In Gaudreault's view, a cultural series is both a mechanical device and cultural practice; it is a base apparatus that is preliminary to the cinema and which exists alongside other series (he lists Reynaud for the cultural series optical toy, Marey and Edison for chronophotography, Lumière for photography, and Birt Acres for the magic lantern and so on). In his view, the cultural series "animation" consists of graphic images that are put into movement. To put it simply, he argues that the photographic is no longer the sine qua non condition of "cinematicity." It is instead animation, or the movement of the synthetic image—which "can now reach an *isolated viewer* without *any form of projection*"[11]—that defines the cinema. Animation, Gaudreault states, is "in the process of recovering its place as the founding principle of all things cinematic."[12] Where Gaudreault is interested in recuperating and centralizing animation's contribution to the history of the cinema, I am interested in asking whether the polyphony of kinematography can include within it a discussion of performance on film. Can we celebrate not just the diversity of the cultural series that gave rise to the base apparatus of the cinema (the optical toy, the magic lantern, and so on) but also the diversity of performances that fed into it? Can we see the theatrical performances of an actress such as Bernhardt on film as part of the cultural practice that ensured the longevity of cultural polyphony, even as the institution of the cinema itself emerged?

Where Gaudreault argues for rupture between two distinct paradigms (kinematography on the one hand followed by the cinema emerging as an institution between 1908 and 1912), I argue that Sarah Bernhardt's films illustrate a performative polyphony working its way into cinematic practice. I am not concerned with the specific cultural industries Gaudreault defines, since these are conceived in terms of their inventors and not in terms of the diversity of performative practices they entailed. Instead, I am concerned with establishing a codependency between visual practices we would not today call "cinematic" and the films Bernhardt made in the midteens when the cinema reached an industrial state of expansion. Indeed, at the point at which the cinema emerged as an institution and began to structure the production, exhibition, and distribution of films in the 1908–1912 period, Bernhardt began to make feature films. Drawing upon existing cultural practices, she appears today to be "too theatrical": she uses the costumes, mise-en-scène, and acting style of the live theater and adapts these to film. But by engaging with the cinema, however, Bernhardt not only made money and expanded her possible audience. She also changed narratives, shortened plays, and accelerated theatrical gesture, ensuring that each shot was visually dense and textually thick. Earlier theatrical productions were referenced, as was the tradition of other famous international actresses playing similar theatrical roles. As I noted earlier, Bernhardt also visually re-creates identifiable paintings, prints, and popular histories in her films, drawing upon the established theatrical practice of the *tableau vivant* (the "living picture," a practice that saw actors physically re-create paintings and statues identifiable and familiar to audiences). In this sense, Bernhardt animates famous pictures in a way that expands Gaudreault's "cultural series animation." In my view, the synthetic and animated image can include within it practices that were first developed pictorially upon the live stage. Rather than see animation usurped by projection or the kinematograph replaced by the cinema, I see Bernhardt's films as proof of what Charles Musser would call "the integrated history of stage and screen."[13] They demonstrate the cinema's capacity to bring together a range of intermedial codependencies even as it developed into a global industry.

Bernhardt's capacity to bring together intermedial codependencies hinges on the experiences she brought to the cinema not just as an actress but as an actor-manager who assumed both performing and executive functions in the theater. Managing the Théâtre de la Renaissance between 1893–1899, Bernhardt began to direct every aspect of rehearsal. After this experience of independent management, she took over the Théâtre des Nations, a municipal theater that was leased from the City of Paris. Renamed the Théâtre Sarah Bernhardt, this theater was managed by Bernhardt until her death in 1923.[14] Acting as manager, producer, director, and star of these venues, Bernhardt fulfilled a role that was not altogether uncommon for the Victorian actor. Indeed, we know that Eliza Vestris, Henry Irving, Wilson Barrett, John Martin-Harvey, Frank Benson, Marie Wilton, Madge Kendall, and Fanny Davenport were similarly engaged in the theater. What Bernhardt achieved, however, was a crossover between theater and film that saw the theater integrated into the cinema. Her roles, costume, physical performance style (with its signature spiral), and visual re-creation of identifiable paintings, prints, and popular histories mean that film did not so much usurp the stage as integrate and adapt it. Was Bernhardt in charge of this adaptation? Did she manage and direct her own performance on film? I argue that although there is no legal or written evidence of Bernhardt's managerial and directorial status in her films, we can determine a codependency between Bernhardt's visual practices on the stage and the films Bernhardt made in the teens.

On the Margins of History

Gaudreault argues that the cinematic institution marginalized animation by emphasizing the Lumière Cinématographe as the device that invented the cinema. He explains that the contemporary digital turn instead sees films that are no longer made of celluloid reach audiences on devices that no longer use projection. Animation, a cultural series that "had never entirely given up the ghost," therefore returns.[15] Using Lev Manovich to articulate and confirm this return to animation, Gaudreault explains that even though the cinema was "born from animation" it "pushed animation to its periphery, only in the end to become one particular case of animation." He continues to explain that procinematic techniques are reemerging as the foundation of digital filmmaking. Again citing Manovich, he states: "What was once supplemental to cinema becomes its norm; what was at the periphery comes into the center. Computer media return to us the repressed of the cinema."[16]

Although my research is not driven by such a broad and theoretical vision of how we might conceptualize technological development, I also believe that we can learn much from the margins of the cinema. Instead of exploring the technologies that are newly centralized in the digital world, however, I explore films that appear to film historians to be excessive and theatrical from an acting (and therefore visual) point of view. Like animation, theatrical films have been marginalized in teleological histories of the cinema. Although a case can be made for the return of excess and theatricality in digital film—think of the *Lord of the Rings* series (Peter Jackson, 2001, 2002, and 2003) or the sets and performances in *Avatar* (James Cameron, 2009)—I am not arguing (as Gaudreault and Manovich are) for a reconsideration of the cinema's debt to animation but for an investigation into cinematic margins that still remain in place today. Indeed, it is because Bernhardt is historically on the margins of the cinema that she reveals much to me. Forced to look in a detached way at intertitles, costumes, gestures, and a relentlessly still camera, I am therefore an observer who sees unintended traces of cultural practices. To put this way of looking at Bernhardt's films into the terminology that Ginzburg uses in his discussion of Bloch and historical method earlier, I isolate "within voluntary testimonies an involuntary, hence deeper, core."[17]

Rather than address the cinema in terms of its base apparatus (or cultural series, as Gaudreault might say), I attempt to make sense of filmic practices that do not fit what we imagine the cinema to be and have been. In an article that has been pivotal to my own thoughts about Bernhardt's films and the historical method I adopt when exploring their fabrication, Ginzburg argues that the historian must share a marginal relationship to what is being observed in order to penetrate and understand it. In his article "Details, Early Plans, Microanalysis: Thoughts on a Book by Siegfried Kracauer" he discusses Kracauer's unfinished posthumous book, *History: The Last Things before the Last*. Arguing that Kracauer develops a cognitive model of the cinema that was first proposed in *Theory of Film*, Ginzburg explains that Kracauer follows

Marcel Proust in *The Guermantes Way*. In *The Guermantes Way*, Ginzburg notes, Proust speaks of "the witness, the observer, with a hat and traveling coat, the stranger who does not belong to the house, the photographer who has called to take a photograph of places which one will never see again." This is the distance that historians need in order to understand their source materials.[18] Going on to give evidence of Kracauer's support for detachment and distance in the writing of history, Ginzburg cites Kracauer's statement that "It is only in this state of self-effacement, or homelessness, that the historian can commune with the material of his concern. . . . A stranger to the world evoked by the sources, he is faced with the task—the exile's task—of penetrating its outward appearances so that he may learn to comprehend that world from within."[19] This is an important context of Kracauer: he himself was an exile.

Ginzburg's reflections are expressed differently—but to the same effect—by Mikhail M. Bakhtin in his "Response to a Question from the Novy Mir Editorial Staff," where he discusses literary scholarship. Although Bakhtin is concerned with the capacity of a literary work to remain relevant to a generation of readers that is not its own, his arguments intersect with Ginzburg's discussion of historical method. They also explain, in a sense, why it might be a historian such as Ginzburg who can help us rethink Kracauer's relationship to film history. Bakhtin states:

> In order to understand, it is immensely important for the person who understands to be *located outside* the object of his or her creative understanding—in time, in space, in culture. . . . In the realm of culture, outsideness is a most powerful factor in understanding. It is only in the eyes of *another* culture that foreign culture reveals itself fully and profoundly. . . . We raise new questions for a foreign culture, ones it did not raise itself; we seek answers to our own questions in it and foreign culture responds to us by revealing to us new aspects and new semantic depths.[20]

I suggest that Bernhardt's films are a litmus case for this mode of historical inquiry. Can we comprehend Bernhardt's world from our position as outsiders to her works today? Can Clair's dismissal of Bernhardt on film provide me with a starting point for historical inquiry? Finally, can cinema's theatrical margins reveal more than history has had us believe?

In *History: The Last Things before the Last*, Kracauer prefaces his discussion of exile and margins with an explanation of how he is interested in "nascent states of great ideological movements." It is in this moment, before the institutionalization of ideas into competing ideologies, that he locates historical truth and integrity. In this sense, an inquiry into historic margins takes place in a moment that is itself on the temporal margins of the events that follow. Kracauer states:

> Roughly speaking, my interest . . . centers not so much on the course followed by the triumphant ideologies in the process as on the issues in dispute at the time of their emergence. I should even say that it revolves primarily around the disputes themselves, with the emphasis on those possibilities which history did not see fit to explore.[21]

Again, Bahktin's ideas resonate here, particularly when he states that "the most intense and productive life of culture takes place on the boundaries of its individual areas and not in places where these areas have become enclosed in their own specificity."[22] In my opinion, Bernhardt's films have long been on the boundaries of film history, excluded from discussions of early film and the development of the cinema. They are, in this sense, doubly marginalized: they emerge in a nascent state and give evidence of "those possibilities which history did not see fit to explore."

Toward an Intermedial History of the Cinema

In Paris, declining theater ticket sales in the legitimate theaters during the early teens were attributed to the growing popularity of film. Bernhardt, the manager of a theater (the Théâtre Sarah Bernhardt), instead maintained that the decline in theatrical attendance had nothing to do with the growing popularity of film. In an article published in *Le Journal* in 1914, she states:

> France is losing its taste for the theatre! But I am not one of those for whom the progress of cinema is a cause for this turn. The theatre and the cinema offer such different kinds of entertainment that it's impossible that the popularity of one impedes the development or success of the other. The two can very easily live side by side, and here's proof: I remember that, in a recent tour I made in America with *La Dame aux Camélias*, our troupe was followed by a cinema company. Everywhere I stopped, and frequently in a theatre right next door to where I was playing, the movie version of *La Dame aux Camélias* was also showing. It so happened that the posters for the two events were sometimes put right up next to each other. However, every night both theatres were full—but in the one you paid only fifteen or twenty sous while in the other it cost fifteen or twenty francs.[23]

Bernhardt maintains that film did not reproduce the legitimate theater. She suggests that to be theatrical in film is not to copy theatrical practices but, rather, to cinematize theater. Many of her contemporaries instead argue that film is a mute document of live stage action. The difference between these arguments is substantial. On the one hand, we have the division (that we are familiar with today) between stage and screen. On the other, we have the cinema viewed as a polymorphous practice that included the theater within it. Bernhardt supported this latter vision of early film, seeing no contradiction in cinematizing theater. The critic M. J. Lefèvre, however, was of a different opinion. Criticizing Bernhardt's involvement in film precisely because she was not audible on screen, he explains:

> The more slavishly the actor reproduces poses, has talent and has authority over the public, the more the silent reproduction is stupid. A Mounet [Sully], a Sarah [Bernhardt], a [Julia] Bartet on the screen are no more than absurd puppets, because their gestures are not enveloped by this atmosphere of art which poetry can alone can create and which they are the interpreters of genius. Their poses, physiognomic expressions, and cadent movements do no more than underline, amplify, and magnify poetry. Gesture is and should be no more than the discreet servant of speech and, because of this, should reveal the thought expressed by the word. Cinema suppresses speech or only reproduces it imperfectly via mechanical means.[24]

In 1915, the American poet Vachel Lindsay reiterates Lefèvre's view that silent film does not properly represent Bernhardt's theatrical skills. In his book, *The Art of the Moving Picture*, he states that Bernhardt's *Camille* could be "compared to watching *Camille* from the top gallery through smoked glass, with one's ears stopped with cotton."[25] It is this view of Bernhardt on film as an incomplete theatrical record that today survives intact. Bernhardt's defense of her capacity to promote two related but different entertainments has long been ignored.

Recent scholarship has begun to redress the view that sees the theater and film develop along two mutually exclusive trajectories. Leading this work is the research of theater historian, David Mayer. For the last two decades Mayer has argued that film historians are surprisingly ignorant of the traditions and practices of the late-nineteenth-century stage and have a tendency to see the nineteenth-century stage supplanted by the advent of motion pictures. In an article written in 1997 he explains that theater historians must therefore ask of film history some searching and "impertinent" questions:

> Is the master-narrative of illusionistic stage into even-more-illusionistic screen a valid historiographic model? Was there a handover from theatre to motion pictures between 1896 and 1910? Was there a total handover or a complete break at any time? Is there (or was there ever) a visible border or frontier between the stage and early motion pictures? Can any developments be described as transitions from lesser to better?[26]

Noting the impact that Nicholas Vardac's 1949 study *Stage to Screen. Theatrical Origins of Early Film: David Garrick to D. W. Griffith* has had on sixty years of film scholarship, he states that "Vardac's concern is with the unidirectional and irreversible transference of genres from live melodrama to mechanical reproduction, almost as if he were recounting a kind of hand-over, the passing-on of dramatic genres like a relay-race baton handed from an exhausted runner to a fresh competitor, from one medium to its inevitable successor." Mayer instead speaks of the way in which the late-nineteenth-century entertainment industry brought inspiration and encouragement to film method and technology that, in turn, stimulated further theatrical change.[27]

The novelty of Mayer's argument lies precisely here, in this idea that two disciplines that are usually discussed as separate entities did indeed engage and interact. In his most recent work, *Stagestruck Filmmaker: D. W. Griffith and the American Theatre*, Mayer demonstrates that D. W. Griffith, the most famous of all silent American film directors, was fundamentally a man of the popular American stage. Again critiquing the hold which Vardac still has over models of film history, he states that Vardac "offers a narrative of separation: of one medium, the stage, failing and being supplanted by a newer, more technically adept medium, cinema, which could achieve the effects and illusions and maintain an environmental 'realism' which allegedly was believed to elude the paint-and-canvas scenery which the theatre offered." Critiquing the teleology that sees a necessary handover of stage to screen, Mayer instead posits "the relationship between the late-Victorian and Edwardian stage and early film as a fluid period of explorations and experimentations, developments, borrowings, and mutual rip-offs.[28] In this context, my work on Bernhardt inverts Mayer's work on Griffith: just as a film director can reveal much about the stage, a stage actress can reveal a lot about early French film.

Mayer is not alone in arguing that an intermedial history of the cinema must take into account the relationship between stage and screen. Although Christine Gledhill's *Reframing British Cinema 1918–1928: Between Restraint and Passion* falls just after the period I am exploring, she similarly argues for a model of cinematic development that takes into account terms of national difference and a significant exchange between stage and screen.[29] In Matthew Solomon's *Disappearing Tricks: Silent Film, Houdini, and the New Magic of the Twentieth Century*, we are introduced not to the question of national film, but to the question of magic. Solomon extends his intermedial approach into the period that Gaudreault would call the "institutional cinema" and explores the exchange between early cinema and theatrical magic. In this sense, "the theater" becomes demonstrably broad. Like myself, Solomon also argues that the dismissal of films as cinematic "failures" reflects less a historical truth than long held presumptions of what is or is not cinematic. He states:

> I . . . extend the intermedial approach into the period of institutional cinema in order to demonstrate how Houdini's films of the late 1910s and early 1920s relate more closely to the trajectory of Houdini's theatrical work than to the latest developments in film history—a disjuncture that has long led to those films being dismissed as failures that were decidedly out of sync with the direction of the Hollywood film industry. . . . A central premise of this book . . . is not only that cinema's relationship to theatre was formative and decisive, but also that traditionally upheld divisions between theatre and cinema were in fact extremely permeable historically. A number of recent film historians have closely analyzed the relationships between theatre and early cinema, but they have tended to focus on dramatic theatre. This book, by contrast, focuses on variety theatre and what I term *presentational modes of performance*—modes of performance that accomplish or demonstrate something, often something wonderful or marvelous—and not on representational modes of performance like acting, which simulates the actions and interactions of characters.[30]

The expanded field in which Solomon writes reviews the limits of institutional cinema just as it emphasizes presentational as opposed to representational modes of performance. In this way, it develops the work of Tom Gunning, who has long argued that early film was visually arresting, eliciting attention through the ability to *show* something.[31] By bringing the notion of the "show" to a later period of time—Solomon is writing about films in the late 1910s and early 1920s—and investing it with its own institutions, organizations, and practices coming from theatrical magic, Solomon develops Gaudreault's model of historiography while extending Gunning's conceptual model of film's nascent visibility. In other words, Solomon traces a history of film that does not "fit" the institutional practice of the cinema in the late teens just as he gives a historical explanation as to why a body of films focus on visual display. My book develops this idea, explaining that the theatrical film based on dramatic theater was as much about presentational modes of performance as it was about representational modes of performance. It emerged, in my opinion, not as a way to record a stage play but as a genre of film that carved its own place within the polyphony of early cinema. As a film genre it is not filmed theater (in terms of the reproduced play) and nor, too, is it uniquely associated with high or low theater. It does not have a unique attachment to either the legitimate stage or (alternatively) with the popular pantomime, music hall, and vaudeville stages. Indeed, Solomon's distinction between dramatic theater and variety theater is hard to sustain with a figure like Bernhardt, who moved between the two after the opening of the twentieth century. Consequently, I argue that an intermedial history of the cinema must regard discussions about the content and context of institutional cinema with some flexibility, and that our understanding of the dramatic theater, how it addressed its audience, and its relationship to the cinema, must be similarly flexible.

Jon Burrows, in a book that has also been important to my own reconsideration of the relationship between the stage and screen, has argued a similar point. In *Legitimate Cinema: Theatre Stars in Silent British Films, 1908–1918*, Burrows explains that the legitimate theater not only signified traditional "high" cultural values. He states:

> [S]ome of the famous stage actors who migrated to the cinema were somewhat contentious figures as far as influential arbiters of national cultural tastes were concerned. Their work was not automatically congruent with conventional definitions of national/canonical artistic values, and several of these performers had a more iconic status in the mass popular imagination than the relationship between stage and screen today might lead us to expect.[32]

Burrows's general point is that we need to better understand the complexity of the relationship between the dramatic theater and film. More specifically, he argues that the use of the British actor on screen was not reducible to a shared national role. We must today learn to accept, therefore, the fluid definitions that can be brought to the association of the cinema with dramatic theater. Addressing the problems this creates in terms of defining a specifically national cinema, Burrows notes that "[i]t would be more accurate to say that the intermedial links between British cinema and the West End stage assisted in the creation of national cinema*s*, not one homogeneous mode of address."[33] Like Solomon and myself, he argues that Gaudreault's notion of intermediality consequently needs to make room for those practices that extend into the post-1910s period. At this point, the cinema might have solidified as an institution but still maintained and developed codependencies with other practices and art forms. Making a case for the inclusion of the theater as a intermedial link that developed within the institutional emergence of the cinema he states:

> [S]ince intermediality has been defined as a process through which different media converge on and explore the new "physical and discursive spaces opened up by moving pictures," it is surely possible to conceive of a later phase of cross-cultural co-dependence after 1910 in which cinema's expanded sphere of influence creates scope for other forms of intermediality. It is in this sense that I will argue that the use of theatre stars in British cinema throughout the 1910s represents a distinctive form of intermedial cinema, which worked

> towards particular cultural goals which would largely have been impossible to imagine or implement if the film industry had not reached a stage of advanced capitalism and expansion.[34]

Like Mayer writing about Griffith and the American stage, Solomon writing about Houdini and the magical stage, and Burrows writing about British film and legitimate theater, my own work on Bernhardt and film is focused within the period in which the film industry reaches advanced capitalism and expansion. I would therefore argue that the theater allows or indeed forces us to speak of intermedial exchange even after Gaudreault's "kinematography" has run its colorful course.

Microhistory

In his work on Griffith, David Mayer argues that we cannot replace one historical paradigm with another. Single historical models create more problems than they resolve. Explaining his decision to focus on a single director and his individual films, Mayer states:

> An overarching paradigm may prove to be inappropriate, and, because the relationships that have governed the creation of each Griffith or rival film are so unsteady and changeable, it is necessary to deal, instead, in individual cases. The historical relationship between stage and screen is far more complex—and far more interesting—than we have granted. Surely, after a century of false and unreliable narratives, we can begin to do justice to the shared history of theatre and film.[35]

This shared history, Mayer implies, emerges only through a close analysis of films as individual case studies.

I agree with Mayer. Without an understanding of why a role was chosen for film and how it was adapted to the screen, we can have no understanding of what it is we are seeing. This point is as relevant to Bernhardt's 50-second *Hamlet* film made in 1900 as it is to her multiple-reel feature films made in the early teens. In this sense, my book is an excursion into what we can learn about the cinema from Bernhardt's films just as it is an illustration of how important microhistory can be to the appreciation of early film. In order to *actually* see and understand what we are watching in Bernhardt's films, we must explore the related fields of art history, music history, theater history, social history, and (often) political history. Indeed, it is precisely because Bernhardt's films emerge at the intersection of so many histories and on the cusp of a new century that I had to research a diverse array of source material. This has not meant, however, that Bernhardt's films illustrate some kind of endless interdisciplinarity so that her films always lead us outside, away from themselves as source material. I argue the contrary: Bernhardt's films are centripetal works. They force us into unique acts of historical interpretation. Rather than illustrating a uniform theatricality, they are textually and conceptually unique.

I can think of no example in any other media or art form where such popular success has been met with such sustained critical and intergenerational silence. As art historians continue to so capably demonstrate, however, visual tastes change: what was popular in one epoch is rejected in another. Highly successful academic painters often need their relevance newly introduced to us just as painters who have been ignored or alienated by these same institutions need their more popular success translated to us. It is microhistorical studies, focusing on the single artist and contextualizing individual artworks, that has today enabled and achieved this. Stephen Bann's 1997 *Paul Delaroche: History Painted* is a case in point: in this study, the historical painting of the French academic painter, Paul Delaroche, is reintroduced to us. As Bann explains, it is Delaroche's capacity to animate historical subjects and his availability (thanks to new technologies of reproduction) that made him one of the most recognizable artists in the West by the mid-nineteenth century.[36] The exhibition that Bann helped to realize at the Musée des Beaux-Arts, Nantes, and the pavillon du musée Fabre, Montpellier—*Paul Delaroche: Un peintre dans l'histoire*[37]—came on the heels of his book and allowed contemporary audiences to review, first hand, Delaroche's overlooked oeuvre. As I will demonstrate, Delaroche is referenced in Bernhardt's films, his famous paintings reenacted as *tableaux vivants* on the screen. For now, however, my point is that Bann asks the same questions of art history that I ask of the cinema. Who was Delaroche? What are we seeing? Through a microhistorical study, how might we revise contemporary understandings of art?

In a similar manner, Alex Kidson revitalizes our understanding of the eighteenth-century English portrait painter, George Romney. A contemporary and rival of Thomas Gainsborough and Sir Joshua Reynolds, Romney was immensely fashionable and popular as an artist. While he received no official accolades, he exerted enormous impact upon the style and development of British portraiture. Within a generation, however, enthusiasm for his style of painting had passed: his depictions of bourgeois women smiling from under broad-rimmed hats was considered secondary to the more imposing portraits of Gainsborough and Reynolds. My study of Bernhardt's films fits here, as part of these recent efforts to acknowledge and revive visual styles that today seem studied, contained, or even excessive in a proto-camp or kitsch kind of way. I join Bann and Kidson in arguing that popular tastes can surprise us. The visual look of a given epoch is often far more varied than we allow. The category of "art" and "the cinema" are inclusive rather than exclusive.

While Kidson, Bann, and Mayer have each provided me with an example of how microhistory can challenge contemporary understandings of a given discipline ("art," "the theater," "the cinema"), T. J. Clark's *Farewell to an Idea: Episodes from a History of Modernism* uses microhistory to ask if we are today capable of properly understanding modernism.[38] Writing his chapters around limit cases drawn from the history of painting—Jacques-Louis David's *Death of Marat* (1793), Camille Pissarro's *Two Young Peasant Women* (1892), Paul Cézanne's *The Large Bathers* (1895–1906), Pablo Picasso's *Man with a Guitar* (1912–1913), UNOVIS (acronym for Affirmers of New Forms in Art) in 1920, and Jackson Pollock from 1947–1950—Clark explores the ways that politics, artistic intent, and social purpose materialize in art. While Clark's case studies seem removed from a discussion of Bernhardt in film—he makes no mention of female artists active in modernism and limits his discussion to painting—he nevertheless concludes his discussion of painting with mention of post–World War II Italian literature and neorealist film. Arguing that Antonioni's *The Cry* (1957) and *L'Avventura* (1960), as well as Visconti's *Rocco and his Brothers* (1960) and Roberto Rossellini's *Paisà* (1946) might also join painting in materializing a (or *the*) breaking point of modernism, he acknowledges the possibility that film might give us the centripetal vision of a modernism that has been otherwise imagined in terms of a centrifugal, outward-reaching force.[39] My study takes up this idea: film, that most expansive and mobile of media that is generally theorized in terms of spectacle and excess, can also return us to a modernism that turns inward, reflectively, upon itself.

As I mentioned earlier, Bernhardt's films are visually dense and textually thick. It has been our incapacity to see this that has resulted in her films being called "filmed theater," as though theatrical excess can explain a visual style we do not understand. In this context, I join Clark in arguing that film lets us see modernism's collective, perhaps even socialist, longing because it emerges within (and so pushes most firmly against) Modernity's vicious, consumerist culture. To deny that an actress such as Bernhardt achieves anything on film, to speak only to her failure to use the formal techniques that today we associate with the cinema (the close-up, the pan, naturalistic screen acting, the intercut), is to concede that modernity's consumerist culture has indeed emptied her films of content. In other words, the capacity to unearth and understand unaccounted practices in Bernhardt's early films brings to light aspects of popular culture that emerge within modernity but which have been otherwise lost in discussions of the relationship between popular and avant-garde culture, celebrity, spectacle, and cinematic language. Even Bernhardt's utopian vision of making herself newly available to poorer audiences through film is hidden in the focus given to her "theatricality." I therefore join Clark in arguing that we can excavate the modernist past and find within it traces of a collective culture that has not yet been fully explored.

It is unfair for me to introduce microhistorical studies only through those scholars who are working in the fine arts, or who are today shaping the course of film studies, theater studies, or art history. My biggest debt as a historian is to Carlo Ginzburg, for famously showing that popular culture has a history that can be recuperated in an intelligent and intelligible way. Menocchio, his Friulian miller in *The Cheese and the Worms: The Cosmos of a Sixteenth-Century Miller*, was not just a unique individual who did not "fit" the way we had thought of and written about traditional peasant culture; he was also a man who was constructed on the basis of the materials that Ginzburg found in the Archivio della Curia Arcivescovile in Udine. Archival research therefore unearthed documents, and these were interpreted and made newly relevant to contemporary debates.[40] Ginzburg demonstrates that a historical study can significantly revise contemporary understandings of abstract categories (popular culture, radicalism, social reform), and that history writing can itself be a form of pragmatic theory. It is on this basis that I develop my work. If I were to believe anecdotal comments about Bernhardt and her films, I would not have a book to write. If, instead, it is accepted that microhistory can serve as a material form of defense, then it is not just our understanding of the cinema that I am expanding but my own capacity to engage in the interpretation of history and popular culture. Bernhardt's films provide me with testimonies that refute a century of scholarly criticism.

Feminist Film History

I have discussed a range of ways in which the margins of the cinema are central to my project. I have also indicated how, methodologically, these very margins help me to derive new information about the cinema. What I have not mentioned, and what must be addressed if any serious discussion of Bernhardt's films is to be undertaken, is the role that feminism plays in enabling us to make sense of her films. We cannot take for granted that an actress of Bernhardt's stature would make films, much less go on to experiment with film in a range of roles across two decades of filmmaking activity. The coincidence of first-wave feminism and the emergence of the cinema should not, in my opinion, be taken lightly: our capacity to speak publicly, to demand visibility, and to represent and articulate our own realities was enabled by the assertion that women are as capable as men in using new technology in a creative and productive way.

It is startling to realize that while Bernhardt has long been celebrated as a precursor to the New Woman, Bernhardt's feminism has never been associated with film. As Susan A. Glenn argues in her book *Female Spectacle: The Theatrical Roots of Modern Feminism*, Bernhardt was an unorthodox and transgressive actress who, by the late 1870s, was famous for joining theatrical spectacle to a unique personality. She also joined serious drama to mass culture. In this sense, she is the transition point between the past and present, tradition and early-twentieth-century modernity. Glenn concludes her chapter on Bernhardt ("The Bernhardt Effect") by noting that Bernhardt's 1907 memoir looks back over a long career. Bernhardt concedes that she was "too much" and "too little." Glenn develops this idea, stating: "It was Bernhardt's genius and those of her contemporaries on the popular stage to turn female eccentricities into commercially viable virtues. It is not surprising to discover, therefore, that "too much/too little" were the critical categories through which the first generation of female comics on the American stage enacted the desires and exposed the dilemmas of modern womanhood."[41] Glenn summarily ignores Bernhardt's engagement with film. Speaking of the emergence of the talkies, she therefore presumes a transition from a spontaneous, intimate, and daring vaudeville stage to the "unreal reality" of the cinema in the 1930s. In this context, Mae West becomes an irreverent reminder of the feminist freedoms earlier enjoyed on the live stage.[42]

Even within the expanding field of "Bernhardt studies," where achievements are quickly claimed, little mention is made of Bernhardt's films. Theater historian Gerda Taranow's otherwise astute and thorough study, *Sarah Bernhardt: The Art within the Legend*, uses Bernhardt's films to verify live theatrical action.[43] In Bernhardt's most recent biography, Robert Gottlieb's *Sarah: The Life of Sarah Bernhardt*, we are told that Bernhardt was "the first international movie star" in 1912 with the successful release of *Queen Elizabeth* by Adolph Zukor. We are also told, however, that Bernhardt "was interested in the new medium but soon realized she would never master it." In Gottlieb's opinion, this is because she "looks over wrought and old-fashioned on the screen."[44] A recent exhibition that made Bernhardt, for the first time, the subject of a major museum exhibition in America—*Sarah Bernhardt: The Art of High Drama*, held at the Jewish Museum in New York from December 2005–April 2006—seems to confirm these ideas. Showing excerpts from her films but giving no indication of their relevance, we can understand Bernhardt's material reach as an international star but not her capacity to reach and mobilize new audiences through film.[45]

It is feminist film history that allows me to speak of Bernhardt's achievements on film and that gives me the conceptual tools necessary to look at her films anew. As much as the work of Glenn, Taranow, and Gottlieb assist me in positioning Bernhardt's achievements in the context of late-nineteenth-century culture, and as much as Gaudreault, Mayer, Solomon, Burrows, Abel, and Ginzburg help me to determine the breadth of my research, it is feminist film historians who bring gender into the discussion of the cinema. Scholars such as Giuliana Bruno, Heide Schlüpmann, and (the late) Miriam Hansen have each argued that women were significant contributors to early film, both as audience members and as filmmakers. Each has convincingly and separately demonstrated that the feature film can indeed actuate and activate the female gaze and that the theatrical film was particularly fruitful for women in the opening decades of the twentieth century.[46] Directors, actors, and fans were forging new links; the emerging feature format was a palimpsest constructed by men as well as eager and inquisitive women.

The work of a younger generation of film scholars has developed this argument. Collections by Jennifer Bean and Diane Negra, one by Vicki Callahan, as well as some exceptional single authored books (for example, Shelley Stamp's *Movie Struck Girls: Women and Motion Picture Culture after the Nickelodeon*) have expanded not just our quantitative knowledge of women and silent film but our awareness of sheer diversity.[47] Supported by scholars such as Christine Gledhill and Jane Gaines, feminist film historians come together around projects such as the *Women and Film Pioneers* project housed at Columbia University and the *Women and Film History International* committee that supports the biennial *Women and Silent Screen* conference.[48] Other forums—significantly, *Cinema Ritrovato* featuring the pioneering work of Mariann Lewinsky—foreground the research and scholarship that archivists and preservationists do on the "frontline" of feminist research. Lewinsky and other archivists such as Karola Gramann of the Kinothek Asta Nielsen and Elif Rongen of the EYE film museum, Amsterdam, have therefore become fundamental to our project, showing us what they have found in the archives and what we can still learn from watching film. It is this fundamental act—of watching a film—that motivates my work. Am I capable of seeing not just age and anachronism in Bernhardt on screen but energy and vitality too? Can I find something other than "filmed theater" to explain Bernhardt's global appeal, since it was an international audience (and presumably a broad international audience) who helped her achieve large box office returns? Finally, can I join my colleagues in recovering a cinema that allows and includes women, not just as celebrated actresses but also as artists who pursued a vision of what the cinema might become?

In Schlüpmann's groundbreaking study of early German cinema, *The Uncanny Gaze: The Drama of Early German Cinema*, she argues that women did indeed impact and drive film production in Wilhelminian society. She states: "[W]omen brought to the cinema a demand that had remained unanswered in theater, namely, to 'see themselves': their desires and possibilities but also their everyday experience, their milieu."[49] With the development of the film drama in the 1911–1914 period, this demand was answered in a new way. For the first time, the actress was free to represent herself and so could emancipate herself from images of women constructed by men on the live stage. As Schlüpmann argues, this meant not just that the film actress embodies modern female characters but that she

> presents femininity as a nonunitary [*nicht Identisches*]—that is, as not identical with her image—and as something that is possible in many roles. The actress was finally able to be mobile in her skills of transformation, just like an actor, rather than being rendered immobile in the beautiful semblance of expressive nature. Finally, she was able to act against the prejudice that as woman she was affiliated with sentiment rather than action and that sentiment has to be real rather than acted; she was able to act against the prejudice that woman cannot actually present herself openly and in public without prostituting herself. In addition to the "mandate" of the audience, she was also supported in her performance by the new medium itself: its mobility met her skills of self-transformation, and the inherent separation of image and real body in the new medium—rather than a naïve belief in cinematic illusion [*Illusionskino*]—supported the fictionality of her physical performance.[50]

I join Schlüpmann in seeing film as a forum that is historically related to but distinct from the stage. I also join Schlüpmann in arguing that film was a new material for female agency. In speaking about this agency, Schlüpmann is careful to identify and articulate the difference between films in the teens and their later institutionalization. In the teens, what characterizes film's aesthetic qualities is its involuntary and ungraspable nature. Schlüpmann states: "[T]hey did not lay claim to being a finished work, nor did they attempt to anticipate their reception in the way that classical film later did. Rather, they anticipated finding an audience with certain experiences and desires, an audience that would do its part to give significance to the film."[51] This capacity of a film to allow and even encourage the spectator to have her own significance and presence resonates with Bernhardt's films precisely because they were inclusive works that appealed to international audiences as well as to an intergenerational public. Those who might have seen Bernhardt on the live stage in the late nineteenth century could return to her anew; those that were born into the turn of the century could be introduced to a celebrity whose renown eclipsed all others.

The historic activation of the female gaze through the cinema is met by Schlüpmann's own pleasure in watching and interpreting early film today. Explaining that her work is therefore still connected to the experience of an early cinema audience, she argues that her interpretation is also speculative. Objective analysis, reception studies, and the mediation of scientific discourses are not her aim. Instead, Schlüpmann hopes "not only to make lost film present 'in the mind of the female spectator,' but . . . to make a lost cinema present in the mind of the reader."[52] I reiterate this aim, stressing only that the films I discuss are not lost in any material sense. They are instead works that have been lost conceptually and perceptually to us. My task is to recuperate Bernhardt's creative passion for film—to demonstrate that there is still a wealth for us to see.

1. *Nullius in Verba*

Acting on Silent Film

Sarah Bernhardt is renowned for her golden voice. Literature tells us that it was her voice that helped her gain entrance to the Paris Conservatoire in 1859, her voice that helped her attract the enthusiasm of a young Parisian audience in the 1860s and 1870s, and her voice that ensures her enduring renown.[1] Theater scholars have long discussed Bernhardt's vocal training, the development of her vocal skills, and the changes that travel, age, and different theatrical venues brought to her live vocal performances. While my work is grounded in the understanding that Bernhardt's voice is indeed important to a discussion of her fame, it asks questions about Bernhardt's transference to the screen. What happens when the most famous theatrical voice of the late nineteenth century is silenced on narrative film? How do audiences understand and interpret Bernhardt's acting when they have no voice to direct them to the emotional meaning of a gesture, series of gestures, or even a scene? How is emotion understood in the absence of words or vocal intonation? What is the role of music in supporting or developing silent gesture on screen?

It is my contention that while Bernhardt's voice was famous on the live stage her gestural acting was of equal importance to audiences. As I will demonstrate, reviews of her performances recognize the importance of her gestures and the unusual use she made of the spiral as a structuring device in her physical acting. I relate this use of the spiral to the development of art nouveau in France at the end of the nineteenth century and use it to show how Bernhardt's acting physicalized and embodied art nouveau's distinctive spiraling tendrils and curved forms. As I argue, Bernhardt's cinematized theater is an industrial art nouveau product that joined her spiraling body to a media that promoted both visual craftsmanship and mass production. Indeed, the very names of the companies with whom Bernhardt was first associated—the Film d'Art in France and the Famous Players Film Company in America—propose that contemporary art is inseparable from the development of modern industry. I argue that Bernhardt's early films join her distinctive theatrical style of acting to a wider art movement that saw artists newly mobilize materials and audiences through novel uses of modern industry.

While Bernhardt's films can be seen as art nouveau theatrical products circulating in a global market, they are also works that must today be interpreted. Rather than follow the traditional position and see Bernhardt silently mouthing her lines on screen in a genre of film usually dismissed as "filmed theater," I follow David Mayer in arguing that theatrical performance can be used to interpret early film. In an article entitled "Acting in Silent Cinema: Which Legacy of the Theatre?" Mayer states: "Conditioned as we are to performance through our late-twentieth-century experience of what we view as more-or-less realistic acting within a more-or-less realistic mise-en-scène, we are unable or unwilling to accept early actors' work as an effective means of explicating narrative, clarifying character relationships, expressing appropriate or valid emotion, or providing aesthetic pleasure. We are conditioned to the camera as an instrument for recording truth and the actor's performance as a means of validating that truth."[2]

It is indeed the camera as "an instrument for recording truth" that we today focus on. This prevents us from seeing Bernhardt's films as anything but cinematographic failures whose unique value lies in their capacity to reveal Bernhardt's late-nineteenth-century stage action. I have entitled my chapter *Nullius in Verba* in order to contest this idea. Meaning "on the word of no-one," *nullius in verba* is the motto the Royal Society adopted in 1662. As I explain later, it was during the Enlightenment period that the Cartesian division between body and soul emerged. The body became the instrument for a universally intelligible language that subsequently made its way into visual literature. Works such as Charles Le Brun's *Méthode pour apprendre á dessiner les passions* (1702) emerged that depicted the passions in detail. Actors studied this work (and others) and used it to shape their expressions and gestures on the stage. When film emerged roughly three centuries later it carried with it this dual history: the idea that in silence the body can express universally intelligible emotions and the artistic practice of visually recording these. In this context, Bernhardt's engagement with the Film d'Art is not just evidence of an emerging art nouveau, it is also a new form of visual literature that, for the first time, can make itself available to a global audience. Bernhardt's use of a static camera and the reliance on the long distance shot is (to rephrase Mayer) a way to explore gesture as a universal language available to all. As the *New York Times* confirms, theatrical impresario Charles Frohman saw Bernhardt's *Queen Elizabeth* in terms of universal legibility and clear accessibility since he "considers his project analogous, to a certain extent, with the book *Tales from Shakespeare* by Charles and Mary Lamb, which provide for children their first and sometimes only really palatable taste of the bard."[3] Bernhardt herself was aware of the availability and appeal of the cinema. When playing *La Dame aux Camélias* to a full theater alongside a full cinema showing her in the same role in America, she states that "in the one you paid only fifteen or twenty sous while in the other it cost fifteen or twenty francs."[4]

With film we have the possibility of testing the legibility of gesture before a broad audience. We also have the possibility of bringing mechanical repetition and theatrical sameness to the definition of theatrical art. Rather than see this negatively, in terms of a loss of creative spontaneity or read this as a product of Bernhardt's repetitive commodification of plays,[5] film allows us to see the theater reproduced in a new way. Bernhardt's films make her theater newly available for mass consumption. Further—and taking into account what Bernhardt said about film being affordable—Bernhardt's films give all spectators the same vantage of her acting, and it does this by presenting her in the same play. There is therefore no "best" seat in the house and no difference in the roles brought to different audiences. Nor is there a difference in the length or content of Bernhardt's performance since it can not be interrupted by applause, scenery changes, or her own idiosyncratic response to audience or venue. Finally, with narrative action now translated into lengthy English intertitles for English-speaking audiences, Bernhardt's body becomes the instrument through which emotions are expressed and empathy solicited. Although we know that musical accompaniment was variable, and that it changed according to the theater in which the film was projected (I discuss this later), music nevertheless retained the function it had on the live nineteenth-century stage. This was to support the emotional meaning of Bernhardt's physical performance. Again, it is her performing body that is brought to film and seen by a new cinema-going public.

Georges Michel, writing a review of Bernhardt's *Camille* in the *Ciné-Journal* in 1912 asks: "My God, what will this hectic cinema do to this gentle figure of charm and pleasure? What is it that Electricity will do to Gesture? to the beauty of gesture?" In response he states: "Admirable mime! Behind her vanishes the hanging sets, the carton furniture, the piano in black wood.

Lips speak and if the public hears nothing, it nevertheless listens."[6] An earlier editorial written by Dureau argues the same point. He states:

> You think perhaps of the "Golden Voice," of the tirades of great scenes, and you say to me: What is there that remains on the screen?
>
> There remains this: that Madame Sarah Bernhardt carries the value of her role so well that its expression does not suffer by the silence. I have understood better than ever, seeing her leave the scene after the farewell letter written to Armand, the poignant emotion of her act and the depth of her love sacrificed for her lover. There is in her tender arms, in her kiss thrown to him in his absence, in her hurried flight, hesitant, held back, a minute of high tragedy which indicates better than words the dreadful torment of a feminine heart.[7]

Moving Picture World reiterated this view when it explained that "The story is revealed as plain as print. 'Camille' was never more pitifully eloquent than in this dumb record."[8] It is in this context that I argue that Bernhardt's films are not failures but instead frame the theater as a vibrant and developing art nouveau that brings Enlightenment thought to the cusp of a new century.

Establishing Physical Fame

As I mentioned earlier, Bernhardt was famous for her voice *and* gesture. Rather than see her films as silent records of a voice we cannot hear, we must recognize that her capacity to express herself physically through costume and gesture had facilitated her renown well before she entered silent film. Indeed, in the role that first shot her to popular as well as critical fame—the *travesti* role of Zanetto, the wandering Florentine minstrel, in François Coppée's *Le Passant* of 1869—it was both her choice of costume and use of her voice that was noted by the influential French theater critic Francisque Sarcey. In his review of the opening night at the Odéon theater he praised the "exquisite elegance" of Coppée's verse and—even before discussing Bernhardt's vocal delivery—notes that she "recalls, by her costume, the Florentine singer by the sculptor Dubois."[9]

Although Sarcey found Bernhardt's body unsuited to this dress, it is significant that he recognized the impact Bernhardt created by visually associating herself with a famous and popular sculpture, Paul Dubois' *A Fifteenth Century Florentine Singer*. This sculpture was identifiable to most in the Odéon audience since it had won a medal of honor just four years previously at the Salon of 1865, had been made into silvered bronze by order of the state, had been installed in the Musée du Luxembourg where the leading collection of modern painting and sculpture in Paris was then housed, and was mass produced (in different sizes) in bronze by the Barbedienne foundry and in porcelain by the Manufacture de Sèvres. As Richard Kendall suggests, *A Fifteenth Century Florentine Singer* was, at the time, "[a]rguably the most critically approved and popularly acclaimed emblem of youth."[10] Bernhardt's own youth, as well as Coppée's status as a young and little-known poet, was therefore reinforced by a theatrical costume that joined physical youth, contemporary art, popular audiences, and industrial reproduction.

Noting that Bernhardt was "celebrated, given curtain calls, and cheered by an enraptured public," Sarcey indicates that Bernhardt was not only a critical success. She was also supported by a loud and vocal audience.[11] In conclusion to his review—he also reviewed plays being performed contemporaneously at the Théâtre-Française and the Gaité—Sarcey defends what he calls "the true public of the theater." This was the public who cheered Bernhardt and who were often denied access to the legitimate theaters. Sincere, passionate, and intelligent arbiters of theatrical talent, they were the critical mass spearheading the growing taste for the theater in Paris. As he observes, their enthusiasm for a player heralded certain fame.[12]

Sarcey's description of the new audience attending the Odéon theater is confirmed by Suze Rueff in her biography of Bernhardt, *I Knew Sarah Bernhardt.* Focusing on *Le Passant* as the turning point in Bernhardt's career, Rueff states that *Le Passant*

> drew to the Odéon the students, the midinettes and the artisans of the *rive gauche* [who were] attracted by the strange music of that voice. These simple folk were among the first to adopt the young Sarah Bernhardt for their own . . . if at any time the press had not been kind to their favorite, these newly-won adherents, *les Saradoteurs*, as Parisians soon designated them, would clap, stamp, and shout themselves hoarse to demonstrate they were of a different opinion.[13]

In this sense, Bernhardt was not only physically representative of youth, she was also part of a youthful engagement in the French theater that brought with it new playwrights, new costumes, new audiences, and new mores to the theater. In her book, *L'Art du Théâtre*, Bernhardt makes much of the comparison between the spectators at the Odéon and the conservatism that still haunted the Comédie-Française. She explains that her supporters at the Odéon were the "poets, dreamers, students, neurasthenics and young girls" while those who attended the Comédie-Française were the "big bankers and hedonists."[14] As Sarcey later remarked in a different context but to the same effect, "theatre is not made for the *pensionnaires*."[15]

When Bernhardt entered film a generation later she was no longer a young actress supported by a youthful audience but an established actress who courted different generations, classes, and nationalities. Film was a commercial product that brought a genuinely diverse public together to watch and consume a single physical performance. Reiterating film's theatrical roots in its advertising campaign, the Film d'Art would cement its connection to the traditional theater by explaining that *La Dame aux Camélias* was "THE TRIUMPH of the Season."[16] Joining the cinema's "theatrical season" to the idea that the cinema might facilitate its own touring road shows through simultaneously different cities, the Film d'Art also publicized Bernhardt's appearance in Bulgaria, Monte Negro, Bucharest, Romania, and Serbia.[17] An audience that might once have been split along class lines and seated in different theaters in urban Paris had become, through film and mass consumption, a global audience that together celebrated Bernhardt's famous acting.

A Signature Spiral

It was Bernhardt's performance as the Spanish Queen in Victor Hugo's *Ruy Blas* at the Odéon in 1872 that confirmed her celebrity within Paris. Performed as the opening work after the theater's closure during the Franco-Prussian War of 1870–1871 (during this time, the theater had been converted into a makeshift hospital), *Ruy Blas* linked Bernhardt to the theme of social reform. The play, which focuses on a commoner who is politically savvy, emotionally sincere, and who kills for social vengeance, troubled the ruling class in Paris when it debuted in the Renaissance theater in 1838.[18] Although now performed to celebrate the return of Victor Hugo from two decades of political exile, it was still considered socially inflammatory. In a note published in *Le Temps* before the play's debut, Sarcey therefore urged the public to listen to it "without political passion" and to see it simply as the "debut of a beautiful work and not a political event."[19]

Sarcey's own review of *Ruy Blas* some days later illustrated this approach. Saying nothing of the political symbolism and metaphor in the work, Sarcey celebrates Hugo's poetic skill and describes Edmond Geffroy (playing Don Salluste) as "a true choirmaster." He then comments on Bernhardt's acting. Stating that her movements are "noble and harmonious" he explains: "When she rises, when she makes a half turn, when she exits, the long folds of her silver spangled dress arrange themselves around her with poetic grace." Although Sarcey then gives his review over to a description of her voice ("Never has delicious poetry been so sweetly spoken," he states),[20] he isolates Bernhardt's use of costume as a key feature of her performance. His attention to the half-turn, a movement that makes Bernhardt's costume spiral around her, indicates the way in which art nouveau literally materializes itself through costume even after being worked physically through Bernhardt's spiraling gestures on the stage.

In 1880, when Bernhardt adopted the role of Marguerite Gautier in Dumas fils' *La Dame aux Camélias*—a role which would go on to become her most performed role in the theater—this signature spiral was newly worked into the play's concluding death scene. When Sarcey saw the play performed in 1881 in London he reported that instead of saying her last words in a soporific murmur while seated (as was traditionally the case), Bernhardt remains standing, defying death. Suddenly she reels, turns her body on a half-pivot, and collapses in "the most elegant and poetic pose imaginable."[21] A few years later, when Louis Ganderax describes Bernhardt's performance in *Théodora* in *Revue des Deux Mondes*, Bernhardt's spiraling turns were as characteristically a part of her performance as her voice. Ganderax states: "[I]t is Madame Sarah Bernhardt, more than Theodora, who twists and turns like a serpent upon the cushions of her throne; it is her who seduces and moves us by the charm and expression of her gestures, as much as by the music and shouts of her voice."[22] In a booklet for a performance of *La Dame aux Camélias* at the Théâtre Sarah Bernhardt in 1908 a bill for the play includes a description of each act. Here, we are told that in the fifth act, Marguerite dies "in the arms of her lover."[23] Action that was once considered original has thus been written into the play itself. Moreover, the booklet states that Bernhardt "aroused the enthusiasm of the crowds of all races, who were captivated and delighted" by her Marguerite.[24]

At the Forefront of Art Nouveau

Bernhardt's turning and twisting body, as well as the spiraling material folds of her costume, were not just an unusual part of her stage performance. They were inseparable with her identity and so worked into the many portraits made of her. Becoming an integral part of Bernhardt's reproduced image, her curved and sinuous body came to symbolize the corporeal shape of art nouveau, its manifestation in human form. Whereas art nouveau is usually associated in France with objects such as Hector Guimard's entrances to the Paris Métro, the furniture shops of Louis Majorelle, or the art objects and interior design of Siegfried Bing's eponymous Maison de l'Art Nouveau, it is important to recognize the importance of this latter point. Art nouveau was a spiraling performance style early realized by Bernhardt on the live stage and, from the 1870s onward, it was worked into many posters, photographs, caricatures, paintings, and sketches made of her.

Most famously, Bernhardt's curving body motivated the graphic art of Alphonse Mucha in the 1890s. Indeed, when Mucha was commissioned by Bernhardt to make his now-famous posters featuring her in theatrical roles in the 1890s (*Gismonda, La Dame aux Camélias, Lorenzaccio, Médée, La Tosca, Hamlet*), he uses the gestural turns of Bernhardt's live theatrical acting to pioneer the graphic art of art nouveau. These posters—popular and mass consumable reproductions that were arresting in their color and long scroll-like composition—give evidence of Bernhardt's body being used as an instrument to materialize a new art form. Mucha's work affirms that art could be produced through the poster and that publicity could be used creatively (see figure 1.1). Mucha's son Jiri, speaking of his father's practice of rendering woman as a flowing, curving form, explains:

> A woman, for him, was not a body, but beauty incorporated in matter and acting through matter. That is why all his figures, however solid, are not really of

Figure 1.1. *La Dame aux Camélias*, Mucha, 1896. Bibliothèque Nationale de France.

> this world. They are symbols, unattainable dreams, like Sarah when she came on to the stage, or died in the role of *La Dame aux Camélias*.[25]

In painting we see this same transcription of Bernhardt's body into a curved female form. Rather than appear in portraits standing frontally or seated facing the audience with a solid torso and limbs, Bernhardt is generally depicted lounging on a bed or couch with her clothes tousled around her. The most famous of these portraits—and certainly the most arresting—is Georges Clairin's 1876 *Portrait of Sarah Bernhardt* (see figure 1.2). In this work, Bernhardt is shown lounging on a plush red couch with a shiny cream-colored dress twisting around her thin frame and falling into a large semicircular fan at her feet. This flourishing tendril is completed by the curved body of a wolfhound and the circular line of his tail as he lounges on the floor beside

Figure 1.2. *Portrait of Sarah Bernhardt*, Georges Clairin, 1876. Petit Palais, Paris.

her. Bernhardt's and the dog's body form the one S-shaped line that falls like a whiplash across the room's dark interior.

Drawing crowds to it when it was first exhibited at the Paris Salon of 1876, Paul Mantz explains how "the picture is clearly sought after, because the beautiful woman and her dog combine their light tones, describing that long serpentine line with which William Hogarth made his delights. These same curves do not appear by chance."[26] This reference to the bright paint as well as to Clairin's use of Hogarth's line of beauty—a relaxed serpentine line that Bernhardt embodies through the sprawling *S* of her undulating form—indicates that audiences saw Bernhardt's art nouveau tendril as part of an aesthetic theory of beauty that was first formulated in Hogarth's 1753 book, *The Analysis of Beauty*. Although some commentators were critical of the colors in the portrait and although this line was often caricatured (in a work published in the same period, Bernhardt is "Skeletal Sarah," her thin body twisted into a satirical knot),[27] it is telling that Hogarth's efforts to make art accessible to the common man was echoed in Clairin's portrait of a theatrical celebrity and in Bernhardt's own subsequent engagement with reproductive media.[28]

In the Victorian era, acting shared qualities with the decorative and applied arts, as Mayer confirms in his book *Henry Irving and the Bells*. Acting not only circulated globally, it was also a repetitious and dependable product reaching the corners of the empire. Moreover, it imparted a similar sense of excess and imbalance through the fact that "dialogue is stretched beyond the norms of daily conversation and human action pushed to the very limits, if not beyond the bounds, of acceptable causality."[29] Mayer develops this point in his more recent work when he notes that the dancer Loïe Fuller's movements were translated into the "pliant, tangled-root lines of art nouveau" and might be further traced into gestural codes of actors working in silent film, into the typographic *AB* of the Biograph company trademark, and into the art nouveau intertitles of David W. Griffith's films (see figure 1.3).[30] In this sense, film is one of the final platforms for art nouveau. Typography, performance, costume, jewelry, and even floral interiors were featured, their curved momentum materialized by a media that was itself based on the principle of circular rotation.

Film industrialized Bernhardt's acting, allowing it to be mechanically reproduced and circulate on a previously unimaginable scale. Film was also considered a durable record of an art form that was otherwise temporal and fleeting. As W. Stephen Bush explains:

> To such a passionate lover of her art, it must have seemed glorious to defy the limitations of space and time and have the whole world as her audience. The

Figure 1.3. *Loïe Fuller Dancing*, Samuel Joshua Beckett, ca. 1900. The Metropolitan Museum of Art, Gilman Collection, purchase, Mrs. Walter Annenberg and The Annenberg Foundation Gift, 2005.

> cinematographe is indeed an "aere perennius"—more enduring than brass and it is far more ornamental and useful as well. The immortality conferred by the motion picture is well worth having.[31]

With Bernhardt as one of its early protagonists, cinematized theater ensures that the theater is made a durable object. It enabled the theater to become, for the first time, an industrial product that could be exported to the far corners of the globe. In this context, film is a material guarantee of the theater's enduring renown.

When Bernhardt's sinuous body entered narrative film, it was framed, advertised, and celebrated as a development in the French Film d'Art. The early teens were also, however, the point at which Siegfried Bing had died (he died in 1905) and a moment in which Cubism was beginning to emerge as the new art form of the twentieth century. Cubism redefined the visual arts, replacing the art nouveau curve for a series of staggered viewpoints whose angles and lines paralleled developments in film language (montage, camera angles, the close-up). For an actress such as Bernhardt, however, it is the gesturing body and not the filmic cut that imparts and determines cinematic meaning. In this sense, our ongoing attempt to read her films through formal developments in film language is mistaken and shortsighted since it misses the importance of her gesturing body. Art nouveau entered film just as it entered the other arts: our obstacle has been to see the static camera as proof of theatrical anachronism rather than an ongoing effort to bring visibility, accessibility, and even longevity to art nouveau.

The Film d'Art

Bernhardt's first films (*Camille* and *Queen Elizabeth*) were made and marketed by the French Société Film d'Art. This was a company established by Paul Lafitte in 1908 that introduced the theatrical "art film" using known stage stars from respected and legitimate theaters (generally, the Comédie Française). Promoting these figures in known stage plays, which had long circulated in the theater and which—if they had not been seen in this forum—were at least familiar through paintings and prints, they tapped in to a source of popular knowledge. Audiences could see stars they might not access in the flesh and could have famous literary and artistic works reenacted in a media they knew and understood. Middle- and upper-class audiences were appeased by the idea that film could be educational rather than shocking and sensational. For the first time, films that encouraged the attendance of respectable women and families in the theater were promoted. In this sense, precisely because the established theater is presented at once as traditional "art" and as popular "film," we can understand that the Film d'Art marketed itself to the broadest possible audience. This is not to argue that the Film d'Art was profitable; rather, it is to indicate that Bernhardt's films were strategically capable of engaging a diverse public.

Publicity for Bernhardt's films made the most of her popular appeal without losing sight of the fact that they were promoting a new art. In a colorful poster for *La Dame aux Camélias*, red type declares: "For the First Time in the Cinematographe."[32] Beneath this is Bernhardt's name and the title of the play at the bottom of the frame. The framed image shows her with her white dress wrapping itself around her thin frame as she lies dead with Armand grieving over her. Unlike Duval Sr. who covers his eyes behind them, we are witness to Bernhardt's famous death flop. With "Le Film d'Art" written across the picture and camellia flowers stretching in S-shaped vines along each side of the frame, we are introduced to film as an art nouveau object. This is a work that might be "art" but which is also intensely moving: as the poster reveals, Duval Sr. covers his eyes in witness to the events depicted.

Queen Elizabeth was produced with money forwarded by Adolph Zukor; in exchange he released the film in North America through the newly formed Famous Players Film Company that sold it on a states' rights basis. The international collaboration that this represents—in terms of an American company profiting from an "art film" proposed by a French company—indicates the extent to which Bernhardt was a commodity linking nations together. It also indicates that Bernhardt enabled collaboration between the nineteenth-century theater and twentieth-century industry. Indeed, as a narrative film that promoted the longer playing feature film format, *Queen Elizabeth* would become the forerunner to Paramount, a company that Zukor soon went on to form. More important, however, is the fact that the success of her appearance in film encouraged other companies to engage and promote established stage stars. And so, just as art nouveau was known under different headings in different nations (the Liberty Style in England, Stile Liberty in Italy, Tiffany Style or Arts and Crafts Movement in America, Jugendstil in Germany, and so on), so, too, did the film d'art manifest itself differently in different countries, becoming associated with (for example) the Società Anonima Italiana per Film d'Arte in Italy and the Autorenfilm in Germany.[33]

L'homme machine

As Clairin's use of Hogarth's line of beauty demonstrates, Bernhardt's sinuous physicality was not just associated with a developing French art nouveau style. It was also a product of an Enlightenment project that made the body newly expressive and intelligible. In his book *The Player's Passion: Studies in the Science of Acting*, Joseph Roach demonstrates how theatrical gesture was rationalized in the seventeenth century when the human body was theorized as a machine. It was René Descartes, in his *Les passions de l'âme* (1649), who decisively proposed that the human body is a machine moved by emotions. Identifying wonder, love, hatred, desire, joy, and sadness as passions that functioned as triggers to external physiological expression, he broke from earlier models by articulating a Cartesian division between body and soul. Later, Julien La Mettrie in *L'homme machine* (1747) argued that "man is a machine." As Roach explains, emotional expression was considered "the mechanical effects of internal physical causes, much like hours showing on the face of a clock."[34] The impact of this thinking on the theater was tremendous. The actor could imagine the body as a formal and regular mechanism with laws that mirrored the physical laws of the universe. S/he could therefore direct the physiological expression of the passions and these could be universally deciphered and understood. The old oratorical style of acting that had associated physical gesture with the animation of spirits that accompanied the songlike chant of verse was replaced by a new emphasis upon the physical body as an expression of rational intellect.

The *homme machine* provided a paradigmatic shift in thinking that ushered in expressive gesture as the new language of theatrical performance. The Royal Society, responding to these changes in scientific thinking that swept away ancient physiological theory, adopted *nullius in verba* as its motto. Roach states:

> In *L'homme machine* ["man is a machine"] of 1747, [Julien] La Mettrie carried to its radical conclusion a scientific revolution begun over a hundred years before. This revolution emerged from the struggle of the new science to view the world afresh, to cast down the idols of received opinion and ancient authority. Its new policy was self-consciously dramatized by the uncompromising motto adopted by the Royal Society in 1662—*nullius in verba*, "on the word of no one." The so-called "mechanization of the world picture," which was the collective achievement of seventeenth-century science and philosophy, presented the universe as matter in motion. . . . Physics and psychology intersect in the study of the human body, identifying emotion with motion.[35]

This thought impacted visual literature. Studies such as the painter Charles Le Brun's *Méthode pour apprendre á dessiner les passions* (1702) depicted the passions in detail. For the first time, Cartesian physiology motivated the artist's study of passions. A modern body of visual literature emerged upon which the actor could draw. The interplay between this literature and acting on the stage is extremely rich. Roach cites Franciscus Lange's *Dissertatio de actione scenica* (Munich, 1727), François Riccoboni's *L'art du théâtre* (Paris, 1750), Roger Pickering's *Reflections upon Theatrical Expression in Tragedy* (London, 1755), and Goethe's *Regeln für Schauspieler* (Weimar, 1803) as examples of the literature that can illustrate this interchange between Cartesian thought, drama, and the visual arts.[36] For my purposes, however, it is sufficient that Le Brun's images still circulate in acting handbooks in the late nineteenth century, even in books that argued that gestural language was not universal but "has its typical features in every nation."[37] In this sense, there is evidence that those actors such as Bernhardt who transitioned from the late-nineteenth-century stage to early film were part of a transition from stage to screen that saw dramatic theory and practice move onto film. Rather than see film as a new technology that engages its own media-specific questions, I see film as a new form of visual literature that is in many respects an early-twentieth-century development of Le Brun's sketches.

Expressing love, anguish, fear, and joy in pictures that now move, the actor transitions between emotions with a fluidity that overcomes the difficulty that haunted the eighteenth and nineteenth century's attempt to choreograph physical movement with pen and ink. The pictures became, in this way, a visual model of the theater. As the *Motion Picture Story Magazine* explained in an article published in 1912:

> With the photographic lens these movements [of Bernhardt on the stage] could be caught, and, with them, the countless others which so glorify a Bernhardt impersonation, and they could be a factor in the training of generations of actresses. Bernhardt, supreme genius that she is, recognizes this and she has already posed for the "little pictures." . . . People do not go to the opera to see the dramatic exposition of the great roles, except in the case of a Mary Garden; they go to hear them sung, and it is for that, solely, that they will buy their phonograph records; with the artists of the drama they will buy their picture reels to see them act, and the dialog will be of as little consequence as it is in the Moving Picture theatre of today.[38]

In my view, it is not by chance that Bernhardt chose to perform the role of Marguerite Gautier in her first narrative film. This female lead must be capable of gaining audience empathy while she experiences and expresses a full range of emotions. As *Moving Picture World* would explain in a 1909 advertisement for Pathé's *La Dame aux Camélias* starring Vittoria Lepanto, "Ambitious actresses aspire to play Marguerite Gautier in 'La Dame,' because it gives a woman on the stage the opportunity of showing off the variety of her histrionic gifts."[39] Indeed, when Bernhardt states that "I never thought . . . that I would ever be a film, but now that I am two whole reels of pictures I rely for my immortality upon these records,"[40] she is speaking of the durability of film *and* to it usurping the status of the visual arts as a record of the range of expressions achievable by an actor. David Garrick, so famous for his control over gesture and dramatic transition on the eighteenth-century stage, was famously painted by Sir Joshua Reynolds, William Hogarth, Thomas Gainsborough, Angelica Kauffman, Henry Edward Dawe, Benjamin Wilson, and many others. There exist ninety-six prints of him in character.[41] Bernhardt, appearing before the camera, had her acting instead recorded for posterity in a way that no previous actor could enjoy.

Personalizing the Pictures

Film was not only the newest and most precise way of recording theatrical expression. It was also, as I mentioned earlier, a way of showing theatrical gesture animated. Earlier photographs taken by Paul Nadar of Bernhardt in the 1870s, 1880s, and 1890s famously depict Bernhardt as Hernani (1876), Fédora (1883), Macbeth (1884), Théodora (1885), La Tosca (1887), Jeanne d'Arc

(1890 and 1893), Phèdre (1893), Gismonda (1894), and Izéïl (1894). Exhibited at the Exposition Universelle of 1889 and 1900 and sold separately as postcards to the press and public, these images depict Bernhardt in the physical language of the late-nineteenth-century stage. Each reveals a precise moment of action, where gesture, glance, and costume together form an intelligible posture.[42] With film, however, these postures give way to animate gesture and are no longer isolated moments in time.

While Bernhardt's films animate theatrical poses, they also reference sculptures and paintings that were popular and identifiable to audiences. I mentioned earlier how Bernhardt's costume for *Ruy Blas* was based on Paul Dubois's *A Fifteenth Century Florentine Singer*. As Martin Meisel explains in his book *Realizations*, this form of physical realization of famous visual art works was a common practice on the nineteenth-century stage. He describes how during the nineteenth century actors newly personalized this practice, embodying "a *particular* painting or engraving, rather than an ideal image in the public domain."[43] Meisel argues that the identification of the pictorial image by spectators was a way to actively engage them in the theater and notes how the increasing availability of the reproduced image facilitated this. Meisel also argues for a photographic origin for tableau realizations in film (as opposed to a pictorial origin by way of engravings after paintings or popular prints on the stage). I instead suggest that Bernhardt's theatricalized cinema incorporates both, bringing the "portrait picture" (the animate portrait photograph) and the "particular picture" for the first time together.

Speaking in Silence

The idea that even (or particularly) as a dumb record film can be celebrated as theater has links to arguments forwarded in the Enlightenment that held that the physical body (and not words) best expresses emotion. Illustrated by Denis Diderot in his *Lettre sur les sourds et muets* (1751), Diderot explains that he blocked his ears in the theater so that he might follow the actors' faces and bodies alone. It was through the calculated manipulation of gesture, pose, and physiognomy that an actor achieved true mastery of the art of acting. In distinction to the critical comments mentioned earlier about seeing Bernhardt on film "with one's ears stopped with cotton," lies this tradition of isolating vocal gesture. As Roach explains:

> Diderot celebrated Lady Macbeth's silent hand-washing as one of those sublime moments of bodily eloquence in which gesture triumphs over discourse. At such a moment spoken language collapses in upon itself, and its meaning can only

escape the soul as a gesture: "The great passions," Diderot notes in *Eléments de physiologie*, "are silent."[44]

When the *New York Dramatic Mirror* relays how in the death scene of *La Dame aux Camélias* Bernhardt—"is standing in Armand's embrace with her face hidden from view by her hand drooping and falling like the flower from which Marguerite's sobriquet was derived"—it is focusing in this type of visual detail. The significance of Bernhardt's rising and falling hand, described as "tremendously impressive and convincing," lay in the fact that spoken language was not needed for a gesture to express emotion.[45] In a similar way, Adolphe Brisson (Sarcey's son-in-law) wrote in a review of Bernhardt's 1912 stage performance of Queen Elizabeth: "We watch Sarah Bernhardt. And Sarah is extraordinary. The incomplete and confused tragedy focuses itself, defines itself, in her pose, in her actions, in the stirring of her hands, in the anxiety in her eyes, in the trembling of her breathless and broken voice."[46] This reduction of the story of *Queen Elizabeth* to the impact of Bernhardt's acting helped the reception of the film. As the London *Times* recounts, events in the film "furnish opportunities for those scenes of passion, remorse, and despair in which the *doyenne* of the European stage shows that she can still excel all juniors."[47] Some long-term critics of Bernhardt jested that her silence on film was an achievement. George Bernard Shaw wrote in a letter to Ellen Terry that he "saw a Queen Elizabeth film, with Shakespear [*sic*] and everything complete, and Sarah Bernhardt as the queen and it was better without her voice than with it."[48]

There is evidence that the legibility of gesture on screen was not unique to Bernhardt but intrinsic to the interpretation of film itself. As *Moving Picture World* explained in a 1911 article entitled "The Eloquence of Gesture," gesture is the "perfection of the histrionic art," it gives "utterance to that, which is too great, too general, too near to be put into language." Stating that while it was true that the French and Italians are "successful beyond other nations because they can and do talk with their hands and eyes," the article explained that Americans were nevertheless at the forefront of gestural expression as they invested each gesture with the fullest of emotion, being "saturnine" and "chary of gestures," clearly trying to establish a racial hierarchy of gestural expression:

> A wave of the hand, a turn of the body, a swinging of the arm means more than a hundred thousand excited gestures of a company of Frenchmen, Italians, or South Americans. There is a suggestion of the monumental about the gesturing of the Northern races. We are reminded of the simple gesture embodied in the marble or iron of the statue.[49]

The Natural

Bernhardt's visual acting had its roots in the Enlightenment idea that emotions were expressed through the external body.[50] As Bernhardt explains in her book, *Art du théâtre*, this includes "the eye, the hand, the position of the chest, the inflection of the head." Going on to state that external physical control is of utmost importance, she describes how "Gesture, like diction, is learned, is made by dint of study, [and] is perfected with time."[51] Bernhardt affirms that gesture must be practiced and studied. She also argues, however, that an actor cannot perform in a mannered and artificial way; it is only by being natural that gesture can move an audience to tears. In her opinion, this is the aim of the actor: to move the public to tears so that they forget they are watching dramatic convention and instead believe they are witness to real drama. In order to do this, the actor must "cry true tears, suffer true pain, laugh true laughter."[52] The separation that Diderot established in *Le paradoxe sur le comédien* between the actor's actions and feelings is therefore refused by Bernhardt. She states "Diderot pretends that the artist should feel nothing. This is an error and I challenge Diderot." As she explains, in Grecian times actors performed aesthetically beautiful gestures before enormous crowds of twenty to thirty thousand people. Their task was to project their voice loud enough to be heard and to focus on the rhythm of their diction. Emotions were voiced by the chorus. It was this group that together expressed the sentiments that the public was meant to feel. In this sense, the actor was merely a living mannequin while the chorus was his emotive and expressive soul. Arguing that today theatrical understanding has changed, Bernhardt states: "Our comprehension of the theatre today no longer permits the abstention of sentiment and personal emotions [in the actor]. Nothing is more exciting than leaving oneself and becoming another."[53]

It is in the context of this argument, forwarded to explain not just the development of dramatic theory but to claim the actor's new stature as a creative individual in the theater, that Bernhardt's engagement with film might be reconsidered. Indeed, when Bernhardt entered the film industry, it was her celebrity and her acting skill that were promoted. I would suggest that Bernhardt's films consequently see a continuity of the theater so that the fame of the most celebrated star of the late-nineteenth-century stage becomes interchangeable with film itself. Film audiences were therefore reassured that film physically captures Bernhardt: in Italy *La Stampa* promoted *La Dame aux Camélias* by stating that "Sarah Bernhardt is in Turin" while in the United States audiences were told that this is "[y]our only chance to see the marvel and miracle of the stage."[54]

Bernhardt's silent acting was a skill that was not enjoyed by all actors: the mere fact of performing for the camera did not guarantee an actor a global audience. As W. Stephen Bush notes in his review of *La Dame aux Camélias*, "The gifts of other noted artists do not shine as well in the motion pictures as they do on the speaking stage. . . . The splendor of Sarah Bernhardt['s] art remains undimmed in the photoplay."[55] In this context, Bernhardt's films become the apotheosis of the "man machine" in the sense that she is an instrumental body that speaks globally to audiences. Better, she expresses genius and records emotion. Here, we join the idealized and universally legible body of the actor to an industrial media that, in true art nouveau spirit, enables the actor to remain a charismatic craftsman driving new definitions of art. The implications are enormous: for the first time, the theatrical star can circulate and be celebrated on a global scale. Rather than presume a split between the stage and screen, we might see an embodied continuity that engages contemporary artistic practices just as it confirms the theater's ongoing use of technology in its production of "the show."

Making Music

In his article "Acting in Silent Cinema," David Mayer argues that music played a fundamental role on the nineteenth- and early-twentieth-century stage and, subsequently, in early film. He states, "(m)usic is to the actor what water is to the swimmer." It provides the tempo, coloring, tonality, force, rhythm, direction, and impulse for gesture. As Mayer goes on to explain, there is evidence that some rehearsals for early narrative film were conducted with musicians. Presumably, this music continued to be played when the actor performed for the camera. Later, when the films were screened, musical accompaniment was provided by the house orchestra or by the piano.[56] In this sense, we must recognize that although Bernhardt is silent on screen, she likely performed for the camera to music just as she was seen on film to the accompaniment of music. It is misleading, therefore, to focus on the incapacity of early film to record and synchronize her speaking voice. We might better imagine Bernhardt's films as works that underscore the gestural legibility of Bernhardt's actions even as they affirm the ongoing association of music and theater.

We know that in rehearsals for her stage performances Bernhardt relied on music and herself directed what was to be heard on the live stage. The London *Sporting Times* therefore recounts the efforts made to time Marguerite's death "to slow music, and with the curtain descending in the very nick of time." It goes on to explain that "From the newly-painted scenery for *Hernani* to the apparently most unimportant orchestral accompaniment to a rollicking song in the first act of *Camille* nothing escapes her; everything is subjected to her controlling judgement and direction."[57] The importance given music in rehearsal indicates its importance in her live performances. As Erin M. Brooks has demonstrated in her dissertation, *Sharing the Stage with the Voix d'Or: Sarah Bernhardt and Music in the Belle Époque*, incidental music was central to her stage productions.[58] In my own research, I have determined that Bernhardt's use of music was important to the reception of her work, with critics drawing attention to the way in which music was embedded within her dramatic action. In *Ruy Blas* of 1872, for example, Sarcey explains that Hugo uses a "marvelous orchestra," which allows him to achieve effects of "surprising strength." Isolating in particular the end of Act 1, he states that the Queen's court forms a choir that sings her praise. At this point, while Ruy Blas asks Don Salluste what he is commanded to do, "the cellos accompanying him lament; and in a hiatus, after a fierce refrain of bassoons, Don Salluste says slowly: 'To please this woman and be her lover.'"[59] In Jules Barbier's *Jeanne d'Arc*, performed with Bernhardt in the title role at the Odéon theater in 1890, Sarcey again speaks of the importance of music. Stating that the play is a "kind of opera," he states: "The music [of Charles Gounod] necessarily plays its part; not only scenic music, softly accompanying the words of the characters, but the music of song . . . the two saints address Jeanne: they sing what they have to say to her while an invisible choir throws from time to time a pressing and tender call on the one note: Jeanne, Jeanne."[60] Commentators reiterate and reinforce this connection between Bernhardt and the operatic stage. In her lifetime she was known not just as the golden voice, but as "the divine Sarah," a term applied otherwise exclusively to opera divas.[61]

What happened, however, when Bernhardt moved to film? While a growing body of scholarship explores the early and productive relationship between opera and silent film, little is said of how this relationship was developed in terms of musical accompaniment. We know, for example, that Edison spoke of the Kinetoscope as "continuous Opera,"[62] that opera gave film prestige, a ready-made musical score, and was "part of cinema's very reason for being."[63] In Paul Freyer's book, *The Opera Singer and the Silent Film*, Bernhardt is woven throughout as an example of an actress who moved between the legitimate and popular stage and as one who successfully moved to film.[64] Nothing is said, however, about the music that was heard when Bernhardt's films were screened. What music accompanied her screening in local theaters? Was, for instance, the orchestral score for Giuseppe Verdi's *La Traviata* played with *Camille* and Gioachino Rossini's opera, *Elisabetta, regina d'Inghilterra*, played with *Queen Elizabeth*? I am not sure. To date I have only found one report—when *Camille* was given its debut in Sydney, Australia—that selections from *La Traviata* were played with the film by a local band.[65]

W. Stephen Bush makes one small mention about the music used for *Camille* when he asks for "music of the right kind," which has "[p]athos as its dominant role."[66] In order to understand this comment, however, we need to know what Bush means by both "the right kind" and "pathos." And while Martin Marks suggests that the composer Walter Cleveland Simon (who crafted piano scores for Kalem) could have composed music for the Réjane/Bernhardt double bill (remember that *Camille* circulated with Réjane's *Mme. Sans-Gêne*), there is no evidence of this musical score.[67] We know, however, that the screening of these two films was accompanied by "appropriate music" and that it was designed as a "complete evening's entertainment of about two and one half hours of the highest standard." Such a program, presented as a special night out, made it akin to an evening at the opera.[68] In an article in *Moving Picture World*, Clarence E. Sinn prints a letter from "our old friend Will H. Bryant" who had been "managing the house and leading the orchestra" in Terre Haute, Indiana. He lists the excerpts he used of familiar pieces of music to accompany *Camille* and indicates the point at which the music was to change. In all, twelve excerpts are chosen. Although Bryant's musical program gives evidence of at least one score used in the screening of *Camille*, it is difficult to interpret the action on screen in relation to music, except to note that action was indeed sustained by a musical score.[69] There is no other mention of music that I have found in relation to *Camille*.

It is *Queen Elizabeth*, with a score written for it by Joseph Breil, which indicates a little more clearly the ways in which music remained part of cinematized theater. Indeed, the Breil score suggests that Bernhardt's film was not just a silent picture play, but a prestigious musical event. Breil was previously the principal tenor in the Emma Juch Opera Company who, as his later film compositions reveal, used opera liberally in his work.[70] Even the length of the film creates a link to opera: with the unusual length of 1100 meters, *Queen Elizabeth* was not part of a double bill nor, clearly, a work that was meant to be divided and shown serially. Rather, it was a feature attraction, one that stood theatrically alone. As I mentioned earlier, the film was imported to America by theater manager Charles Frohman and film entrepreneur Adolph Zukor through their new distributing company, the Famous Players Film Company. It was given a private debut at the Lyceum theater in New York in July 1912. A legitimate theater usually reserved for theatrical plays, the Lyceum not only guaranteed the quality and prestige of the film, but also encouraged a respectable middle class. Launching the film through a private audience publicized *Queen Elizabeth*'s status as a prestigious theatrical event.

When *Queen Elizabeth* was given its public launch at the Powers Theater on the 12th of August, 1912, this same aura of class and privilege was maintained. The theater was a legitimate theater, seats were sold on a reserve seat basis, and the *Chicago Post* reported that "there is a new sort of picture audience" that was "quiet, attentive, and very well dressed."[71] At this screening, *Queen Elizabeth* was accompanied by Breil's music. Publicity for the opening emphasized this, declaring: "Special music written by Mr. Joseph Carl Breil with complete orchestration that will play the production to the music of success."[72] Martin Marks recounts, however, that there is little public comment about the score beyond an article in *Music News* that noted that the film was accompanied by a piano. Emphasizing the ongoing importance of music to drama, the review states that Breil's "especial score" is

> of great elaborateness as well as being accurately descriptive to the most minute detail. At Powers [theatre in Chicago] it is given with piano only but even in this attenuated shape it shows marvelous care on the part of the composer, and the movement of the play is followed very accurately.
>
> There is considerable "leit motif" used, and the stress and accent of the music follows the line of the story in surprising degree. . . . Between the parts of the play a young woman, wearing a Chicago Musical College medal, sings some old English songs very prettily.[73]

We do not know how often Breil's score was used in the screening of the film nor whether lectures, songs, and other forms of entertainment became a habitual part of the show. Beyond this, nothing has been said about how the film "sounded." What is interesting, however, is that Breil emphasized the Wagnerian aspects of his music. According to him, the work was orchestral, dramatic, and dignified, and each principal character in the film was given a motive or theme. The use of music to flesh out the emotions of the actors was developed. As he explains:

> I realized at once that trivial music would not do, and set to work to write a score that would portray human emotions from a truly dignified point of view. With the limited means of a small orchestra put at my disposal then, I set to work and wrote a dramatic score built very much upon the motif lines set down by Richard Wagner. That was about six years ago . . . and the score to *Queen Elizabeth* was the first original score ever composed (in the world) for a "movie."[74]

Leaving aside the mistaken claim to *Queen Elizabeth* being the first score ever composed for film (Camille Saint-Saëns and Walter Cleveland Simon preceded Breil), what is interesting is Breil's emphasis upon Wagner. This recalls the youthful group of musicians—*les Jeunes*—who had founded the Société Nationale de Musique in Paris in 1871 on the heels of national defeat in the Franco-Prussian War. Musicians such as César Franck, Jules Massenet, Gabriel Fauré, Charles Gounod, and Saint-Saëns sought to remove themselves from the decadence of Second Empire France and the music with which this was associated, namely Offenbach's operettas and the spectacles of the Opéra. Seeking an intellectual and moral revival in music, the Société sought to incorporate Schumann, Liszt, and Wagner as models, finding inspiration above all in the grand opera of Wagner. When Saint-Saëns left the Société in 1886, concerned with the militant Wagnerism of its younger members, he nevertheless remained committed to the ideal of French musical renewal.[75] We know that Saint-Saëns went on to score the first original music for the Film d'Art's *L'Assassinat de Duc de Guise* in 1908. We know, too, that the theater was being reborn at this time as a more popular, industrial, and accessible pursuit through its links to film. Breil's score for *Queen Elizabeth* fits in here, as an attempt to ensure that music was used in the reform of the theater. Its aim was not merely to accompany film, but to portray, elevate, and dignify emotions. It would seem that the charge of theatricality so often levied at Bernhardt's films ignores the ongoing efforts that were made to ensure the legibility of her gesturing body on screen.

2. *Hamlet*

A Short Film, 1900

In 1900, Bernhardt made her first film, just four years after the Lumière cinematographe was given its official public launch. Part of Paul Decauville's program for the Phono-Cinéma-Théâtre at the Paris Exposition, Bernhardt's film featured the dueling scene of *Hamlet*. She had played (and toured) *Hamlet* successfully on the live stage the previous year. In this way, the film pointed backward just as it pointed forward, to a known theatrical show and to invention, to mechanical mediations that brought with them new ways of presenting and promoting theater. Indeed, with the Phono-Cinéma-Théâtre Bernhardt was recorded by both film and the phonograph (or, to be more precise, by the Lumière cinematographe and Henri Lioret's Idéal phonograph). Both were part of the screenings at the Exposition. While her recorded sound consisted only of the sound of clashing swords, it is important to realize that Bernhardt was presented to audiences as a theatrically polymorphous body. Live musicians, the phonograph, and hand-colored film all contributed to Decauville's initiative and hence to *Hamlet*. In my opinion, the Phono-Cinéma-Théâtre was not, however, just a spectacular technological event. It was a theatrical and performative event, referencing and using the traditions of the live stage. Indeed, insofar as it relied on the coming together of theatrical performers, live musicians, and visual and acoustical effects at a single event that might be repeated but could never be duplicated, it referenced the theater. Part of an eclectic program of forty short films, Bernhardt was integrated into a varied program that presumed and even promoted the theater just as it promoted experimentation and change.

Until relatively recently, the Phono-Cinéma-Théâtre has been largely remembered as a failed attempt to join recorded sound to film. Considered a technological experiment in the march toward properly recorded sound, it was not until the Pordenone Silent Film Festival projected a restored copy of this initiative in 2012 that we were able to properly consider the richness of the project. As Laurent Mannoni notes in the accompanying catalog:

> Phono-Cinéma-Théâtre is an attraction which mingles several different genres: sound films synchronized with the phonograph (songs, monologues, extracts from plays), but also dances and pantomimes which were simply accompanied by a pianist or orchestra. There was also a sound effects man and possibly also a bonimenteur (narrator).[1]

In this chapter, I focus on Bernhardt's appearance in *Hamlet* as a case study and so shift attention away from the overall program itself. I nevertheless keep a focus on the program's mix of genres, entertainments, and technologies. It is my belief that even within a single film we might unpack different genres and entertainments while also acknowledging the changes that film brought to these. Indeed, *Hamlet* was at once a short vaudeville skit, reference and excerpt of a longer play, as well as evidence of the modern woman who used sport to maintain an athletic and svelte figure. I argue that Bernhardt's short film was therefore a calculated response to the new media and to its possible future. Bernhardt did not just adapt her stage work for the screen; she was a savvy businesswoman aware that cinematized theater could attract new audiences to her.

On the Cusp of a New Century

In 1900, Bernhardt was an internationally renowned star. She had recently toured America, Australia, and most of Europe. She had performed in an array of venues before audiences who often did not understand French. She was consequently uniquely Parisian and famously worldly. She was also a patron of the arts and a woman who was engaged in her own commercial reproduction. The fact that Bernhardt extended this reproduction to film is telling, since it draws attention away from the idea that she was a stage actress who belatedly (and mistakenly) came to film with the release of *La Dame aux Camélias* in 1911. Her *Hamlet* also draws attention back to a transitory moment that bridged the nineteenth and twentieth centuries. As the official guide for the Exposition would explain, the Exposition was both "the synthesis of the century that has finished, the beacon of the dawn of the twentieth century."[2]

That cinema was part of this vision of a possible future (and was therefore still very much an experimental undertaking), indicates the extent to which Bernhardt continued to engage with new cultural and technological developments. As Emmanuelle Toulet explains in her article, "Cinema at the Universal Exposition, Paris, 1900," the Phono-Cinéma-Théâtre joined other experiments in film such as the Lumière Giant Cinématographe and Gaston Manceaux-Duchemin's Animated Voyages. Although these undertakings met with little success when compared to the success of other spectacles at the Exposition—Decauville's receipts did not, for example, cover costs while The Hall of Illusions (in which a play of light was reflected in a huge hexagonal room) was visited by 2,772,600 people[3]—the appearance of film at the Exposition was important. Characterizing its appearance as a "parenthesis without immediate consequence, an episode both glorious and marginal"[4] Toulet explains:

> It was glorious because of the official recognition that it brought to the role of the Lumière brothers and their invention; because of the individual spectacles, new and varied, that appeared there; and because of the vast and varied public that it attracted. Nevertheless, at the same time, it was marginal. After the event had run its course, the palace and pavilions were, for the most part, destroyed and the center of a momentarily transfigured Paris was returned to its previous state.[5]

I argue that Bernhardt's *Hamlet* at the Phono-Cinéma-Théâtre is Toulet's parenthesis in microcosm. This was an episode without immediate consequence yet an episode that was both glorious and marginal. It was glorious because it formed part of the first major publicization of an art form that would, in its later development, join sound with action, performance with technology, the star with an international audience. On the other hand, Bernhardt's *Hamlet* was marginal because it was but a film contained within a program of many other short feature films. It was also an attraction at the Exposition that did not boast huge crowds. As I mentioned earlier, it was also later characterized as a failed experiment in recorded and synchronized sound.[6]

The Phono-Cinéma-Théâtre's slippage between terms—marginality and centrality, the past and the future, a local public and an international audience—is linked to the fact that it was Léopold and Georges Maurice, the sons of Clément Maurice (the projectionist of the first public Lumière showings at the Grand Café in 1896) who served as projectionists for the program.[7] A family that is famously associated with film "proper" yet who was involved in a project that drew upon the live theater, Léopold and Georges Maurice make explicit the productive exchange between theater and film. As Laurent Mannoni has recently explained, although the Phono-Cinéma-Théâtre company was dissolved on November 26, 1901, the show continued in Paris and toured Switzerland, Sweden, Spain, Germany, Austria, and Italy during

1901–1902.[8] It is in this spirit of exchange that *Hamlet* represents a turning point: it is an image of the past (the legitimate stage of the nineteenth century) as well as a conjecture about what it might become (cinematized theater that circulates globally). The cinema that *Hamlet* anticipates is, I argue, a cinema that celebrates the agency of theatrical performance as well as the blurring of artistic, social, and sometimes even national boundaries.

Posing for the Poster

The posters used to promote the Phono-Cinéma-Théâtre advertise the blurring of acting and film, performance and reproduction. In these, we see a woman facing forward, her right hand pointing a cane diagonally downward and her left hand holding aloft an unfurled banner. The banner lists featured performers. In one poster (reproduced on the cover of David Robinson's *Music of the Shadows: The Use of Musical Accompaniment with Silent Films* and included in Toulet's article), the woman leans on the cinématographe and the cane points down to a phonograph that rests besides her feet (see figure 2.1). We read that Bernhardt is the opening attraction, followed by the likes of M. COQUELIN Aîne, M. Victor MAUREL *de l'Opéra Comique*, Mme. REICHENBERG *de la Comédie Française*, and Mme. RÉJANE.[9] As the names and titles suggest, this is a program that not only joined the stage star to reproductive media, but that drew upon the range of spectacles available to contemporary audiences (the boulevard theater, the classical theater, the variety theater, the circus, and the opera).

In another poster, reproduced in Georges Sadoul's *Histoire générale du cinéma*, the phonograph and cinématographe are absent and the woman leans instead against a wooden sideboard. Again, she points, cane in hand, to a list of feature attractions. Bernhardt is here listed in bold, providing final climax to FOOTIT et CHOCOLAT, COSSIRA, Melle. Félicia MALLET, LITTLE TICH, POLIN, and COQUELIN AINE.[10] In both posters, the woman, costume, and cane remain identical.

While these advertisements foreground Bernhardt's participation in the Phono-Cinéma-Théâtre, it is the woman depicted on the poster who best illustrates Bernhardt's importance. This figure, with pointed black shoes, yellow dress, rounded feathered hat, and diagonally held cane, is identical to François Flameng's *Portrait of Sarah Bernhardt as Tosca*. Reproduced in Sotheby's 1995 *Arcade Auction Catalogue of Old Master and 19th Century European Painting, Drawing and Sculpture*, Flameng's image is dated 1908.[11] Whether this is wrongly dated or is a later reproduction that capitalizes on Flameng's earlier image (he is, after all, the artist who designed the poster) is unclear. What is certain, however, is that contemporary audiences, familiar with the visual cues of Bernhardt's *Tosca*, could identify the actress and the role. As Gerda Taranow explains in *Sarah Bernhardt: The Art within the Legend*, Tosca is the first role in which Bernhardt uses a cane.[12] This prop is accordingly foregrounded in sketches and paintings of the actress.[13]

Figure 2.1. *Phono-Cinéma-Théâtre programme*, 1900. David Robinson, private collection.

Bernhardt's pointed shoes and dress in the advertisement similarly coincide with descriptions of Bernhardt's appearance in *Tosca*. As *Le Figaro* states in its review of Bernhardt's *La Tosca*:

> From her head to her toes, it is a century that, on the stage, walks before us. There is no detail that is indifferent and the shoes are as important as the costume. . . . Everything, from the pointed Empire shoes in green satin embroidered by palm leaves to the mix of black Peking satin and yellow is impeccably authentic.[14]

Depicted in the advertisement as Floria Tosca who introduces herself as Hamlet in the program, Bernhardt highlights the performativity of the proposed show. As La Tosca, Bernhardt also highlights the importance of sound, her cane pointing diagonally downward to the phonograph at her feet (see figure 2.2). Clearly, the Phono-Cinéma-Théâtre was an intermedial attraction

Figure 2.2. *Phono-Cinéma-Théâtre* poster, 1900. Cinémathèque Française.

that presented the actress's capacity to expand and develop our perception of theatrical "play."

The Talking Pictures

What is significant about the poster for the Phono-Cinéma-Théâtre is that, from any number of roles, Bernhardt is depicted as Floria Tosca. Tosca, an Italian opera singer, was a figure created by playwright Victorien Sardou in a work expressly written for Bernhardt and first performed in Paris in November 1887. In this context, Bernhardt is pointing back to her own fame as an actress with a *voix d'or* (golden voice) since it was this that encouraged Sardou to write a play in which she incarnated an opera singer. As Sardou knew, Bernhardt's voice was so famous that she was early engaged by the phonograph industry. For example, in December 1880, on her first tour of North America, Bernhardt was recorded on Edison's tin foil phonograph. In 1896 she made two cylinders for Gianni Bettini in New York. Although she would go on to make many more recordings, Bernhardt was unusual in introducing both recorded sound and the recorded image to an international public. The use of Bernhardt to appear as Tosca to publicize the Phono-Cinéma-Théâtre was also topical: *Tosca* had only recently been brought by Puccini to the operatic stage (Puccini's *Tosca* debuted in January 1900). Past and present as well as sound and image are thereby brought together in Bernhardt who gestures toward a list of recorded performances.

This focus on a list of familiar performances suggests that the Decauville's program (like Bernhardt's *Tosca* earlier) is legible to a broad and international audience. Sliding between categories—Tosca was Italian but performed by a French actress, an opera diva characterized in terms of dramatic gesture, and a figure from the eighteenth century introduced to the nineteenth century—Bernhardt expands her mediation of the phonograph, cinematograph, and live performance to other terms and categories. As a play whose climax is the moment in which Tosca watches her lover die, unwittingly believing that his death was being staged, Bernhardt similarly indicates the possibility of an exchange between the real and the represented, the event and the performance. This, in turn, suggests that the films presented by the Phono-Cinéma-Théâtre might be equivalent (if not more spectacular) to the theatrical productions of the plays themselves.

Changing the Cast

This slippage between terms and emphasis on the spectacular and performative nature of film is highlighted by the way the poster presents Bernhardt as an Italian diva introducing herself cross-dressed as Hamlet, the Danish Prince. This was not *Lorenzaccio*, the Florentine Hamlet of Alfred de Musset, where Bernhardt initiated the new acting category of the *premier travesti rôle*.[15] Nor, too, was it *l'Aiglon*, the "white Hamlet" of Edmond Rostand, which was enjoying enormous success after its debut on March 15, 1900. Instead, it was the "black Hamlet" of William Shakespeare. Opening at the Théâtre Sarah Bernhardt on May 20, 1899, and commissioned by Bernhardt herself, this play demonstrates the control Bernhardt held as manager, producer, and actress in her own theater. As Taranow relays:

> In her capacity as producer, Bernhardt requested Marcel Schwob and Eugène Morand to prepare a new translation of the play. When she performed the Schwob-Morand text, she was the first in the French theatre ever to have offered the public a translation rather than an adaptation of Shakespeare's tragedy. . . . Gone were the rhyming alexandrine couplets used in the stage adaptations that preceded the Bernhardt Hamlet, and gone were the alterations in plot that had characterized theatrical adaptations of Hamlet since 1879. In place of previous adaptations was a prose translation based upon scholarly sources in English, French, and German, and presented with so few excisions that the performed text was fuller than any of those used by then contemporary English Hamlets.[16]

It is interesting to note that the Ghost, the grave-diggers, the players, and the fencing match had appeared in French versions of *Hamlet* only within the preceding fifty years, and that it was not until 1886 that Hamlet would first die on the French stage.[17] What must be attenuated, therefore, is the very originality of Bernhardt's commission. Not dictated by questions of decorum and sensibility (which had seen the exclusion of these scenes) and based on an unadapted English text, Bernhardt's *Hamlet* is best conceived as an intervention, if not a challenge, to French classical drama. Evidently, while Bernhardt as Tosca was endorsing a spectacular cinema, she was doing so conscious of the polemical and political nature of spectacle and performance. She was also conscious of her own importance to this role and its interpretation: Decauville might have given her a context in which to show, but it was Bernhardt who determined the play, her role, and the moment that was to be seen and filmed.

Speaking Strangely

Although the phonographic cylinders for the Phono-Cinéma-Théâtre's *Hamlet* consisted only of the clashing of swords, it is significant that Decauville's program challenged the sounding of film in much the same manner that Bernhardt's staged *Hamlet* challenged the "sounding" of the stage. A dual challenge might therefore be heard: on the one hand there was the assumption that sound (and recorded sound) was part of theatrical performance, and on the other there was a refusal of the literary form that usually defined the classical couplet. It is therefore fitting that it is Bernhardt as Tosca, an excessive and expressive opera singer, who introduces herself as Hamlet in the Phono-Cinéma-Théâtre's program. This was a forum in which the actress continued to develop and extend both her polymorphous body and what we might expect of the theater.

In his introduction to *Hamlet*, Schwob explains that his aim was to capture the flavor and imagery of Shakespeare's language. His removal of the rhyming alexandrine couplets was based on linguistic criteria and textual analysis alone.[18] Schwob's discussion contains, however, evidence of another theatrical challenge: surveying the pre-Shakespearean accounts of the play, he argues that Shakespeare used a 1570 French translation by François de Belleforest of a thirteenth-century Saxo Grammaticus chronicle as inspiration for his *Hamlet*.[19] As Romy Heylen notes in *Translation, Poetics, and the Stage: Six French Hamlets*, this positing of Old French literary models and practices as antecedents to Shakespeare's text reclaimed *Hamlet* not only philologically but culturally as well.[20] In an effort to preserve meaning and form, Schwob and Morand also translate *Hamlet* into the language of the period corresponding to the source text—they provide, in effect, a historical French equivalent of Elizabethan English. They insert into this allusions to late fifteenth-, sixteenth-, and early-seventeenth-century French literature. Heylen states that they

> seemed to be attempting to reappropriate (at least in part) *La Tragique Histoire d'Hamlet* back into the native, oral tradition whence they believed it came. . . . Although they "historicized" the linguistic and textual/narrative material of the source text, they decided to "naturalize" all space and culture-bound elements in Shakespeare's dramatic text, thus striking a blow for French literary imperialism.[21]

It is within the context of these claims that the reception of Bernhardt's play abroad can be situated. While advance tickets of the production would sell so rapidly in London that the number of performances jumped from eight to sixteen, and while the prices at the Adelphi Theatre (and later in New York) would be unusually high,[22] criticisms were nevertheless directed at the French prose. Exemplary of these is a review in the London *Times* which, while recognizing that Schwob and Morand had provided Bernhardt with an "entirely new version of the play," noted further: "Of course their prose sounds bald after the magic phrasing and the musical glamour of

Shakespeare's lines. There is even a touch of the ludicrous to the English ears in such a matter-of-fact rendering."[23]

John Hansen, writing in the American *National Magazine*, levies the same criticism. He states:

> To an English ear accustomed to the flow of Shakespeare's verse the prose version sounds rough, unadorned and insufficient, not to say ridiculous, in spots where the rendering is particularly matter-of-fact, as, for example, "The funeral baked meats did solidly furnish forth the marriage tables," converted into "Le roti des funerailles a été servi froid aux tables de noces." But the expression, bordering upon farce comedy, is born where Hamlet exclaims in the play scene: "Wormwood! Wormwood!" which the Frenchman turned into a cry of "Absinthe! Absinthe!"[24]

Schwob and Morand were not ignorant of cultural context. Predicting such a response, they explain:

> We translated old mole by *vieille taupe* and *wormwood* by *absinthe*. To the English imagination, these words conjure up the Boulevard, its cafés, and its passers-by. But in French literature, thank God, a mole remains a mole and *absinthe* a bitter herb . . . In a few years when apéritifs will no longer be fashionable and when our argot will have changed, even in England, *taupe* and *absinthe* will accurately convey what they are supposed to represent *sub specie aeternitatis*.[25]

Referencing a play whose language brought attention to French theatrical tradition and whose very script refused Shakespeare authorship of *Hamlet*, Bernhardt's film underscored the importance of sound to any theatrical production. In my view, the Phono-Cinéma-Théâtre was less an experiment in sound than confirmation of the centrality of music and voice to theatrical performance.

Filming a Fragment

Schwob and Morand's fidelity to François de Belleforest's translated text resulted in an extremely long play. Indeed, the French première ran for over five hours. Although 885 lines and three tableaux were cut for the London production, reviewers still relay how "the wag in the gallery who whistled 'We won't go home till morning' during the last entr'acte was felt to have neatly expressed the feeling of the house."[26] This length enabled the inclusion of scenes never seen on the French stage (i.e., the dumb show)[27] while it also reveals the time it took to arrange the elaborate scenography on stage.

As Taranow explains, the production "required more shifts of scenery than any of the elaborately designed spectacles that Sardou had written for Sarah Bernhardt."[28]

In this context, Bernhardt's film is a veritable interval: at once part of a series of short films, it is also a section of its larger, staged "whole." Perhaps more importantly, the film presents—in compressed form—visible evidence of the challenge Bernhardt's *Hamlet* levied at the traditional performance of the play. Relevant here is the fact that Bernhardt's film not only staged Hamlet's death, but provided document to Bernhardt's introduction of the standing death.[29] This death, itself a reference to Bernhardt's famous elaborations of deaths on the Boulevard stage, was later featured in Bernhardt's longer running narrative films *Camille* and *Queen Elizabeth*. Here, the Phono-Cinéma-Théâtre was again poised between past and future: allusion to a projected cinema, it was also witness to Bernhardt's stage practices.

Manufacturing Meaning

It is within the context of *Hamlet* providing introduction to a spectacularly conceived narrative cinema that the filming of the duel scene might be considered. This scene, it should be remembered, contains both the sword fight and Hamlet's death. Taranow contextualizes:

> [Bernhardt] approached Hamlet from a background of two traditions—classicism and the Boulevard—and undoubtedly recognized that although Shakespeare's dramaturgy had points of contact with both, it had greater affinities with the popular tradition of the Boulevard. While the soliloquies of the Prince of Denmark could satisfy any classicist who savoured the tirades of Corneille and Racine, the Ghost, the mad scene, the grave yard scene, the fencing match, and the death scene must have seemed like indigenous fare to audiences at the Théâter Historique where the Dumas-Meurice Hamlet was performed in 1847 and to those at the Porte Saint-Martin where the Cressonnois-Samson Hamlet was performed in 1886.[30]

As with her standing death, Bernhardt's performance of this "indigenous fare" stood in contrast to the customs of the legitimate stage. Struck by the venom on Laertes's sword, Bernhardt relays the physical effect of her wound with her back to the camera/audience. This reiterates and literalizes Bernhardt's turn from stage tradition (where performers traditionally faced the audience).[31]

Bernhardt's turn from tradition is also evident in her eschewal of Hamlet's traditional hat and plume. While in the stage production of *Hamlet* Bernhardt was costumed in a hat and a blonde Fechterian wig, it is the absence of the black plume that warrants attention. As Taranow, again describing the stage production, explains:

> The most significant aspect of the hat was that it lacked, intentionally, that signature of Hamletism which was inextricably associated with the graveyard scene: the black plume. Sarah Bernhardt's entire production can be regarded as a repudiation of the hamletic Prince of Delacroix, Manet, Baudelaire, Laforgue, Mallarmé, and Mounet-Sully, the absence of the black plume represented a literary and theatrical statement. The unadorned hat announced boldly that this Hamlet was liberated from the delicacy, pallor, pessimism, and irresolution which characterized the young Prince of Hamletism.[32]

It can be suggested that the absence of the hat on the film represents a negation of the romantic Hamlet's presence. In other words, Bernhardt's Hamlet is unable even to carry the plume: his turn from tradition is resolute, final. This turning from tradition is reinforced by the way in which Bernhardt's image overlaps with the fashionable figure of the dandy. Indeed, her visible and thin legs, plumeless hat, and pageboy haircut visually intersected with this new category of masculine identity.

The liberation of Hamlet from his traditional characterization as an irresolute, melancholy prince, paralleled the changes in the Schwob-Morand text. Bernhardt's performance was a translation: it challenged what had been traditionally presented on the stage, and its difference was ascribed national characteristics. For some, this represented a change for the better. Clement Scott, drama critic for the *Daily Telegraph*, describes Bernhardt's Hamlet as one of the "best" (with the Briton, Charles Fletcher) since she displayed "that dominant note of comedy, that rare vein of humor, that eccentric capriciousness which are in the very veins of Hamlet." Scott continues: "I begin to think, on the whole, that the French temperament is better for the play of Hamlet as acted before an audience than the philosophical German, the passionate Italian, the alert American, or the phlegmatic Englishman."[33] The French *Annales du Théâtre* similarly speaks of Bernhardt's performance in terms of a "tour de force."[34] In England, however, Bernhardt's Hamlet was regarded as "little less than an invasion of national property,"[35] a "gain for the French stage—not English."[36] It was suggested that "the ardent, ambitious, and marvellous artist may be congratulated on her energy and her pluck, and upon the financial result of an experiment in trading upon English sheepishness and ignorance of and contempt for art."[37] John Hansen contextualizes:

> As Paris differs from London so does Madame Bernhardt's Hamlet differ from Shakespeare's as it is understood by the English mind. . . . The chief point of attack in Madam Bernhardt's performance, judged by British standards, is a

> lack of proper philosophical melancholy, the critic forgetting that whereas the northman would say "To be or not to be" with tears in his voice, the southman utters the same sentiment with the same wondering heartache, but with a smile on his lips. Few outside France understand the French smile or French philosophy, and certainly one could hardly expect a Londoner to comprehend a Hamlet brooding over the why and wherefore of creation unless he punctuated his reflections with lugubrious tears and sighs. Therefore, the British critics while admitting Bernhardt's poetic, forceful, magnetic impersonation accuse her of frivolity in her conception of the part, of creating "a pleasant, humorous, very gay prince, who in happier circumstances would have been the life and soul of the court," to quote one high dramatic authority present at that important first night in London.[38]

Like Schwob and Morand before her, Bernhardt defended and rationalized the changes she introduced to the production. In a letter to the editor of the *Daily Telegraph* on June 16, 1899, she responds:

> I am reproached for being too lively. . . . I know that Hamlet is a scholar. . . . I am reproached for not being stunned and frightened enough when I see the ghost;[39] but Hamlet went expressly to see the ghost, he went looking for it. . . . I am reproached for not being courteous enough to Polonius; but Shakespeare makes Hamlet say all sorts of stupidities to Polonius. . . . I am reproached for getting too close to the king in the chapel scene; but if Hamlet wishes to kill the king, it would be necessary for him to get close to him.[40]

Anglo-Saxon critics, castigating Bernhardt for her lack of restraint, tied this to her "southern origins." They also suggest that Bernhardt, as the star performer, was unable to properly relay the subtlety of Hamlet's character. Referring to the attention Bernhardt drew upon herself as Hamlet, Hansen notes that "Ophelia flits in and out of Hamlet's life a pathetic shadow—no more; in fact all the other people are reduced to subsidiary themes woven about the grand motive of a star part."[41] More vitriolically, *Atheneum* comments: "It is a French euphemism, which we have to a certain extent localized, to speak of an actor as 'creating' a role. A juster or apter term would be manufacturing."[42] Bernhardt is cast as a foreign (and female) intrusion into an established art form. Implicit in this criticism is the idea that the actress, in her encroaching age, was unable to appreciate what was appropriate to the stage.

That excess was an interpretative tool used by Bernhardt to render dramatic character and to justify narrative development is overlooked. That Bernhardt (as the producer, principal director, and performer of Hamlet) was also representative of emergent twentieth-century feminism (that would go on to claim the right to self-representation and the right to interpret things "differently") is similarly overlooked. Hence, just as Bernhardt has been largely excluded from film history, so too has her acting been denied its productive meanings.

Staging the Scene

Bernhardt's decision to stage and film a play that boasted a long history indicates the extent to which she was prepared to take on the role of female antagonist. Even the choice of theatrical role (she chose, for instance, to perform Hamlet and not Ophelia) demonstrates Bernhardt's awareness that she was at once producer, director, and actor, and so very much involved in the interpretation and presentation of a theatrical spectacle. As Silvia Bigliazzi explains, "Hamlet is both actor and director, he is the first stage presence with an acute awareness of what it means to be staged."[43] This awareness was articulated in the scene Bernhardt chose to record on film. Hamlet's fight with Laertes is, after all, a staged and performed fight, one that differs from Shakespeare's other duels—Edgar and Edmund in *King Lear*, Roderigo and Cassio in *Othello*, and Macduff and Macbeth in *Macbeth*. The bout is therefore introduced in the following manner: "His majesty . . . sends to know *if your pleasure holds to play* with Laertes"; "The queen desires you to use some gentle courtesy to Laertes before you fall to a *play*"; "I . . . will this brother's wager frankly *play*."[44] Even when the duel threatens to become "real" (i.e., Hamlet realizes the sword is poisoned), the tragedy is still contained within reference to its spectacular and dramatic nature: "[G]ive order that these bodies / *High on stage be placed for viewing*"; "[B]ear Hamlet, like a soldier, *to the stage*."[45] As Lisa Hopkins explains: "One of the primary effects of this insistent emphasis is to link this exhibition of fencing skills less with the anger-driven fights of the other tragedies than with the play-within-the-play of Hamlet itself . . . the staged rather than impromptu quality of the duel underscores a motif already very markedly present in the play: of the fragility of the line separating illusion from reality."[46]

Filming Fencing

This interconnection between illusion and reality is also implicit in the film's status as excerpt to a longer play and document to a live performance. As a film that features a fencing duel, *Hamlet* similarly oscillates between narrative performance and sporting display (see figure 2.3). Hopkins, addressing the status of the fencing duel on the stage, notes it is "specifically conceived of as a largely academic exercise of skill, designed to test the combatants and, incidentally, to provide a show of spectacular entertainment suitable

Figure 2.3. *Bernhardt in Hamlet*, Phono-Cinéma-Théâtre, Gaumont Pathé Archives.

for the amusement of the courtly audience (and, by implication, for the real one too)."[47] Since the film does not include any other scenes and the Queen and King (Hamlet's attendant audience) are absent from view, *Hamlet*'s duel was one which presumes the engagement of a watching public. This focus upon the fencing match, particularly in the context of a female protagonist, indicates the extent to which Bernhardt engaged in (and predicted) contemporary social trends.

By the mid-1880s in Paris, the display of fencing skills was a fashionable undertaking. Or, rather, fencing was fashionable for those "belles mondaines" with the money and leisure to pursue it. An article in *La Vie Parisienne* in 1884, which detailed the sport's burgeoning popularity, explained that fencing reduced weight while it also provided a form of emancipation from traditional "feminine" pursuits:

> The practice of different sports each day becomes more of a female Parisian custom. Their physique and their self-esteem are equally accounted for; the habit of exercise, especially masculine exercise, helps to put them in "good form," to make them more seductive. It is, at the same time, for them a sort of emancipation.

Of all the sports, the most favoured by our *belle mondaines* after horse riding is fencing. Nothing, in effect, is more efficient in combating this modern sickness of neurosis which they all more or less suffer, for accentuating the elegance of a slender waist, or for reducing the exaggerated opulence of the bodice. And then there is the vest, this provocative vest, a delicious cross-dress which is a thousand times more varied in cut and more becoming that the abominable "tank tops" of the beach, its tightness allowing the pretty woman to effortlessly appear in all her serpentine grace while she fences with agility.[48]

While Bernhardt's thinness had earlier prompted caustic comment, especially in the anti-Semitic press, by 1900 this was harbinger to a movement that would see increased attention paid to the smallness and suppleness of the female body. That Bernhardt would wear a midthigh-length tunic in the film—and Pierre Magnier, as Laertes, a knee-length coat—is illustrative of this shift in the conception of the female figure. At a time when female costumes were, however, still often ankle-length, the exposure of Bernhardt's legs was hardly innocent. As Taranow remarks: "Bernhardt's costume appears to have remained the same throughout the play, with the length of her tunic extending only to midthigh so that her figure would seem elongated by the exposure of her legs."[49]

What is also interesting is that the article in *La Vie Parisienne* finds "serpentine grace" desirable and travesti dress "delicious." Again, this indicates changes in the approach to the female form, since these were earlier considered transgressive. It also positions Bernhardt as a progenitor of female trends. Explaining that fencing was first introduced via the actress on the stage, the actress becomes representative of a fashionable avant-garde.[50] That Bernhardt was clearly part of this avant-garde—her fame was associated with her thinness, her tendriled art nouveau curves, and that she fenced on the stage—is often overlooked. Particularly in film history, where she is characterized as a theatrical anachronism, Bernhardt's challenge to the nineteenth century remains absent from discussion.

By the turn of the century (and thus in conjunction with *Hamlet*'s appearance), popular women's presses would be detailing the availability of fencing classes in Paris. Fencing was also available to working-class women. This parallels the idea that the staging of Hamlet's duel and subsequent death was "indigenous fare." The popular French journal, *Femina*, discussed the joining of fencing classes with the dance and music classes offered at "Mimi Pinson's School" in Paris:

Everyone now knows the Charity of Mimi Pinson. Founded in 1900, thanks to the initiative and tenacity of M. Gustave Charpentier, the famous composer of music, this initially proposed to offer theatre seats to the female workers of Paris thanks to some particular donations and to the graciousness of the theatre directors. But, since this, the aim has been enlarged and M. Charpentier has founded for the young female workers of our great Paris popular classes in music and dance to which, two months ago, was added fencing lessons. . . . He had first dreamt of gymnastics, but the delicate body of the female does not generally accommodate its brusque and uncoordinated movements well. These violent and strong exercises tend not only to deform women's slender proportions, but provoke all sorts of physical disorders, dizziness, flutters of the heart etc."[51]

This practice of female fencing—and its accompanying rhetoric—was not unique to Paris alone. An article in *Harper's Bazaar* (appearing in 1900 and entitled "Fencing as an Exercise for Women"), explains:

> Time was when this most graceful and healthful of exercises was confined entirely to the sterner sex. Now all this has changed. The fashionable woman of today is quite as expert with foils as is her brother or husband. . . . A man is usually satisfied to do one thing well: not so a woman. She must have various accomplishments. Its main value is in charm of person and grace of motion. . . . Fencing gives a natural poise and grace to the body. . . . It makes the body supple and sinuous. . . . So important is good judgement that fencing by experts has often been claimed to be more the work of the head than of the hands.[52]

Stressing the body's sinuous charm, this article indicates that it is the female body that incarnates the tendrils and curves of art nouveau. Further, the association of fencing as an activity of the mind as much as the body provides echo to Bernhardt's characterization of Hamlet as an active yet reflective youth.

An oscillation between the two terms—"Hamlet play" and "female fencing display"—is evident in the attention paid to the details of the duel on the film. While Bernhardt wore gloves, she had no protection on her trunk, face, or head, and thereby held to the theatrical tradition of performing the match in a costume suited to the needs of the stage. Bernhardt also did not use her cloak as a defensive alternative to the dagger but instead employed it as a costume embellishment.[53] At the same time, however, we can see the coincidence of her actions with the etiquette of the sport of fencing. As Taranow states:

> Although stage fights tend to depart substantially from the formal rule of fencing, the match in the Bernhardt *Hamlet* adhered with far more usual fidelity to prescriptive fencing regulations. What occurs at the opening of the match is

> an abbreviated version of the grand salute. . . . The opponents enter from opposite sides of the stage. . . . They cross, salute the King and Queen . . . return to their original positions, salute the King and Queen again, then turn and, face to face, salute each other . . .[54]

Transvestite Theater

The crossing of boundaries between the play and female "play" was not received favorably in the press. In criticism of Bernhardt's apparent inability to sustain her performance of masculinity on the stage, *North American Review* states: "[T]here is no moment in the drama when the spectator is not fully and calmly conscious that the hero is a woman masquerading, or is jarred into sharp realization of the fact by her doing something that is very like a man. It is a case where every approach to success is merely another insistence on failure."[55] Almost but not quite: Max Beerbohm—the drama critic of *Saturday Review*—accordingly entitles his review of the play "Hamlet: Princess of Denmark."[56] *Atheneum* explains that "It is a full-blown truism to say that where everything is necessarily wrong nothing can possibly be right. Madame Bernhardt's Hamlet has not even the negative advantage of showing us what to avoid. . . . The suggestion of *Punch*—offered, of course, as badinage—that Sir Henry Irving shall play Ophelia to the new Hamlet, seems, beside the present experiment, not wholly outrageous."[57]

These reviews ignore the idea that Bernhardt might have sought to keep her gender visible to the watching public. What they also elide is that, in emphasizing the performativity of gender, Bernhardt was also associating herself with a long and productive history of the theatrical stage. From the ancient Greek theater and the public theater of the English Renaissance through to the roles essayed by such women as Charlotte Cushman in the mid-nineteenth century, cross-dressing was an integral part of the theatrical stage. Involving both men and women, cross-dressing was a visible custom that unsettled gender, as a social and cultural norm, in a public and open manner. This disruption highlights the challenge that the theater brought to its audience. Although entertaining and providing popular relief from quotidian life, the theater also undercut and disrupted the categories that structured normative reality. The theater's status as an art form, which dealt with the problem of representation and reenactment, was therefore joined to a critique of the constructed and artificial nature of reality. Bernhardt's "failed" *Hamlet*, introduced by a loud and self-publicizing Tosca, works to unsettle the natural transparency of social and cultural categories.

The criticisms of Bernhardt's performance of masculinity were carried into her performance of youth. John Hansen reviewed *Hamlet* in *National Magazine* in 1899:

> Physically Bernhardt's unusual lines of figure proved of assistance in rendering her impersonation sexless if not altogether masculine. Even now, with a contour rounded out considerably since the days when the supreme dramatic genius of our times was better known to the American public, Bernhardt, costumed in the traditional sables of the Dane, does not belie the part by strong suggestion of femininity except facially; there she comes up against a stumbling block—that elderly unique face, haunting at any time, becomes a nightmare, a specter in opposition to her faithful simulation of a youth's body.[58]

Bernhardt responded to these criticisms by explaining why and how she essayed Hamlet. In an article published in *Harpers Bazaar* entitled "Men's Roles as Played by Women,"[59] Bernhardt contends that male roles were more difficult to perform than female roles and that it was this challenge that prompted her to perform *l'Aiglon* and *Hamlet.* Going on to argue that performativity is not a specifically female prerogative, she reminded her public of the constructed nature of both genders:

> Much of the success of the usual woman's role lies in the feminine charm and magnetism with which the actress is capable of investing the part. It is contended that in assuming a man's role she is obliged to part with her strongest weapons, and that therefore more skill is required to achieve success. This is only partially true. Skill is undoubtedly demanded, but it is the skill which can assume and depict the masculine charm and magnetism which exists just as surely as does the feminine. It is not sufficient to look the man, to move like a man, and to speak like a man. The actress must think and feel like a man, to receive impressions as a man, and to exert that innate something which, for want of a better word, we call magnetism, just as a man unconsciously exerts it.[60]

Fencing Films

Bernhardt's film not only directs attention to sport and to Bernhardt's choice of a theatrical role. It also illustrates a practice common to the popular theater, where duels were a recognized genre of entertainment and were one of the ways in which touring actors exhibited themselves or gave encores. This practice emerged in the 1840s, as variety theaters spread across Europe and America and legitimate actors appeared in music halls or vaudeville, performing their known duels. As David Mayer explains in his article "*Fights of Nations* and National Fights," few people anywhere saw complete performances of Shakespeare plays; Shakespeare was generally known only in excerpts. Literature confirms this: as Mayer notes, Mark Twain parodies the practice of presenting Shakespeare as an excerpted duel in his novel *Huckleberry Finn.* Hence, when Huck and Jim meet the con men–rogues "the King" and "the Duke" they decide, at one point, to make money and gull rural hicks. They put on a play *The Royal Nonesuch* in which they perform "the Duel from *Richard III*" and bash at each other with improvised swords.[61]

The arrival of film saw these duels become part of the film segment of the music hall and vaudeville program. While Mayer discusses Billy Bitzer's Biograph film, *Fights of Nations* (1907), as an example of a film that brings at least four dueling episodes from the variety stage to screen (the film is comprised of six dueling episodes), he also mentions that filmed excerpts of a duel could help promote the theater. Hence, Biograph's *Duel Scene "By Right of Sword"* (A. E. Weed, 1904) was an excerpt that was filmed eleven days ahead of the performance of Arthur Marchmont's play *By Right of Sword* in New York. Bernhardt's filmed duel does not promote a forthcoming appearance in Hamlet; as I noted earlier, the play preceded the film. Instead, the film confirms her awareness that a popular audience might be familiar with the duel as a theatrical genre. Furthermore, Bernhardt's film is both part of a program specific to the Phono-Cinéma-Théâtre and part of a filmic genre that includes *Fights of Nations* and *Duel Scene "By Right of Sword"* as well as other fencing films such as *A Gypsy Duel* (Biograph, 1904).[62]

Other short dueling films help to illustrate the contextual complexity of Bernhardt's *Hamlet*. For example, the short film *Duel in Macbeth* (Biograph, 1905) is one of the six episodes contained in the film mentioned earlier, *Fights of Nations. Duel in Macbeth* showcased the noted English actor Frank Benson who was on tour in America when the film was made. Revealing that film was indeed used to promote theatrical plays and that Shakespearean duels were part of the variety film program, the film also indicates that filmed duels worked their way into longer film formats. Although Bernhardt's *Hamlet* is specific to the Phono-Cinéma-Théâtre, it would be misleading to completely separate it from the later development of the cinema.[63]

Courting the Challenge

As Bernhardt's demand for intellectual challenge makes clear, her performance of Hamlet levied a broad critique at the roles that were available for women to play on the stage. When she states: "Most women's parts are mere play. The characters are required to look pretty, to move gracefully, and to portray emotions natural to the average woman,"[64] Bernhardt makes clear the changes and challenges she was introducing to the stage. That these changes and challenges would, after the turn of the century, be incorporated into the demands of an emergent feminism reveals the importance a performer such as Bernhardt played in the development and formation of twentieth-century feminist thought. As Susan A. Glenn explains:

> As a figure of transition between traditional and modern values, Bernhardt constitutes . . . a perfect starting point for understanding how the theatre helped Americans explore and redefine femininity in the years between 1880 and 1910. At a time when actresses and female performers exhibited the unorthodox and increasingly fashionable qualities that would come to be associated with women's revolt against tradition, Bernhardt proved to be a highly elastic symbol of female irreverence. Because of that, she became a touchstone for a number of ambitious American women in as well as outside the theatre: from female comics in vaudeville to activists in the woman suffrage movement.[65]

While Glenn restricts her comments to the stage and an American public, the effects of Bernhardt's transgressions were felt across the arts and before a broad and international audience. What needs to be emphasized, therefore, is that Bernhardt's *Hamlet* was part of an international event that suggested some of the possible futures for film. It was, in other words, a forum that enabled experimentation. Film, yet to make a claim to its uniqueness and separation from other media and art forms, was still very much a new technology that incorporated and projected different ways of looking at and thinking about the world. The theater, directly involved in the marketing and production of film, was yet to be separated as an art form whose established traditions retarded or at least suspended the "natural" development of the filmic medium. The phonograph, only just beginning to be sold as a leisure pursuit, was not yet part of the history of private entertainment. In other words, Bernhardt's belief that she could participate in the cinema had not yet been marginalized as a theatrical and mistaken intrusion into the development of film. My task as a historian is not just to recuperate Bernhardt's contribution to the Paris Exposition. It is to ask that we explore and appreciate the liberties that the Phono-Cinéma-Théâtre once offered.

3. *Camille*

The Ladies of the Camellias

La Dame aux Camélias was a film made by the French Film d'Art in late 1911 and released to French, American, and English audiences in early 1912. With a length of 2,275 feet, it ran for roughly forty minutes. In America, Canada, and Mexico, it was released as *Camille* and sold with Madame Réjane's *Mme. Sans-Gêne* on a states' rights basis as part of a double bill. As a two-page advertisement in *Moving Picture World* announced, the program was a "Complete Evening's Entertainment of About Two and One Half Hours, Presenting the Divine Sarah, the World Renowned Emotional Actress, and Mme. Rejane, the Famous French Comedienne, at Their Best."[1] While other feature films had preceded this double bill in America, the impact of this program cannot be ignored.[2] Not only was it rare for an actress of Sarah Bernhardt's caliber to appear on film, it also was rare for a film to be marketed to a middle-class audience as an evening's entertainment. *Camille* was therefore at the forefront of two related movements. It helped to expand the filmgoing public to include women and a more traditional theatergoing audience while it also offered a respected theatrical venue and program for an entertainment that had been largely associated with short films, the mass public, and the variety stage.

Camille not only helped expand the demographic of the filmgoing audience, it also enabled spectators from around the globe to watch the same actress in the same film almost simultaneously. This was an achievement that the live theater could never enjoy. While the theater furnished the actresses and their "original company," film cinematized them, making their theater a product that was widely available. In my view, the French art nouveau movement is evident here, in this circulation and celebration of French cultural achievement as an industrial and commercial product that could be enjoyed and integrated by a global audience into their daily life. Indeed, with Bernhardt at its helm, cinematized theater became an art nouveau product par excellence. It joined other French art nouveau products (the theater, costume, furniture, and so on), expanding French presence and visibility abroad. *Camille* also expressed the tendriled curving lines of the art nouveau spiral in Bernhardt's physical acting. Indeed, the fact that Bernhardt's famous death scene remains intact in the film is important. We see Armand enter her bedroom, their final embrace, and Bernhardt spiral to her death with a white gown billowing around her. Even after she has come to a standstill—when she is stretched out dead on the floor—her legs are encased in a swath of twisting material (see figures 3.1–3.3).

The taste for art nouveau in late-nineteenth-century France emerged hand in hand with the growing availability and taste for Japanese arts and crafts, particularly the Ukiyo-e print, with its curved lines and undulating forms. In this context, I argue that Bernhardt's use of the spiral in physical action and her taste for oriental colors and objects (the yellow of her Tosca costume discussed in Chapter 2, her use of the umbrella and the fan, for example) is also evidence of the broader impact that *japonisme* was having on the fine arts in France. With film, Bernhardt brought *japonisme* into new circulation: she animated the colors, composition, and bold form of the Ukiyo-e print (developed by artists such as Claude Monet, Vincent van Gogh, and Edgar Degas in the preceding decades),[3] bringing its turns and spiraling costumes back afresh onto and into the reproduced and globally circulating print. I consequently argue that the different classes, generations, and national audiences that celebrate *Camille* are proof of Bernhardt's international fame just as they are evidence of her capacity to realize and express popular taste. While we cannot argue that *japonisme* was at the forefront of Bernhardt's mind when she made *Camille*, I nevertheless identify it as a style that is articulated on her film.

We must understand, as her contemporaries certainly did, that in 1911 Bernhardt not only had contemporary tastes and styles to negotiate. She was in her late sixties and suffering from the pain that would cause her right leg to be amputated in 1915. At this point, if Bernhardt had to stand or walk in performances, she did so with the help of props or cast members. As Forest Izard states in his 1915 book, *Heroines of the Modern Stage*:

> In 1912 she made a visit to America, playing—as before and since in London—in the vaudeville theatres short scenes from her former successes. There were circumstances in her acting that puzzled the beholders. She would take a fixed position and maintain it for long periods. When she moved across the stage, it was usually with another's support. . . . As time went on she gradually modified

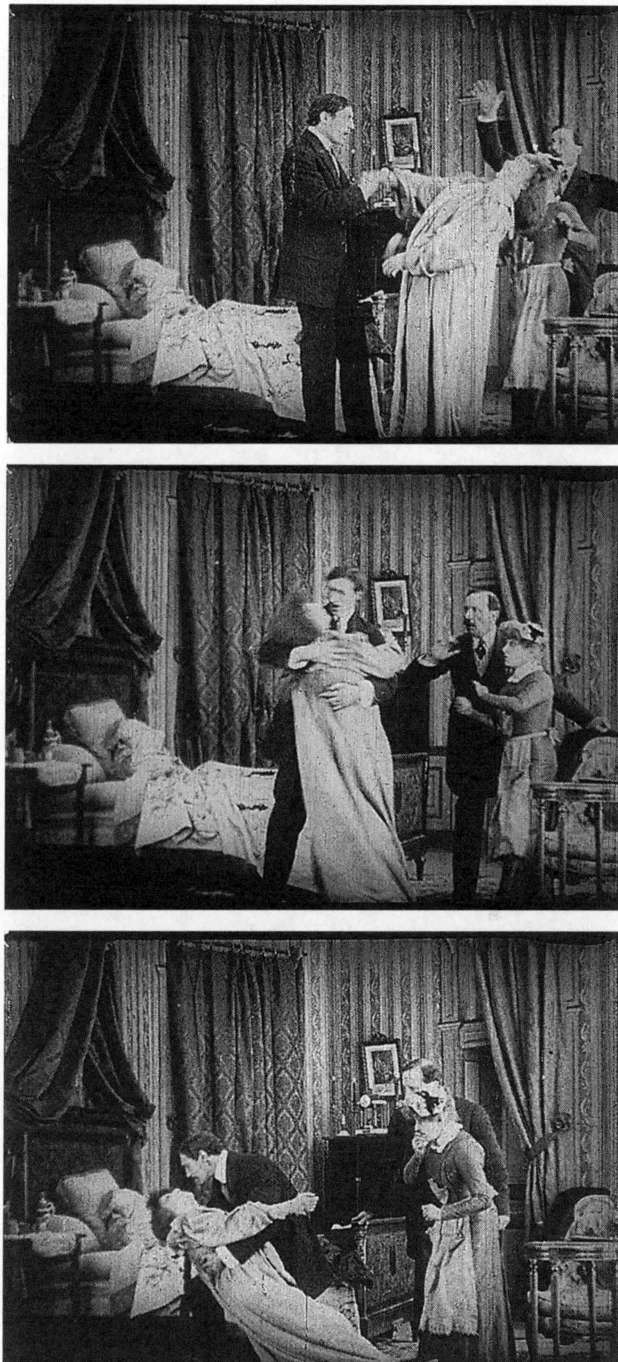

Figures 3.1–3.3. Bernhardt spirals to her death, *Camille*, 1911. National Film and Sound Archive of Australia.

> the business of her parts—and even had plays written to suit her limitations, as in *Le Procès de Jeanne d'Arc*, in which she stood in court all during one act and in another remained seated at the side of her bed.[4]

Camille therefore made the impossible possible since it allowed Bernhardt to present a longer theatrical work to an audience. She could include acts that had otherwise been eliminated from her live stage performances. Film also allowed her to travel and engage people she could never physically meet. As I will explain, *Camille* therefore ensured that Bernhardt maintained and even developed her international fame at a point in her life when she was older, physically weaker, and less able to sustain the rigors of a full-length theatrical show.

Was *Camille*, consequently, a substitute for live performance? Was it a record of the action she would otherwise perform, had she the assistance and time to move between scenes and sets? It was not. As I argue in my introduction, Bernhardt's film presented theater cinematized. It was a spectacle that was very different from what was seen (and heard) on the live stage. Indeed, at a time in which Bernhardt had isolated *Camille* into a single death scene on the music hall and vaudeville stage, her film instead presented a developed narrative. Action was not, however, the Dumas play that she had performed since she first adopted the role of Marguerite on her first tour to North America in 1880. Rather, *Camille* adapted and changed the speed, structure, and meaning of her live play. As I will demonstrate, *Camille* referenced the theater but was not the theater: audiences could watch *Camille* as a unique product, one that created a coherent and engaging narrative in and of itself.

La Dame aux Camélias

Camille was based upon the scandalous mid-nineteenth-century novel, *La Dame aux Camélias*, by Alexandre Dumas fils about a prostitute (Marguerite Gautier) who dies of consumption. The story was familiar to most people at the opening of the twentieth century. Briefly, what Dumas recounts in his novel is a tale of a woman with a past who is ill and who falls in love with a young man (Armand Duval). Armand is from a rich and established Parisian family. Deciding to relinquish her work, Marguerite abandons her paying lovers and moves into a country house in Bougival with Armand. She secretly sells her possessions in order to maintain their modest lifestyle. When Armand discovers this he asks his lawyer to transfer his income to Marguerite. The lawyer informs Armand's father, Duval Sr., who is concerned about the social implications this relationship will have for his family. Concerned particularly for his daughter (who is engaged) he asks his son to leave

Marguerite. Unsuccessful, Duval then meets Marguerite alone. Explaining to her that she will irreparably harm Armand's future were she to remain with him, he explains that the decency of his family is at stake. His daughter, engaged to a desirable suitor, will lose thc possibility of a respectable marriage if Armand does not cut all contact with Marguerite. An ex-courtesan—no matter how changed her ways—is not socially acceptable.

Marguerite, responsive to these arguments and seeking redemption from her immoral past, agrees to leave Armand. Writing him a farewell letter, she departs and returns to her life as a courtesan. She is then treated cruelly by Armand. Taking her friend Olympe for his lover, he torments her whenever he meets her. Unable to bear the pain this causes her, and becoming increasingly unwell, Marguerite pleads with him to leave her alone. They enjoy one final night of passion together. Armand is, however, furious that Marguerite is not his own. He cruelly leaves money on the doorstep to pay for her services and goes abroad. Marguerite remains in Paris and slowly dies of consumption. She writes a diary that Armand reads posthumously, where she explains the reason for her actions and the sacrifice she made for him.

It is believed that Marguerite was modeled upon the Parisian courtesan Marie Duplessis who allowed Dumas fils to have an affair with her as an *amant de coeur.* Duplessis died of consumption in 1847, at the age of 23.[5] Dumas published his novel—the most famous of his works and the one that launched his fame—in 1848. When Bernhardt first appeared as Marguerite in London, the *Sunday Times* made this link, stating that "a real woman, Marie Duplessis, is supposed to have supplied the portrait."[6] Later this link between Bernhardt and Marguerite as Dupleissis was more explicitly articulated. When playing at the Coliseum in London in 1913, the London *Times* tells us that before the performance of the death scene "An interesting description of Marie Duplessis, the prototype of Marguerite Gautier, and the way in which she faced death, was thrown on the screen."[7] In the *New York Times* some years later, we are told that Dumas gave Bernhardt the original farewell letter he had written to Marie Duplessis, and that she sent this to Ethel Barrymore as a gesture of support for her performance of *Camille.*[8] Clearly, both English and American audiences were aware of the intertwined histories (both fictional and biographical) that helped maintain popular interest in *Camille* in the early twentieth century. To speak only of a strict novel-to-screen transition is to miss these different and changing ways that Bernhardt's *Camille* was presented, publicized, and interpreted by audiences.

It was the theater, however, that saw *La Dame aux Camélias* reach a wide international public. Adapted for the Théâtre du Vaudeville in 1852, Dumas' original novel became a five-act play that changed the novel's details. In the play, Armand does not enjoy a final night of passion with Marguerite but instead sees her at a gambling party hosted by Olympe. Throwing his winnings at her in contempt, Armand is challenged to a duel by Marguerite's rich new lover, the Baron de Varville. In the final act, we learn that Armand won this duel, that the Baron was wounded in the encounter but survived, and that Duval Sr. seeks Marguerite's forgiveness. When Armand visits Marguerite in her modest bedroom in Paris, having been recalled to Paris through an explanatory letter from his father, he declares his love for Marguerite. Marguerite is, however, on her deathbed. With two friends beside her and Armand crying out her name, she dies.

Dumas' play had a great impact upon French audiences and subsequently on the development of the nineteenth-century theater itself. The realism of Dumas' social drama was considered shocking: Marguerite was a contemporary courtesan, she spoke in ordinary prose, and she was a figure considered socially unacceptable to the French middle class. Moreover, her role was performed so realistically by Eugénie Doche that theater critic Francisque Sarcey would say that she was "to the last breath, a courtesan."[9] Dumas would later make the demimondaine a heartless and deceitful character who uses trickery to marry into a respectable family: in his 1855 play, *Le Demi-Monde*, Suzanne d'Ange is quite different from Marguerite since she is a grasping opportunist. For all these differences, Marguerite nevertheless inaugurates the modern comedy of manners.[10] As an erring woman whose task was to negotiate her difficult relation to society, Marguerite therefore spawned many plays. For example, there is Théodore Barrière and Lambert Thiboust's *Les Filles du Marbe* (*The Marble Maidens*, 1853), where the marble maidens remain motionless when promised fame but come to life when promised money.[11] There is also Émile Augier's *Le Mariage d'Olympe* (1855), which joins *The Marble Maidens* in attacking Dumas' original assumption that a courtesan is capable of noble love.

Most famously, Dumas' play was brought to the operatic stage in Giuseppe Verdi's *La Traviata*, which debuted in Teatro La Fenice in 1853. When the French American Film Company released Bernhardt's film to an American audience in 1912, it drew on this history of the work, explaining that "The story is too well known to need any synopsis. For a generation it has been enjoyed by old and young both in the book form and in Verdi's masterful adaptation known to the operagoers as 'La Traviata.'"[12] While opera was a way to make film respectable and to attract a middle-class audience, it also indicates that *Camille* was part of a history of "masterful adaptations." Rather than filming theater, cinematized theater engages in the opera's own task of adapting literary works and making them newly available to a wider theatergoing public.

The Ladies of the Camellias

A busy history of Anglo-American adaption followed the debut of Dumas' *La Dame aux Camélias* and Verdi's *La Traviata* on the stage. In England, where *La Dame aux Camélias* was censored until 1881 because it "ennobled immoral behavior, glorified harlotry, and profaned the sanctity of death,"[13] it was Bernhardt who introduced the role to audiences on her first tour as a solo artist in 1881. As Sarcey states, until Bernhardt's performance it was "prohibited ground." Sarcey indicates that the censor might still have impacted what he saw on the London stage (reviewing the London performance of the play, he notes that "some scenes had been cut here and there without great damage to the work"). Nevertheless, Sarcey also notes that the play was a chef d'oeuvre, "a cry of passion."[14] This is significant since it was Bernhardt who chose to perform this role on leaving the Comédie Française. Her identity as an actress and as an international celebrity was forever linked to climatic death scenes and to the figure of the beautiful, young, passionate yet noble woman who is a social (and often cultural) outsider.

While *La Dame aux Camélias* was censored until Bernhardt performed it in London, other plays and performances anticipate its introduction to England. These were produced on both the legitimate and popular stages. On the legitimate stage, Helena Modjeska's *Heartsease* was understood to be a weak adaptation of the Dumas play when it was performed in London in 1880 at the Court theater.[15] Sarcey comments on this when he states that the censor had "miserably massacred this work [*La Dame aux Camélias*], of which almost nothing remained."[16] More significantly, *La Traviata* circulated in England on the operatic stage from 1856 onward; this was permitted because the libretto was considered secondary to the music and because few were thought to understand Italian. Verdi's opera was nevertheless translated into English as *La Traviata, or, The Blighted One* in 1857 at the Surrey Theatre since censors presumed that it would be watched only by a restricted, upper-class audience.

The appearance of contemporaneous works on the more popular burlesque stage indicates, however, that a broader audience was engaging with *La Traviata*, and doing this in ways that made fun of the original work. Colin Hazlewood's *The Lost One/La Traviata*, Leicester Silk Buckingham's *The Lady of the Cameleon*, and W. F. Vandervell's *Our Traviata* parodied its characters and narrative. Even if some audience members were indeed from the upper class and therefore familiar with the work in the legitimate theater, others had no knowledge of Italian opera and so responded to the comedy of the burlesque itself. In *The Lady of the Cameleon*, for example, characters play in cross-dress and sport names such as "Vile Letty, a fish seller" (for Violetta, Verdi's Marguerite), "Alfresco, a 'pavement artist'" (for Alfredo Germont, Verdi's Armand Duval), "Gus Stone, a shoe shiner" (for Verdi's Gastone), and "Doleful, a beggar" (for Baron Douphol). This indicates the extent to which Verdi's opera (and, consequently, Dumas' original play) was appropriated and parodied well before it was introduced by Bernhardt to the legitimate English stage.[17]

In America, where there was no Examiner of Plays to block the licensing of *La Dame aux Camélias*, Dumas' work was first played by Jean Davenport in September 1853. Adapted from the French, it was newly entitled *Camille, or the Fate of a Coquette*.[18] Davenport became famous for introducing "English proprieties" to the role. Her Marguerite did not have the same impact, however, that Matilda Heron enjoyed when she appeared in her own translation of the role just two years later in 1855.[19] Heron went on to tour America with the play until well into the mid-1860s. She became so famous for her interpretation that she became the reference point for subsequent American actresses playing *Camille*.[20] Celebrated for the "startlingly realistic" way she performed the emotional anguish and physical illness of Marguerite, Heron inaugurated "the social sensational drama" in America with this role.[21] Heron was also famous for her capacity to engage an audience. As Merle L. Perkins describes in an article about Heron as Marguerite, "Her mood was contagious. Women sobbed and cried, and men were not ashamed to weep."[22] When Clara Morris adopted the role of Marguerite in 1876, she relied on Heron's interpretation of the play.[23] As a journalist would later note, Morris was "a woman who had immense resources of an intangible and unnatural sort, who does not reach the hearts of her hearers, but plays madly upon their animalism, the human sympathies and emotions with a wizard touch of spiritualism which is almost demonic."[24]

In New York, two generations of actresses had therefore essayed the role of Marguerite by the time Bernhardt performed the *La Dame aux Camélias* in 1880. We are consequently told that *Camille* was "known almost by rote to most playgoers in the Metropolis who can count a score of years."[25] Unlike London, where the history of Marguerite's appearance on the stage was tied to Doche's initial appearance in the role, Bernhardt was compared to her popular American predecessors.[26] Actresses such as Matilda Heron and Clara Morris provided points of comparison. It was therefore explained that "(t)he hollow cough of the consumptive heroine [used in their performances] was not one of the marked features of "La Dame aux Camélias" last night, and in the death-bed scene the actress did not awaken horror, as well as pity, among the audience."[27] Later, this point is repeated: "The last scene was quiet and pathetic; as has been already said, the actress did not rely upon physical suffering to gain sympathy, the cough was infrequent, and the fall by the window, a favourite piece of business with former Camilles, was omitted altogether."[28] Acting "without hysterical gasps for breath or any display of violent emotion" Bernhardt performed a "beautiful and memorable piece of art, and at the close of the act [in which she renounces her love for Armand] Mlle Bernhardt was three times summoned forward by the cheers of the audience."[29]

The frequency with which Bernhardt was recalled by an enthusiastic New York audience indicates the success of her performance. Action within scenes was even interrupted: after Bernhardt's parting with Armand we are told that the audience "interrupted the play, and thrice recalled the actress." Even without these interruptions, the entr'actes were said to be unusually long and the play "not finished until a late hour."[30] This indicates that Bernhardt was not merely launching a successful career after leaving the Comédie Française; she was successfully engaging an upper-class audience and challenging interpretations of Marguerite on the American stage. Her acting was described in terms of its variety, womanly passion, sincerity, and sensuous emotion. Performing in French, presenting productions that ran longer than normal, and celebrated by a wealthy, established class of people who watched with "scarcely a dry eye in the house," Bernhardt used *Camille* to develop her identity as an empathetic and emotionally engaging actress.[31] With Bernhardt, Americans saw "an idealization of the character, and yet it is not felt to be to any point unreal." Her Marguerite eclipsed all of her predecessors with "a charm so completely its own, and a beauty so winning and expressive, that it is almost impossible to compare its effect with that of any other acting."[32]

In both the English and American Bernhardt productions, all dialogue was kept to its original French and tickets were relatively expensive. This indicates that Bernhardt was publicized and received as a highbrow French attraction.[33] Even at this point, however—and almost thirty years after the play's debut in France—the London *Times* would state that "it says much for the advance of the spirit of toleration on our own stage that even in its foreign dress the play should be presentable at an English theater."[34] In America, similar sentiments had already been voiced. As Grace Greenwood stated in an 1875 discussion of the play, Marguerite was a role unsuited to "any true English or American woman, pure and loyal. It is a contradiction, an anomaly, a moral monstrosity."[35] As late as 1905, the *New York Times* still speaks of "the dubious ethics involved in the familiar Dumas play."[36] Bernhardt might adopt a literary and theatrical role and claim it as her own, but the celebrity she achieved is far more nuanced than the "legitimacy" she has today come to represent.

Playing Differently

While debate about the morality of *Camille* continued, Bernhardt's debut in this role also mentioned the novelty of her performance. At its opening in London, *The Times* would note how

> Mdlle. Bernhardt introduces a curious novelty. She dies standing. Madame Doche, whose name is identified with the part of Marguerite, was accustomed to sink down upon a couch and die holding her lover's hand, but Mdlle. Bernhardt remains standing till the last, and falls forward upon the bosom of her lover, who, with a cry of alarm, lays her down straight and stiff upon the floor. It may be presumed that Mdlle. Bernhardt has fortified herself with some physiological authority for this unusual action.[37]

Relevant to Bernhardt's reception in London is also the reference made to Doche: the thirty years in which the burlesque, operatic, and even legitimate stage in England had re-presented and reworked Dumas' play are ignored, or at least elided.

I mentioned earlier how Bernhardt incarnates the art nouveau tendril, basing her actions around the spiral. The "curious novelty" that the London *Times* reflects upon is not just Bernhardt's fall to the floor, but the spiraling way in which this was achieved. Francisque Sarcey, reporting on Bernhardt's London performances to a French public, explains more fully:

> Mme Bernhardt stands—it is the movement imprinted, stamped in the [theatrical] program—but instead of sitting herself down again for her last words, and murmuring them seated, as was the tradition, she remains standing, breathing life in with all the strength of her being, defying death. Then, using herself as a pivot, she reels and makes a half-turn and, as if finally vanquished, she falls from her height in the most elegant and poetic pose imaginable.[38]

What this introduces is a visual motif that, as much as Bernhardt's musical voice, determines the meaning and impact of her performance. Indeed, while Sarcey describes Bernhardt's proficiency in sounding cantilenas, saying that she modulated her voice in certain passages so that it arrives like far-off music, he also gave great attention to the youth, variety, and energy of her physical performance.[39] What he details is not a languishing woman but one who refuses performative conventions. Even in 1894, after fourteen years of playing the role on the stage, reviewers would note that "She has changed the whole stage business, working out the story with new methods. . . . Sarah is progressive."[40] In this context, Bernhardt's spiraling fall becomes a reminder that art nouveau was not merely a decorative visual style associated with the tendril and curving lines, but a structuring device in theatrical performance that represented youth and a possible departure from traditions.

Maguerite for the Masses

Bernhardt continued to play Marguerite into the 1880s and 1890s. A bill of play for London's Lyceum Theatre in March 1889 lists the full five acts of *La Dame aux Camélias* and Bernhardt's husband, the Greek aristocrat Aristides Damala, as the actor who played beside her as Armand Duval (see figure 3.4).[41]

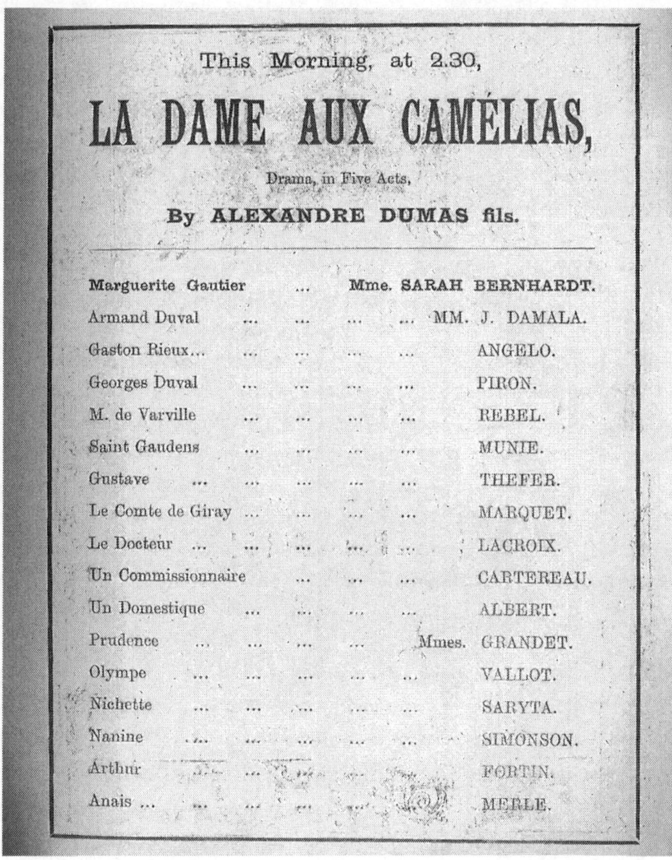

This Morning, at 2.30,

LA DAME AUX CAMÉLIAS,

Drama, in Five Acts,

By ALEXANDRE DUMAS fils.

Marguerite Gautier ...	Mme. SARAH BERNHARDT.
Armand Duval	MM. J. DAMALA.
Gaston Rieux...	ANGELO.
Georges Duval	PIRON.
M. de Varville	REBEL.
Saint Gaudens	MUNIE.
Gustave	THEFER.
Le Comte de Giray	MARQUET.
Le Docteur	LACROIX.
Un Commissionnaire	CARTEREAU.
Un Domestique	ALBERT.
Prudence	Mmes. GRANDET.
Olympe	VALLOT.
Nichette	SARYTA.
Nanine	SIMONSON.
Arthur	FORTIN.
Anais	MERLE.

Figure 3.4. Inside of Lyceum playbill, March 8, 1889. Author's own.

By this point, however, interest in Bernhardt's play was also due to the fact that she was playing alongside a husband who was twelve years her junior.[42] Damala died in 1889 from an overdose of morphine. In 1901, exactly twenty years after Bernhardt first essayed the role on the English stage, the *Times* describes Bernhardt's performance as "an affair of solemn ritual."[43] In 1902, *Atheneum* repeats this sentiment when it states that "Madame Bernhardt is going through a round of the characters in which she is constantly seen. Her appearances as Marguerite Gautier and Fedora are always welcome, but are so familiar that no further word remains to be said concerning them."[44]

While Bernhardt's *Camille* was increasingly familiar as a spectacle on the international stage, it was also regarded as a popular form of entertainment. Although generally described in terms of charm and idealization, her most outspoken Anglo-Saxon critic—George Bernard Shaw, a staunch advocate of a more "natural" and restrained form of acting—found her performance of Marguerite in the 1890s sensationalist. The occasion that gave rise to his comments was the famous competition between Bernhardt and her contemporary, the Italian actress Eleonora Duse. In a well-publicized duel between the two in 1895, they played *La Dame aux Camélias* and Hermann Sudermann's *Heimat* against one another at Daly's Theatre and Drury Lane, London. On this occasion, Shaw wrote an often-cited comparison of the two performances, stating:

> In "La Dame aux Camélias" . . . it is easy for an intense actress [Bernhardt] to harrow us with her sorrows and paroxysms of phthisis, leaving us with a liberal pennyworth of sensation, not fundamentally distinguishable from that offered by a public execution, or any other evil in which we still take hideous delight. As different from this as light from darkness is the method of the actress who shows us how human sorrow can express itself only in its appeal for the sympathy it needs, whilst striving by strong endurance to shield others from the infection of its torment. That is the charm of Duse's interpretation of the stage poem of Marguerite Gauthier. . . . Duse's range includes these moral high notes . . . [so] that her compass . . . immeasurably dwarfs the poor octave and a half on which Sarah Bernhardt plays such pretty canzonets and stirring marches.[45]

Shaw's horror at the lowbrow and spectacular nature of Bernhardt's Marguerite had, perhaps, some foundation. We know that a more popular audience in America was given access, in this same period, to Bernhardt's Marguerite in variety performances. An 1897 advertisement for a Saturday program of shows at the Jefferson Theater (Charlottesville) listed, for example, Bernhardt as the key attraction in a program that included shadowography and "Jean Duval and company" arranging a series of *tableaux vivants*.[46] The variety spectacle presented short acts that enabled audience members to see such diverse performances as a harpist, contralto, and violinist as well as Bernhardt in the final scene of *Camille*. As the climatic act of the play this was a logical choice: love, suffering, and death were all contained within the one scene. Even without knowledge of the play, action was therefore legible. This legibility was reinforced by the fact that the act remains unnamed and unnumbered. Character names alone indicate, therefore, the scene to be played. Reduced to the one finale, Bernhardt is a climatic endpoint to a variety program. Indeed, on both the Saturday matinee and Saturday evening bill, she is listed as the last act. While I do not know if similar programs were played contemporaneously in England, Shaw's comments suggest that already (well before she entered the music hall or vaudeville), Bernhardt was considered an engaging and popular act.[47]

In the opening years of the twentieth century Bernhardt continued to play *Camille* in its entirety to audiences in established venues. A booklet for a performance of *La Dame aux Camélias* at the Théâtre Sarah Bernhardt in Paris 1908 provides the bill for the play and includes a description of each act. Here, we are told that in the fifth act Marguerite dies "in the arms of her lover."[48] Action that was once considered original has thus been written into the play itself. Moreover, the booklet states that Bernhardt "aroused the enthusiasm of the crowds of all races, who were captivated and delighted" by her Marguerite.[49] The foreignness that Bernhardt represented as an actress who performed abroad became part of her appeal for audiences in Paris.

In America, particularly on her 1905 tour when she was in contract with Lee Shubert, who had declared independence from the theater syndicate, Bernhardt was forced to play in a variety of different venues. First appearing in the Lyric Theatre in New York (this was then leased by the Shubert brothers),[50] she was forced into more popular and unusual venues. As Stephen M. Archer explains in his article "E Pluribus Unum: *Bernhardt's 1905–1906 Farewell Tour*," Bernhardt performed "in several miserable venues: conventional halls, skating rinks, a combined swimming pool–auditorium in Tampa, a summer theatre five miles outside Little Rock, [and] a boathouse in St. John, Missouri."[51] Because of the difficulty in engaging theaters, Bernhardt also had a special tent constructed for her performances. Although enabling a large audience of 6,000, this presented problems of its own:

> Reports suggested that after the tent filled no one past the tenth row could hear a word, and those who could hear did not understand French. After a time, patrons in the rear tired of pantomime and began to invent other means of amusement, filling the air with peanuts and paper wads. Some of the audience

began to abuse the actors, bedlam broke loose, and police were called in to quiet the audience during a halt in performance.[52]

The venues in which Bernhardt performed in England also indicate her growing popular appeal. As an article in the *Manchester Guardian* in 1910 explained, discussing Bernhardt's possible engagement in the music hall:

> The salary is tempting . . . but then to act at a place where the curtain that falls on one's performance is covered with advertisements—how very undignified! And to have the passion of Phèdre or Adrienne Lecouvreur followed by the antics of the acrobat or the inanities of the Sisters this or the Brothers that, is not it a conjunction somewhat too violent both for the actress and for the ardent lovers of her art who will crowd to see her?[53]

Concluding with the observation that Bernhardt helps foster change in content and audience for the music hall, we are reminded that the music hall "contains in it the seed of some of the most hopeful developments in the future of dramatic art."[54] Some months later Bernhardt did indeed enter the music hall. Paid a wage of £1,000 a week, she appeared alongside the famous comic singer, Yvette Guilbert, as well as with troupes of acrobats and jugglers at the Coliseum in London.[55]

The following year, when Bernhardt performed on the vaudeville stage in America, she became the spokesperson for the effort to legitimate vaudeville as an entertainment industry. Associated today with a bawdry humor, it is important to realize that vaudeville targeted middle- and working-class audiences from 1895 on. It was not, therefore, necessarily a stepping down in terms of the theater and the public she was attracting. Rather, it was a way for Bernhardt to continue to expand her audiences and to ensure circulation in theatrical circuits she might otherwise not have had access to. In other words, the short acts and condensed dramatic excerpts performed before audiences in vaudeville ensured an ongoing cultural relevance while maintaining the entrepreneurial hold she had as a performer in America. As the brochure to Bernhardt's opening at the Majestic Theatre in Chicago, 1911, explained: "She was convinced that to appear at moderate prices was to afford an opportunity of presenting herself to the vast multitude of play lovers to whom, on account of the fees charged for her previous performances here, Bernhardt has been but a glorious name. . . . The progressive policy of vaudeville, of course, made Madame Bernhardt's desire to appear before the great majority possible."[56] While it is realistic to cite financial reasons for Bernhardt's entrance into vaudeville (in vaudeville she could command a weekly salary of $7,000, which was double that of any previous attraction and higher than that commanded on the stage),[57] it must be recognized that a changed theatrical context brought her a new public. Six years later, on her ninth and final tour to America in 1917, Bernhardt abandoned her refusal to appear on bills with blackface artists. She also performed "opposite cockatoo imitating a cornet" at the Brooklyn Academy of Music.[58] These acts, while different from the classical musicians who shared her bill in the 1897 Jefferson program, indicate a capacity to embrace the opportunities that the theater offered her.[59]

From the legitimate stage to the popular stage and on to the music hall, vaudeville, and finally film: by 1912, when Bernhardt released *Camille*, there was a rich history of her playing Marguerite before a global audience in a range of venues. What, then, could film achieve? Certainly, it could not record her performing exactly as she did on the live stage. There are just too many theatrical venues and too many forays into popular theater to realistically presume that, in 1911, Bernhardt saw the legitimate theater as a single point of shared reference for an international public. Moreover, audiences were now long familiar with the role; there was no hint of scandal to motivate audiences to see a play that had been performed for so many years on the live stage. Instead, film ensured that a wider audience had access to Bernhardt as "the foremost living female interpreter of human emotions on the stage."[60] The play remained in her hands an expressive vehicle for theatrical acting. In this context, cinematized theater ensured that the fame of a nineteenth-century actress be given a new lease on life in the early twentieth century. In other words, it was Bernhardt and her performance of character and emotion, rather than Mercanton as film directors (or even the Film d'Art as a commercial undertaking), that prompts a resurgent interest in her play.

Cinematizing *Camille*

The 16-mm print held in the Australian National Film and Sound Archive, Canberra, is the most complete version we have of *Camille*. In this we see evidence that although the film drew upon the narrative of Dumas' original theatrical play, it modified and changed events. In this sense, Bernhardt's cinematized theater was neither a record of the single acts or abbreviated works of *Camille* that Bernhardt was performing on the popular stage nor a complete record of an extant play. Indeed, rather than open with the play's first act (in which Armand and Marguerite meet at a supper party, an episode intended to establish the frivolous world of the demimondaine), we open to a scene in Marguerite's living room. Armand visits but is soon told to leave. To Armand's concern, Count Giray arrives in a horse and carriage as he exits. Upset at his dismissal, Armand rushes to Prudence and writes a letter to Marguerite, explaining that their friendship is over. He then returns to her, begging forgiveness. In the DVD copy of *Camille* available commercially today, the film opens here, at the point where Marguerite is visited by Duval Sr.[61] Although this scene is missing from the more complete National Film and Sound Archive print, this longer print nevertheless includes the preceding scene, where Armand Sr. receives a letter from the father of his daughter's suitor, explaining that Armand is jeopardizing his sister's happiness. It is this letter that Duval Sr. extends to Marguerite when he makes his request that Marguerite leave Armand. In the following scene, Armand discovers Marguerite's departure when, watched at a distance by his father, he reads her farewell letter.[62] Armand subsequently sees Marguerite with the Count of Varville at an evening party at Olympe's house. Misunderstanding her motives for leaving him, he throws his prize money at her. Film action then moves on to the brief scene in which the Count and Armand prepare to settle their differences with a duel and concludes with Armand (at his father's prompting) reconciled with Marguerite as she dies of consumption in his arms.

Changes to *Camille* on film are, I argue, specific to the transposition of theater onto screen. We see, for example, Count Giray arriving at Marguerite's house in horse and cart. Marguerite's life as a demimondaine is thereby relayed not through a party but through the carriage of a client on a street. The fencing scene—only alluded to in the play in the final act through Armand Sr.—is included on film as a performed event. Moreover, we see Bernhardt perform Marguerite from a vantage point impossible to witness in the live theater. While Bernhardt is never in close-up, she is also never filmed at a distance. She is instead always full-bodied and in full frame. We therefore see her dress curving around her legs when she sits with her suitors, we see her pensively reading Armand's letter, we see her writing the farewell letter, and so on: in each scene Bernhardt is not dwarfed by sets but instead uses her entire body to express her emotions. When the set does become significant, it is included to amplify emotion: Bernhardt happily arranges flowers in a vase before Duval Sr. visits her; her body arches backward onto the couch at Olympe's party after Armand's money has been thrown at her. In these moments, the objects around her amplify the emotions she is experiencing, becoming intimate props.

The popular appeal of *Camille* was fast proclaimed. It was advertised with *Mme. Sans-Gêne* by the French American Film Company in America in March, 1912, as "Making New Records for Selling States Rights"[63] and "The Fastest Seller Ever Offered States Rights Buyers."[64] With one Chicago venue having a tiered entrance fee of 10, 15, 25, and 50 cents during the day and 25 and 50 cents after 6 P.M., the film was clearly a "class" event that was available to a wide public.[65] In order to capitalize upon her accessibility, advertisements explained that Bernhardt was the "WORLD'S MOST FAMOUS EMOTIONAL ACTRESS."[66] In other publicity, Dumas' work was also described as an "Emotional World Classic,"[67] a "soul shaking emotional drama,"[68] and an "Emotional Masterpiece."[69] It was Bernhardt's capacity to interpret Marguerite in an engaging and emotional way that was publicized and promoted, and that seems to have driven the film's success in North America: *Camille* was launched as work that gave audiences access to an actress that engaged the passions and made spectators empathize with her character. Previous knowledge of Dumas, or even of the legitimate stage, was evidently not necessary in this pitch to human emotions.

Reviews of Bernhardt's stage acting in *Camille* in 1910, just two years earlier, reiterate her capacity to move audiences. As the *New York Times* explains: "After seeing the French actress at intervals for thirty years in this piece, her acting in it has become as familiar as the sun." Nevertheless, "There were many tears when the final curtain fell, and there was no lack of evidence that the actress had again moved her people as she has done many score times before."[70] In contrast to the image we have in film studies of an out-of-touch, aged, and anachronistic Bernhardt recording her theater for film, I suggest that *Camille* was a popular film that engaged a variety of audiences in an emotional way that characterized her earlier involvement with the vaudeville stage. Indeed, each of Bernhardt's "great scenes" was included in the film. There is "the scene with the elder Duval," "the scene by the card table," and the "death itself."[71]

Camille was famous for the emotions it brought forth, both in Bernhardt's playing and in audience response. As Bernhardt explains, it was the death scene that particularly impacted theatrical audiences since "powerful situations requiring the greatest expenditure of nervous and physical force generally occur in the last acts."[72] Prior to this scene, however, the film also included the scene that one reviewer of her stage performance in 1880 describes: "The intense and terrible agony of the scene with the elder Duval in the third act [that] left scarcely a dry eye in the house." On film, Bernhardt also performed this scene: "The meeting with Armand in the ball-room [that is] always a powerful scene with actors even of ordinary merit." Finally, the film ends with the "quiet and pathetic" death scene, where "the artist did not rely on physical suffering to gain sympathy."[73] In this context, a reviewer's suggestion (in 1901) that the first two acts of the play as well as the fourth (where Armand throws his bank notes in Marguerite's face) be removed so that "the interview with old Duval and the death scene [be] presented as "Popular Selections from *La Dame aux Camélias*" is refused on film.[74]

Rather than replicating the original stage play or presuming prior familiarity with the Dumas narrative, *Camille* focuses on new details in the telling of the Dumas narrative. With close-ups provided of the letter that Duval Sr. receives threatening cancelation of his daughter's marriage and the one Marguerite sends, a renewed focus is given the reasons for the separation between Marguerite and Armand. We clearly understand Marguerite's capitulation to the will of the father, Duval Sr. We clearly see (also in written form) arguments about propriety, social acceptability, and morality presented to a woman who selflessly (and at great personal cost) concedes Duval's argument. Given the concern—particularly in America—about cinematic content and the efforts made to protect "those of limited means" against "the evil influences of obscene and immoral representations,"[75] *Camille* exposes and enacts emotions while presenting a kind of a guarantee for the maintenance of social order. The working classes can enjoy a product that engages them emotionally as spectators but that reinforces the separation of the classes. Reconciled with Armand (and his father) only at the moment of her death, Marguerite does not live to enjoy the social acceptance she is finally granted.

There is evidence that W. Stephen Bush prepared and provided accompanying lectures for the screening of *Camille*. Along with lecture notes on *Madame Sans-Gêne*, together typewritten and selling for one dollar, these were sold as "Lectures on Special Films" and were "limited edition" products that could develop an exhibitor's program. While we do not know what these contained, they were sold alongside three other lectures: "How to put on the passion play," "How to put on the crusaders, or Jerusalem delivered," and "Key and complete lecture on Dante's 'Inferno.'"[76] Clearly, Bush's intent was both commercial and educative. *Camille* might very well have been able to stand as a self-enclosed work that could be seen without prior knowledge of French literature or the legitimate stage, but it might also be discussed, contextualized, and watched as part of a longer program that included the voice of a knowledgeable educator. As Bush explained in a review of the Bernhardt/Réjane double bill (and he is speaking in relation to *Mme. Sans-Gêne*), "the charm and considerable meaning of the story" can otherwise be "lost upon the average audience."[77]

The Fastness of Film

As I noted earlier, the narrative told in *Camille* was a changed version of the longer stage play. Reviews note this: the *New York Dramatic Mirror* indicates, for example, the "picture's art" was compromised in the duel scene because it became a "fragment" and not the depiction of a longer fencing duel. As it explains, the duel scene "may have been cut down to a mere indefinite indication of the end of the duel, to avoid fancied interference of troublesome censors. In this, however, the producers were probably too cautious at the expense of the picture's art."[78] The extent to which these cuts in Bernhardt's work intersect with the demands of censors is difficult to determine. It is clear, however, that *Camille* did not reproduce stage action. The *New York Dramatic Mirror* emphasizes this, stating:

> Fortunately the picture adaptation of *Camille* has been modelled with considerable success after the technique of the photoplay as developed by the experience and genius of those who have led in the growth in this new art. Had the adaptation been merely or even largely a reproduction of the action of the stage play minus the words it must have proved disappointing even with Mme. Bernhardt's great ability and prestige. But this pitfall has been avoided. The story is told by the photoplay method and told quite clearly.[79]

An article in *Motography* reiterates this view, explaining under the heading "Bernhardt and Rejane in Pictures" that "In each case the play has been somewhat revised to meet the requirements of the new conditions under which they are given."[80]

Noted in reviews of *Camille* is not just that theater is adapted to film, but that the speed of action also changes. I mentioned earlier that Bernhardt's live performances were interrupted with applause from the audience. Her entr'actes were also lengthy: reviewers speak of these being "unusually long" and how "the performance was not finished until a late hour."[81] These interruptions were not part of the film. Moreover, physical action on screen was quick. When *Moving Picture World* states, "Someone has said that the pictures fairly crackle with life and send wireless messages to the spectator,"[82] it indicates that the work was legible and that action was immediate and fast. In another discussion, *Moving Picture World* explains how "'Camille' was rehearsed a few times with the watch in order to get it timed right . . . [and] the result is a long series of photographs that are staccato in their expressiveness."[83] Other reviews note the "hurried flight" and "a minute of high tragedy" in the third act of the film, when Bernhardt painfully leaves the house she shares with Armand. This is described as a "precious synthesis."[84] As *Le Cinéma* states: "Rapidly, it unwinds on the screen. The supper; the passion that was born, that blooms; Duval Sr.; the flight [from Paris]; the ball scene; the simple, grand, noble, tragic, death of Marguerite–Sarah Bernhardt, inseparable beings."[85]

Comments about the speed with which narrative action unfolds on screen are not unique to Bernhardt's film. As Armand Bour states in *Le Cinéma* (he is writing in 1918, seven years after the release of *Camille* and so at a point at which the novelty of fast action on screen might have worn off), the spectator of film is party to "a sort of new visual language." Bour states:

> All of a sudden, pfutt! The image disappears. Another replaces it; it takes me to another place, towards some other events. Perfect. I begin to be interested in these new events. After *scarcely a few seconds* pfutt! My spirit is once more violently dragged along another trail.[86]

While the speed of Bernhardt's action is therefore not unusual, the change this represents in terms of Bernhardt's live performance is significant. In order to understand why this is so, we must briefly return to her voice and appreciate its use on the live stage. Bernhardt's voice was—as I explained in my first chapter—considered an important part of her performance. Audiences at the opening of the twentieth century were galvanized by her expressive use of voice. W. B. Yeats, describing Bernhardt's importance to the Irish stage in 1902, therefore explains how

> it was in *Deirdre* that [the Irish National Theatre Company] interested me the most. They showed plenty of inexperience, especially in the minor characters, but it was the first performance I had seen since I understood these things, in which the actors kept still enough to give poetical writing its full effect on the stage. I had imagined such acting, though I had not seen it, and had once asked a dramatic company to let me rehearse them in barrels that they might forget gesture, and have their minds free to think of speech for a while. The barrels, I thought, might be on castors, so that I could shove them about with a pole when the action required it.
>
> The other day I saw Sarah Bernhardt and De Max in *Phèdre*, and understood where Mr Fay, who stage manages the National Theatrical Company, had gone for his model. For long periods the performers would merely stand and pose and I once counted twenty-seven quite slowly before anybody on a fairly well-filled stage moved, as it seemed, so much of an eyelash. The periods of stillness were generally shorter, but I frequently counted seventeen, eighteen, or twenty before there was a movement. I noticed, too, that the gestures had a rhythmic progression. Sarah Bernhardt would keep her hands clasped over, let us say, her right breast for some time, and then move them to the other side, perhaps, lowering her chin till it had touched her hands, and then, after another long stillness, she would unclasp them and hold one out, and so on, not lowering them until she had exhausted all the gestures of uplifted hands. Through one long scene De Max, who was quite as fine, never lifted his hands above his elbow, and it was only when the emotion came to it climax that he raised it to his breast. Beyond them stood a crowd of white-robed men who

> never moved at all, and the whole scene had the nobility of Greek sculpture, and an extraordinary reality and intensity.[87]

Yeats was trying to eliminate action on stage in order to return a lost, common voice to the theater.[88] His comments are useful since he tells us that Bernhardt held a pose in a performance in 1902 for up to 27 seconds as she spoke. What must be remembered, therefore, is that a silently mouthing Bernhardt who moves quickly, rapidly, and is in constant action on film is not equivalent to Bernhardt performing on the live stage.

For Yeats, Bernhardt's voice is a tonic to the mechanical restlessness of industrialization. As statements indicated earlier, however, film is instead "crackling with life," sending "wireless messages," and an industrial product that might even be experienced negatively in terms of the violence of modern life.[89] Other advertisements explain that Bernhardt's film is "AS VIVID AS LIGHTNING."[90] Perhaps more tellingly, her film places the photoplay "in competition on equal terms with the living Stage of Stars."[91] In this context, Bernhardt's *Camille* promotes the actress as a figure that is equivalent yet quite different to the actress on the theatrical stage.

The speed of Bernhardt's acting on screen changes the language used to describe performance. It does not, however, change the attention given to details of physical gesture. Like Victorin Jasset explaining that Charles Le Bargy's performance in the Film d'Art's *The Assassination of the Duke of Guise* (1908) was "a revolution to attentive eyes,"[92] reviewers of *Camille* also highlighted details of Bernhardt's physical movement. The *New York Dramatic Mirror* relays, for example, how Bernhardt "is standing in Armand's embrace with her face hidden from view by her hand drooping and falling like the flower from which Marguerite's sobriquet was derived." The importance of this rising and falling hand, described as "tremendously impressive and convincing," lay in the fact that it condensed narrative meaning into the one gesture.[93] A comment by W. Stephen Bush about the gesture used by Bernhardt to indicate Marguerite's illness in the opening scene of the film similarly illustrates that viewers were attuned to such nuance. Noting (perhaps) the way she wipes her brow when she is seated at home he states: "How subtle is the touch by which she gives us the first hint of the fatal nature of her malady, when the first reel has scarcely begun. This marvellous power in developing the tragic element is finely sustained throughout until it culminates in a veritable triumph of acting in the last scene."[94] When I speak of lost cinematic practices, I also believe that cinematized theater allows me to recuperate this practice of condensing Marguerite's character into small

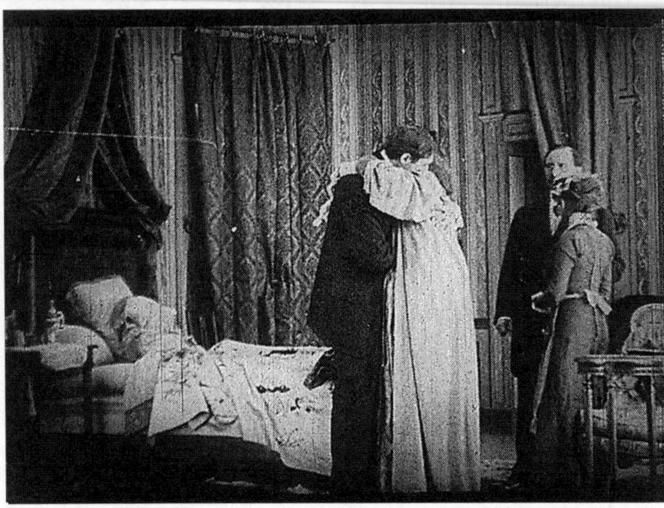

Figure 3.5. Bernhardt waves a white handkerchief on Armand's shoulder, *Camille*, 1911. National Film and Sound Archive of Australia.

gestures (see figure 3.5). Just as nuance was recognized by viewers a century ago, so too can we interpret and elaborate Bernhardt's gestures today.

Commerce and Colonialism

I argue that film engaged a global public, that film adapted live stage action, and that Bernhardt remains a figure who directed how a character was performed and interpreted on screen. The publicity that surrounded *Camille* did, however, change. Unlike the shared trailers, posters, and publicity used in the promotion of film today, in 1912 *Camille* was promoted differently to different national audiences. This might be a simple point to make, but it reminds us of the mobile and changing ways that Bernhardt's film was seen in the early teens and of our tendency today to compact film history into a single narrative of historical reception. Whereas American trade presses focused (as I noted earlier) on the emotional impact and popular accessibility of the film, in France the film remained entitled *La Dame aux Camélias*, was publicized by the Film d'Art, and formed part of a broader national effort to aristocratize the craft industry. A brief comparison between these two campaigns can reveal two separate ways of looking at and interpreting Bernhardt's cinematized theater. While today *Camille* has been consolidated by film historians into a film that features Bernhardt as an aged star of the legitimate stage, when it was launched its audience and meanings were many and mobile.[95]

In America, *Camille* was publicized by the French-American Film Company in New York. Selling states rights to exhibitors, the film confirmed the artistic and commercial ties that joined the two nations. Instead of seeking to elevate film to the level of "art," however, the French American Film Company sought to make film respectable. The criticisms levied by civic reformers in America were therefore forcing change: seeking regulation and censorship of the film industry, moral crusaders had already won much ground. For example, the Illinois Supreme court in 1907 defended its censorship ordinance that required police permits for films shown in nickel and dime theaters with this explanation:

> The ordinance applies to five and ten cent theatres . . . which, on account of the low price of admission, are frequented and patronized by a large number of children, as well as by those of limited means who do not attend the production of plays and dramas given in the regular theatres. The audiences include those classes whose age, education, and situation in life specially entitle them to protection against the evil influences of obscene and immoral representations. The welfare of society demands that every effort of municipal authorities to afford such protection shall be sustained.[96]

Like the publicity that accompanied Bernhardt into vaudeville, the publicity for *Camille* argues that film made art newly available to a mass audience. As one advertisement states, audiences do not have to await "her brief, sensational, immensely costly visits."[97] A double-page spread published in *Moving Picture World* in 1912 declares: "Like the Noonday Sun Alone in Blazing Majesty Giving Light and Life to Art MADAME SARAH Bernhardt Illuminates the whole Motion Picture World Through Her Stupendous Genius Revealed in Her First and Only Photo Play Dumas' Heart-Gripping Drama 'CAMILLE.'"[98] With no mention of the Film d'Art, *La Dame aux Camélias* translated into *Camille*, and the play described as "heart-gripping," attention moves from French art to the American motion picture industry and Bernhardt's international fame. As the advertisement states, Bernhardt was "Illuminating the whole Motion Picture World," "Her Drawing Power is Stronger that that of all Other Stage Stars Combined." A smaller caption, playing upon the well-known fact that Bernhardt was one of the first women to forgo the use of the corset, preferring instead to allow her clothes to turn themselves around the curves of her lean body, stated that she was "taking the nations by storm and making a girdle of her pictured glory around the globe." The informal tone of this statement, directing itself to an audience that was aware of Bernhardt's popularity and her transgressions from social norms, indicates the way in which the film industry was courting respectability while emphasizing the film's continuing popular appeal.

Another advertisement in *Moving Picture World* for *Camille* boasted that

> World Famous Emotional Actress Sarah Bernhardt in "Camille" is the greatest money-making proposition in the history of motion pictures. Her great name is famous in every part of the world. Her art is unsurpassed. Superior to any actress on the stage. She has chosen one of her greatest successes, Dumas' "Camille" which shows every fiber of talent in this wonderful woman . . . you require only a machine and a picture screen in giving a production of merit of the highest class. An entertainment for all classes.[99]

Again, the Film d'Art is absent in the focus given Bernhardt and her international renown. Again, *La Dame aux Camélias* is given its English translation, and once more the affective resonance of Bernhardt's work is highlighted (like Dumas' "heart-gripping drama" in the advertisement discussed earlier, Bernhardt is an "Emotional Actress" who facilitates spectatorial engagement). As with the focus given the "Motion Picture World," Bernhardt is also "World Famous," "famous in every part of the world," and "superior to any actress on the stage." This emphasis on Bernhardt's global marketability guarantees the film industry a broad and popular audience. It also obfuscates the elitist and nationalist claims of the French Film d'Art. Rather than elevating the film to the level of the established arts, Bernhardt's art is "entertainment for all classes," "a production of merit" and the "greatest money-making proposition in the history of the motion pictures."

Bernhardt was not promoted alone. I have explained that in North America she appeared with the French actress Réjane in *Mme. Sans-Gêne* on a double bill. Richard Abel, in *Americanizing the Movies and "Movie-Mad" Audiences, 1910–1914*, has noted that this five-reel package "could be exhibited either as one or in consecutive programs."[100] In this sense, the film was not an isolated product but part of a show that was varied and changing. This variety is implicit in the doubling up of two very well-known French stage stars. Indeed, W. Stephen Bush states that "Madame Réjane is good foil to Sarah Bernhardt, just as Madame Sans Gene is a good foil to Camille."[101] Whereas Réjane is a comedienne known for being "greater in comedy than heroics" and known for playing "the realities of life,"[102] Bernhardt is a tragedienne famous for her sentimental and emotional appeal. Victorien Sardou's play *Madame Sans-Gêne* recounts the story of a laundress to Napoleon who rises to fortune through marriage but who was outcast by him when he fails to recognize her at court. *Camille* tells a far more tragic tale of a woman on the margins of society who did not live to enjoy her reintegration into official (and social) favor. While narrative differs, the two theatrical stars are easily coupled. As a *New York Times* article explained, just a year before Réjane debuted her hugely successful play in America, "Her talent is her own, of self-creation, and it delights the poet, the dreamer, and the gamin. No one but Sara [*sic*] [Bernhardt] so pleases the spectators of the upper gallery, and none enjoy the same control of the fashionables and the men about town. She will be a craze always."[103]

In France, the promotion of *Camille* was very different. The first advertisement for *Camille* that I have found (dated January 6, 1912) features a large photograph of Bernhardt turning left toward the camera, her arm resting casually on her hip. Above this image and directly below a large Film d'Art title is written "SOON *The greatest Artist of the époque*." Below this and in bigger titles is Bernhardt's name, beneath which is written "FOR THE FIRST TIME IN THE CINEMA."[104] Here, we have three assertions: that Bernhardt is an artist, that she is the most important artist of her generation, and that she is in the cinema.

In February, this same Agence Générale Cinématographique at "16, Rue de la Grange-Batelière, Paris," again advertised the release of *Camille*. The film was given a release date ("C'EST LE 8 MARS que paraitra LE FILM D'ART") and linked with French literary renown. Bernhardt is once more shown photographed from the chest upward in the role of Marguerite Gautier, staring pensively off into space. The portrait is captioned, on each side, with two phrases: "La Dame aux Camélias" and "Interprété par Madame Sarah Bernhardt." Beneath this it is explained that the film featured "the most famous drama" and "the most famous artist."[105] Since both player and play are French, the Film d'Art is highlighting its investment in French culture and celebrating the international renown of French artistic enterprise. A handwritten and autographed statement, "It is a great pleasure to be a friend of the film d'art," is also included beneath Bernhardt's portrait. This indicates that Bernhardt is both patron of and participant in film as an artistic enterprise. It also demonstrates that a personal and subjective voice is not lost in the medium's mechanization. In this sense, film is not a record of the theater but instead a new craft medium that (like the more traditional arts) bears the imprint and signature of its maker.[106]

This joining of film with French artisanal supremacy is played out in the advertisements that list the concessions and representatives for *Camille* abroad. For instance, a January 1912 advertisement in *Cinema Journal* states that "La DAME AUX CAMELIAS the Chef d'Oeuvre of Alexandre Dumas fils played by Mme SARAH Bernhardt edited by LE FILM D'ART will be put on Location in the Oriental countries from the 16th of February." Beneath this is listed the "Exclusive Concession" for the Balkans, Turkey, Greece, and Egypt, the "Franchise holders" for Romania, Bulgaria, Serbia, and Montenegro, as well as the "Representatives" for Turkey and Greece.[107] In another advertisement, a two-page spread in *Ciné-Journal* appearing in February, the franchise holders for these same countries (except the Balkans) are again listed.[108] This listing of different locales and countries brings a very literal meaning to the motion pictures. Whereas previously we have noted that Bernhardt sold quickly in America (on a states rights basis), now we can appreciate the film's momentum as a globally circulating product.

The publicity given a uniquely French product circulating commercially abroad underscores Debora Silverman's contention, made in *Art Nouveau in Fin-de-Siècle France*, that the French art nouveau movement is unique within Europe in that it focuses upon a "shared nationalist ethos," which was more about national renewal than it was about a youthful counterculture. As she states: "Rather than seek to democratize art and to recover it for the people, French art nouveau sought to aristocratize the crafts, to extend the hierarchy of the arts to include the artisan. Finally, in the French art nouveau movement a shared nationalist ethos superseded antitraditionalism and generational conflict."[109] Within France, the function of Bernhardt's film thus relates to the traditional arts. G. Dureau accordingly states, in review of Bernhardt's film, that "I said to myself with some pride that . . . millions will see, thanks to the Film d'Art, the most beautiful glory of our French theatre in Dumas' immortal masterpiece."[110] It is also within this context that a 1914 article in *Ciné-Journal*, speaking of the contributions French artists make to film, again relates Bernhardt's performance to the "masterpiece of Alexandre Dumas fils."[111]

Film and Fashion

We know Bernhardt expanded her public through film, and we know that she did this by presenting *Camille* as a new form of cinematized theater. Part of Bernhardt's ongoing success lay in her capacity to join the legitimate theater to its apparent nemesis: to the masses, to silence, to speed, to mechanical reproduction, and to industry. Part of her success also lay, I believe, in her capacity to harness contemporary tastes and fashion. One of these tastes, particularly at the turn of the twentieth century, was *japonisme*. While I do not argue that *japonisme* was a conscious fashion adopted in the making of *Camille*, I argue that along with flowers, decorative interiors, and spiraling art nouveau acting, *japonisme* is a practice that we can identify and see in the film today.

We know that Bernhardt was part of an avant-garde group of artists, collectors, and writers who became obsessed with Japanese pictorial art between

1860 and 1890. She joined Siegfried Bing, Philippe Burty, Édouard Manet, Claude Monet, the de Goncourt brothers, Paul Gauguin, Edgar Degas, Henri Toulouse-Lautrec, and Jules Chéret in absorbing and adapting Japanese art (the Ukiyo-e prints as well as lacquers, bronzes, fan, ceramics) into France. Her taste for this fashion is well documented: in Marie-Désirée Bourgoin's 1879 portrait of Bernhardt painting in her studio, for example, we see Bernhardt painting a model dressed in a kimono, seated before an oriental screen. Even an 1881 portrait of Bernhardt as Marguerite in *La Dame aux Camélias* features her in white period dress resting an oriental umbrella on her right shoulder. Later, in Georges Antoine Rochegrosse's *Portrait of Sarah Bernhardt Reclining in a Chinois Interior* of 1894, Bernhardt is dressed in a colorful kimono-styled gown, lounging upon cushions as she stares back at a group of hanging oriental masks.

By the late nineteenth century the taste for *japonisme* was increasingly popular. Already in 1868, Edmond de Goncourt laments its vulgarization when he complains that "[I]t is now spreading to everything and everyone, even to idiots and middle-class women."[112] W. S. Gilbert and Arthur Sullivan celebrated the spread of *japonisme* in the opening lines of their popular 1885 operetta, *The Mikado*: "If you want to know who we are / We are gentlemen of Japan / On many a vase and jar / On many a screen and fan." Film brought *japonisme* to an even bigger audience. While Japanese subjects were seen in actuality films, they were also implicit in the swirling costumes of some of our most famous early dancers on film. In (most obviously) the films of Loïe Fuller, the female body disappears in a flush of material color. This returns us to the color, costume, and bodies disappearing beneath the layered patterns of the kimono dress so common to Japanese woodblock prints. Bernhardt's death flop in *Camille* physically describes a sinuous turn, recalling the serpentine figures in these prints as well as the spiraling action intrinsic to the Kabuki theater. Again, Bernhardt is not the first person to introduce *japonisme* to film; she is instead one of its most visible, famous, and popular ambassadors.

Although Bernhardt never states that she was indebted to *japonisme* for her choices in costume and movement, her biographer and friend Reynaldo Hahn mentions in his book *La Grande Sarah* how (in contrast to the Chinese) Bernhardt found the Japanese "so artistic, so intelligent."[113] That Japan was esteemed culturally and artistically by the actress is suggested by the fact that Bernhardt met the Japanese actor Otojiro Kawakami in Paris in 1893. Kawakami, a Japanese actor trying to modernize the content and stylization of Kabuki drama in the late nineteenth century, traveled to Paris to study French theater. He wanted to bring some of the best traditions in Western drama to Japan.[114] After seeing Bernhardt perform *La dame aux Camélias*, he met with the actress and decided to translate the play and have it staged as the first Western drama to be adapted for Japanese audiences in that same year.[115] Because of this, we might guess that the most famous play he staged in France and America when he returned to tour with a Japanese troupe in 1899–1900—*The Geisha and the Knight*—was not just a hybrid of Kabuki plays but also had some connection with Bernhardt in the Dumas play.[116]

We know that Kawakami was also innovative in shortening the performance time of Kabuki theater and in making Sada Yacco (who was both his wife and a former geisha of the first rank) a star performer in his troupe.[117] Never before had a woman performed in Kabuki theater, and never before had legitimate Japanese actors performed in the West. Critics in Japan decried Kawakami's experiments while the public in America and France made the "Japanese Players"—and above all, Sada Yacco—a celebrity. Her unfamiliar spiral dancing, her graceful poses, and her lithe curving movements were seen as physical incarnations of the sinuous, curving bodies that decorated imported Japanese curios and prints.[118] When Sada Yacco went to Paris for the 1900 Exposition, she performed in the Théâtre Loïe Fuller and eclipsed the popularity of Fuller herself. As Shelley Berg explains in a discussion of Yacco's tour to France in 1900, Yacco was so popular with audiences that she became "the principal attraction of the Exposition."[119] Berg also explains how Yacco became the embodiment of the art nouveau spirit through her mixing of oriental difference with feminine, organic, floral, and serpentine form.[120]

Bernhardt saw Yacco perform in a special matinee organized in 1900 at the Comédie Française. She also, apparently, appeared disguised at Yacco's performances so that she might develop her own death scene in *L'Aiglon*, which she was playing to great success in Paris at her Théâtre Sarah Bernhardt. Commentators compare the two actresses in their spectacular death scenes, finding in Yacco "death as not even Sarah Bernhardt has shown death."[121] In a photograph taken from the death scene in *The Geisha and the Knight* published in *Le Théâtre* in 1900 we can see the reasons for this comparison.[122] It was not just that the characters in their most famous plays—a geisha and a courtesan dying in the arms of their respective lovers—were similar. It was that Yacco dies in the arms of her lover in much the same way that Bernhardt drops to her death while she is held by Armand. Moreover, Bernhardt was famous for her serpentine form and lithe body, and for turning her back on the audience in performances. While it cannot have been Yacco who influences this choice of movement in the 1880s and 1890s, we might guess that *japonisme* created new ways of seeing and interpreting Bernhardt's engagement with film.

With the help of Fuller, Yacco returned to tour Europe in 1901 to 1902. In 1907, she returned to France for the last time. On this trip, she went with

Kawakami to Auteil, just outside Paris, in order to study the acting methods taught at the Paris Conservatoire. It was in this same year that Bernhardt was made a professor at the Conservatoire; without this she could not be eligible for the cross of the Legion of Honour.[123] Whether the two met or spoke here I do not know. We know, however, that when Yacco and Kawakami returned to Japan in 1908, they opened an actor training school. Yacco went on to stage *La Dame aux Camélias* in Japan. In 1914, three years after Kawakami's death, Yacco also appeared as Tosca—a role explicitly written for Bernhardt—at the Imperial Theatre in Japan. Yacco retired from acting in 1918.[124] As we know, Bernhardt instead involved herself with the film industry. Her *Camille* came on the heels of the craze for Sada Yacco and for things Japanese in France. In this context, I suggest that Bernhardt brought serpentine motion to film and that film, in the new millennia, was important to the meanings and development of the reproduced print.

Open Endings

Bernhardt is neither a lone pioneer nor an eccentric provocateur. She instead works with *Camille* as she had worked on the stage and in the arts more generally, using one art to synthesize and engage others. Our difficulty today in watching *Camille* is not only that visual references are unfamiliar to us, but that we have difficulty in seeing how film diverges from Bernhardt's live performance on the stage. Comments by theorists such as Vachel Lindsay do not help our task: taken literally, they imply that Bernhardt recorded her stage performance when she brought the Dumas play to film. Those who are instead enthusiastic about Bernhardt's film write anonymously in the trade presses or write reviews in the press. The aim of these publications is to encourage audiences to see the work and to promote film to the broadest possible public. The fact that this aim is achieved—*Camille* was a box office hit in America and reached a global public—indicates that Bernhardt did tap new markets and reach new audiences.

What, however, did the public go to see? How did they watch the film? I would guess that only a few went to see a famous theatrical actress speak silently. It is here that *Camille* is of interest to me, because it was the changes brought by cinema that reinvigorated theater for the public. While I concentrate on the most obvious aspects of *Camille*'s appeal—emotional engagement, mechanical speed, and *japonisme*—there are probably other tastes and fashions that can help explain the success of her work. Although *Camille* therefore appears as an open type of text, I do not agree that meanings are endless or that my task as a film historian is playful.

4. *Queen Elizabeth*

A Moving Picture, 1912

Sarah Bernhardt, Adelaide Ristori, Nance O'Neil, Fanny Davenport, Minnie Maddern Fiske, Eleanora Duse, Ellen Terry, and many other actresses of the late nineteenth century worked from a common core of plays by playwrights such as Paolo Giacometti, Shakespeare, Victorien Sardou, Alexandre Dumas fils, and Edmond Rostand, some of them introducing new dramas into the repertoire (as with Sardou and Bernhardt), but all of them holding a number of roles in common. Of all these great diva actresses, only Bernhardt was sufficiently adventurous, daring to put elements of this repertoire before the camera. Ristori, of course, finished playing before movies came into existence and so couldn't, but all of the others were of an age where they could reach a new public with film but chose not to. Duse's *Cenere* is a role outside this core. In my view, *Queen Elizabeth* is consequently not just the most famous of Bernhardt's films. It is also a feature film that gives testimony to the diva, her roles in the late nineteenth century, and to Bernhardt's insistence that these could remain relevant to audiences in the twentieth century.

First shown to an audience of exhibitors and representatives from the press at Broadway producer Daniel Frohman's prestigious theater, the Lyceum Theatre, in New York on the 12th of July, 1912, *Queen Elizabeth* was the inaugural attraction of the Famous Players Film Company. The Famous Players was an initiative that Frohman, New York exhibitor Adolph Zukor, and Edwin S. Porter formed in order to market and produce prestige feature films. As Michael Quinn explains in his article "Distribution, the Transient Audience, and the Transition to the Feature Film," the three financed Bernhardt's film because they wanted to convince the American film industry of the value of the feature.[1] In this way, Famous Players helped finance a work that was produced in London by J. Frank Brockliss, the London distributor and European representative of the Lubin Company, for the Histrionic Film Company.[2] Given U.S. distribution rights for the film, Famous Players then offered exhibitors a feature film with a longer-than-usual run time, a high rental price, and an increase in admission prices. The film was an enormous success. As Quinn states:

> The success of the premiere was not the only reason for the film's popularity, however, for Bernhardt's participation gave Famous Players' first release enormous credibility. Her popularity was a major factor in the opening of the legitimate theatre exhibition market; because of Bernhardt, Famous was able to book *Queen Elizabeth* outside the standard motion picture and small-time vaudeville theatres. After its premiere, *Queen Elizabeth* played in opera houses and large legitimate theatres at a top rental cost of $50 per day, quite a sum considering that the GFC's [General Film Company] most expensive film rented for $15 at the time and Vitagraph charged only $50 a day for its best features in 1915.[3]

Queen Elizabeth enjoyed a similar success when it opened at Powers Theatre in Chicago, was released at the Palace Theatre in London, and was released by Eclipse in France in January 1913.[4]

In histories of the cinema, however, *Queen Elizabeth* is a film consistently referred to as an example of "filmed theater."[5] As Charles Musser astutely notes, recognizing the paradox between the film's popular success and our later marginalization of the work, this film is also one that can be considered a "chasm." It is a "gap" or section of history that still sparkles, precisely because it has yet to be assimilated into established narratives of the cinema.[6] While Musser explores the ways that Bernhardt uses film and other media and popular entertainment to transform and revitalize her career during the 1910–1913 period, I instead explore the cinematic practices that *Queen Elizabeth* reveals. Demonstrating how Bernhardt's film draws upon the long and rich history of Queen Elizabeth's appearance in the theater, the visual arts, and the popular presses, I argue that Bernhardt's film was an intelligent and creative response to the theatrical possibilities of the cinema and to the tastes and fashions of her day.

It is the chasm between the film's popularity and our own tendency to criticize it as filmed theater that I want to understand. How can we look afresh at this film? We know that *Queen Elizabeth* adapts Emile Moreau's 1911 *La Reine Elisabeth*, a four-act play, and that it was played for the first time in the Théâtre Sarah Bernhardt on the 10th of April, 1912.[7] It played only ten times and was removed from the theater on the 21st of April.[8] While film could bring new audiences to the play and so enable Bernhardt to recoup the losses she apparently incurred through the failed theatrical production,[9] this does not explain the film's success. Further, a four-reel film demanded an engaged audience. With admission prices raised to anything from 25 cents to a dollar, audiences were also paying more for a film.[10] How can we explain this? What can we see that can today help us appreciate its appeal?

There is only one recent and relatively short article on *Queen Elizabeth*, Jean-Marc Leveratto's "Sarah Bernhardt dans *Queen Elizabeth* (1912), du théâtre (français) au cinéma (américain)."[11] Otherwise briefly mentioned in histories and theories of the cinema, it is not generally explored. Scholars describe what they see: a still camera, action introduced by twenty-six intertitles, elaborate costumes, and a gesticulating, silent Bernhardt. Note is made of the two documentary close-ups inserted into the film—the 2nd Earl of Essex, Robert Devereux's original Irish commission and his death warrant—both of which are available at the British Museum. The final scene where Bernhardt dies, falling to the ground in long bell-shaped sleeves, is also often mentioned. It is generally conceded that this epitomizes Bernhardt's emphasis upon spectacle (rather than narrative) in the development of the film.[12]

I agree that *Queen Elizabeth* is a spectacular film. I also agree that players are theatrical in a manner that is easily criticized today: they are separately introduced to us at the opening of the film, they mouth words we cannot hear, they are elaborately costumed, and they (rather than a mobile or fluid camera) articulate narrative meaning. Finally, I agree that Bernhardt's final fall onto a pile of cushions is excessive, even funny. This was a point that was noted by contemporary reviews.[13] The fact that she immediately returns to this same set (now cleared and cleaned) in order to acknowledge applause reinforces this view. At the same time, however, my question remains. How did a Tudor Queen return to renew Bernhardt's hold not just on the Empire (now newly conceived in terms of film)[14] but on the affection and loyalty of an international public?

A New Player Queen

As I noted earlier, Queen Elizabeth was not an unusual subject on the stage or in popular culture at the opening of the twentieth century. Like *Camille*, there was an ongoing awareness of the role on the international stage. So, too, was there interest in Tudor England. For example, a report in the *Times* in London that was published around the same time that Bernhardt's play was staged in Paris explains, under the heading "Queen Elizabeth's Ring," that among the items auctioned at Christies was "the Essex ring." Explaining that this is the "identical ring given by Queen Elizabeth to Essex," that it descends from Essex's daughter in unbroken succession from mother to daughter, and that it sold for the enormous sum of 3,250 guineas, the article presumes general knowledge of the ring's significance. The article also mentions that the ring had been exhibited at the Tudor exhibition of 1890. Clearly, readers were engaged in this Queen and her epoch.[15] As proof of this—at least (again) within London but this time reported in the America press—is the fact that Shakespeare's England was reproduced at Earl's Court in 1913, replete with narrow streets, wooden houses, and the Globe Theatre. This hosted the performance of relevant Elizabethan plays; there was also the spectacle of Queen Elizabeth dining "in state in a banqueting hall, with all her courtiers about her."[16]

Joining these shows of Elizabethan England were the plays that narrate an aspect of Elizabeth's life. Famously, the American actress Nance O'Neil and her company toured America (in 1906) in *Queen Elizabeth*, a "five-act classical tragedy written around the life of Elizabeth, Queen of England, by Paolo Giacometti."[17] In 1905, this play went on tour to Australia and New Zealand. O'Neil's tour was itself a return tour after her success in bringing *Queen Elizabeth* (and other roles) to audiences in America, Australia, and New Zealand in 1901 (she also took it to London in 1902).[18] When O'Neil first played *Queen Elizabeth* in Australia, note was made of the fact that it was new to audiences. Still, readers were reassured that "*Queen Elizabeth* will seem as an old friend to many from the mere fact of its historical foundation."[19] We are therefore reminded that local audiences are familiar with the Tudor Queen. We are also reassured that "the play was written for [Adelaide] Ristori, and by an Italian [Giacometti], but was easily adapted to be rendered in English."[20] Even having forgotten that the play had already toured in English translation abroad, *Queen Elizabeth* was considered an accessible role for English-speaking audiences.[21]

It is the international renown of Adelaide Ristori, even more than Bernhardt's contemporary Nance O'Neil, that explains the significance of Bernhardt's *Queen Elizabeth* in 1912. Rather than presume that Bernhardt adopts *Queen Elizabeth* because she reaches an Anglo-American audience that had seen the role performed by O'Neil, we must recall that *Queen Elizabeth* has a long history on the live stage. This reaches back (at least) to 1681.[22] As the *New York Times* notes, even on Ristori's first tour to America in 1866:

> The story of the plot is an old one. It has been served in many forms and always successfully. It is simply that of Essex who, receiving a ring from the Queen in her favor, and knowing that it will give him pardon, freedom and life, refuses these boons . . . in his indignation at her coquettish cruelty.[23]

Queen Elizabeth was familiar to audiences, but it could also be transformed. It is this process of transformation, whereby actresses competed or played against each other (in much the same manner that Duse and Bernhardt played against each other in *La Dame aux Camélias*) that is relevant to the role. Indeed, I argue that Bernhardt seeks comparison between herself and Ristori. Difference is then established, as well as generational succession. Given that Ristori was the contemporary of the world famous French actress Rachel, and that she had traveled to Paris in 1855 to successfully perform what was seen as a challenge to the great actress, it is not surprising that Bernhardt essays one of her main roles (Mary Stuart was Ristori's other signature role).[24] I argue that Bernhardt facilitates this comparison since it was Ristori (and not Rachel) who had undertaken world tours within the public's living memory: Ristori's final tour to America, where she played *Queen Elizabeth* in English, was in 1884–1885.[25] Ristori's final performance in England was also *Queen Elizabeth* performed (again in English) in Manchester, 1883.[26]

What is interesting about Bernhardt's use of Ristori's role is that the emotionally expressive style of acting that is associated with Ristori—that stood, in the public's mind, in contrast to the control and self-possession of Rachel—is also associated with Bernhardt. Bernhardt's Queen is described in the following manner: the "subtlest moments of craft and cunning give place in brutal suddenness—which yet seems natural—to paroxysms of rage and grief or to times of delirium."[27] Such description is similar to Ristori's own account of the need to incorporate character transitions in her depiction of the Queen.[28] It is also in accordance with the reception Ristori enjoyed on her American debut: "So majestic in action, so graceful in motion, no attitudinizing, no statuesque poses, but the living, breathing Queen . . . Queen of art and hearts! The subtle expounder of the human passions in their varied phazes [*sic*]."[29] In this sense, the criticisms levied by film scholars at Bernhardt's theatrical anachronism are paradoxical since she, like Ristori, abandons theatrical choreography for more emotionally spontaneous and impulsive action on the stage.

Bernhardt not only adopted a role that was closely associated with Ristori, she also followed her practice of studying and presenting historical figures and scenes with meticulous care. The importance given the representation of history in the second half of the nineteenth century is illustrated by the criticism given Mrs. F. W. Lander's (actress Jean M. Davenport) 1867 production of *Queen Elizabeth* at the French Theatre, New York. While her acting was applauded, the mise-en-scène was described as being "both badly and carelessly put upon the stage; the scenery being old, tawdry, and inappropriate."[30] This comment could never be directed to Bernhardt: as the photographs of her play reveal, great care and attention were paid to details of costume, the authenticity of furniture and wall hangings, as well as the verity of the painted backdrops that create first the scene at camp, then Richmond Park, and finally a succession of palatial interiors.[31]

Starting with the Story

Accounts of Moreau's *Queen Elizabeth* were published in American presses.[32] As Martin Marks notes in *Music and the Silent Film*, some details of reports were incorrect: the plot synopsis contained in *Literary Digest*, for example, was wrongly attributed to theater critic Henri Bridon (rather than Henri Bidon) of the *Journal des débats politiques et littéraires*, and Emile Moreau was mistakenly introduced as Amiel Moreau.[33] More significant than misspellings, however, is a point Marks does not mention: that the translation of Bidon's April 1912 synopsis of Bernhardt's theatrical action on the French stage was reprinted under a banner declaring "Bernhardt IN MOTION PICTURES" in August 1912. Just before recounting the narrative of *Queen Elizabeth*, it is explained that "to many it will doubtless be a surprize [*sic*] to learn that no less an artist than Sarah Bernhardt has entrusted her art to the films, and that she will be seen this season in the United States in a historical photoplay. Twenty-one scenes are adapted from Amiel Moreau's 'Queen Elizabeth,' a new drama in which the actress made her first appearance and scored a fresh triumph only last April."[34] Going on to quote Bidon's "full account of the plot, which is based on the tragedy of Elizabeth's relations with Essex," *Literary Digest* is an early example of how the plot for the film *Queen Elizabeth* was mistakenly confused with the narrative of Moreau's stage play. Indeed, the simple description of theatrical narrative in *Literary Digest*'s review removes not only Bidon's original (and quite critical) historical contextualization of an aged Queen Elizabeth and her reinterpretation on the stage,[35] but it translates Bidon's narrative of theatrical action, removing all comments and contextualizations. In so doing, it implies that the story of *Queen Elizabeth* on film was identical to that of the stage.

Bidon's translated and much edited account of the play is valuable since it tells us what was performed on the live stage and how this was described to audiences abroad. As he explains, the play opens with the Queen and her English army on the night of August 6, 1588. They are

> crouched in a crevice of the cliffs. The scene is admirable. This niche has been worn by nature in the high chalk bluff. The queen's tent, to the right, whips in the southwest wind which has risen towards the end of the night. Gray clouds scud across the sky. The sea dashes its gleaming waves against the rocks. In

> the midst of the roaring and sobbing of wind and sea the words now of the soldiers and then of the Queen enlighten us as to the anguish of the hour. An enormous Spanish fleet is bearing a hostile army to the English shores. It has reached Calais. What can the little English squadron do against it? On land nothing is ready. The Queen is in despair. Then a gloriously handsome young man with a magnificent faith gives her courage. It is Essex.

Skipping the historical details that Bidon then gives about James VI and his inclusion in this scene, *Literary Digest* continues:

> Lights and noises announce the battle is joined. The sea throws up wreckage bearing both English and Spanish dead. Who has won? The Queen is frightfully disquieted. The aid of the Scotch soldiers may be necessary. James demands only that Elizabeth recognize him as her successor. . . . This is repugnant to her, but she is about to sign when the victorious English marines arrive in glad tumult.[36]

We are then told:

> Blackened and bare of breast and arm, pipe in teeth, but superb, Drake recounts the battle. Amid the general enthusiasm the handsome Essex falls on his knees, exclaiming "How beautiful you are, Madame, in this aureole of glory, and what a misfortune not to be able to shed one's blood for you." . . . Then crying "Long live the Queen," he and Drake bear her off in a litter to review the marines. This young lover will remain for Elizabeth the embodiment of the glorious days of victory.[37]

Literary Digest again eliminates details from Bidon's account of stage action since Bidon notes that Moreau has replaced, in this scene, the more traditional "idyllic meeting in the garden" between the Queen and Essex (long depicted in paintings, as I discuss later) for the spectacular arrival of the Armada. It is in this outdoor scene—where in the theater a cyclorama represented this cliffside vigil—that Essex and Elizabeth fall in love. It is also here that Essex does not merely lay his cloak on the ground for her to walk on, but "draws his sword, throws his hat, crying 'Long live the Queen!'"[38]

Other American publications recount the opening narrative action of *Queen Elizabeth* in a similarly schematic way. For example, the *Boston Evening Transcript* introduces Essex with no discussion of his famous laying of the cloak, and states only that Queen Elizabeth "roughly brushes Leicester aside, and accepts the offer of a young man, Captain Essex, to lead the military forces against the enemy."[39] When the Armada is vanquished we learn that "Elizabeth, with a disdainful glance at James Stuart, throws to the ground the parchment she has not yet signed, and is carried triumphantly by her soldiers to the water's edge to see the remains of what Drake calls 'the enemy's cathedrals.'"[40] Clearly, with no mention made of how Essex's actions might confirm or depart from historical accounts of his meeting with the Queen, we can presume that Bernhardt's play opens onto a self-contained narrative that might stand theatrically alone.

As *Literary Digest* states, the second scene is of the Queen in Richmond Park in 1600. This is a documented part of play.[41] It is also discussed by Adolphe Brisson in *Le Temps*, where he explains that the Queen relaxes here with her court, maids, and greyhounds and that she engages in light talk with Shakespeare.[42] *Literary Digest* tells us that Essex is combating rebels in Ireland and is much missed by the Queen. She confides her love of Essex to Lady Howard. Suddenly, Essex appears and proposes home rule; Elizabeth is called elsewhere. Essex and Lady Howard (Essex's cousin) are alone together and audiences of the play now understand that they are in love. Returning to find the two lovers together, Elizabeth is furious. She dismisses Lady Howard, summons her court, and accuses Essex of having made a pact with the Irish. He denies this, and she throws a glove in his face. He then draws his sword and the act is fatal: the Queen has him arrested for treason. It is this last act—the drawing of the sword against the monarch—that is recorded in photographs of the scene and that explains Essex's subsequent death sentence. Again, in Bidon's longer description of the play in *Journal des débats politiques et littéraires*, details are included that are elided in this abridged citation of stage action. Most notably, Bidon indicates that it is absurd to have the Queen's own confidant as Essex's lover. He also sustains that with the French, passion is not deceitful: in his opinion, Essex's amorous duplicity is an indication of the coldness of the English race.[43]

Literary Digest tells us that in this scene "we are not alarmed" for Essex since Elizabeth has promised that should he return her ring, a gift she gave earlier to him, she will pardon him for any act of treason. As Bidon again contextualizes for his French readers, the story of the queen's ring was taken from Corneille's *Comte d'Essex* that was taken, in turn, from French novelist and dramatist M. [Gauthier] de la Calprenède's earlier play, *Comte d'Essex* (1638).[44] Explaining the differences between the two plays, he states that whereas in the former a sweet Lady Howard keeps the ring and later confesses this to the Queen, in Moreau's play there is instead the "sinister old man," Lady Howard's husband, who announces to the Queen that Essex has refused to send her his ring. The Queen waits, hoping that the bells will not ring to confirm his death, but at the end of the act they do.[45] A publicity photograph shows Bernhardt holding open a curtain, arms outstretched in a gesture of distress as she hears the bells ring.[46]

In the final scene of the play, Bidon recounts a collection of "disparate traits" that are not included in *Literary Digest*: the Queen is dressed in an ermine cloak, she keeps Essex's sword (unsheathed) near her, she unsuccessfully offers her crown to Lord Seymour, and Lady Howard confesses to her that Essex returned the ring to ask for pardon. Lady Howard explains her jealous husband took the ring from him and, instead of giving it to the Queen, cut his throat with a dagger. Hearing this, the Queen recalls the prediction that a gypsy once gave: that she will die as Lady Howard dies. Finding out too late that Essex asked for a royal pardon, Elizabeth demands with "a savage cry" that Lady and Lord Howard be tortured. She then speaks tenderly of Essex, declares that she carries one crown of glory and one of sorrow, and stumbles on her feet. Dismissing everyone with a tragic shake of her hands that is "truly regal," she then dies, tortured by anger, regret, and despair as she suddenly falls face forward, dead.[47]

The *New York Times*, recounting only this last scene in its review of the Parisian play, explains that the Queen is "so shaken by the hurricane of passion" that she experiences after hearing Lady Howard's confession "that death can no longer be held away." It concludes: "When Mme. Sarah Bernhardt falls forward from the throne the audience is relieved; not till then can they really appreciate the volcanic energy shown in this complex scene, in which the subtlest moments of craft and cunning give place in brutal suddeness—which yet seems natural—to paroxysms of rage and grief or to times of delirium."[48] The photographs in the Bibliothèque Nationale de France confirm this range of emotions: in one, Bernhardt stands hands raised, with her eyes shut before a pile of cushions, in another she is standing with the cushions behind her, eyes shut, with one hand clutching her face and the other raised above her head, in yet another she stands regally addressing her ladies and court.[49] Some of these images (and particularly those of the final scene) were reproduced in Anglo-American newspapers such as the *Graphic* in London and available to readers as summations of narrative action, which is significant.[50] It indicates that even if the play was not taken on tour its key scenes were familiar to readers some time before the film *Queen Elizabeth* was released.

Shifting the Story to Screen

The film is considerably different from Moreau's stage play. It opens with an intertitle that explains: "The Queen, anxiously awaiting news of the Spanish Armada, is struck by the enthusiasm and noble bearing of Earl Essex, who alone is confident of success. Drake arrives and announces the total defeat of the Spaniards." While there is general narrative overlap between the scene we then see on film and the one recounted and photographed on the stage, film action is certainly different. Indeed, there is a compression and condensation of meaning in the film that suggests not just that actions and exchanges have been greatly accelerated, but that the scene itself is of less narrative importance to the film than it is in the first act of the play. In other words, while descriptions of the play give attention to the sea battle and to the complicated network of interests that were then surrounding the British Queen, on film the focus is instead given to Essex and his arrival. Lasting just over two minutes, this is but a short prelude to a tale that is to unravel.

What can we see today, as viewers who might not know the play in the detail that Bidon recounts? We are inside a tent. There is Essex, who can be identified by his youth and his plumed hat and cloak. The Queen is literally announced as she arrives. When she enters the scene, Essex gallantly throws his cloak on the ground for her to walk on, removes his hat, and executes a deep bow, with one knee on the ground. By watching carefully, we can see that the Queen has an exchange with a man at court. Who this person is, in his dark hat and court attire, we do not know. We can also see the Queen in dialogue with a man with a beard, moustache, and ruffled collar. Although some might guess that this is the future James I of England and that he is asserting his right to the throne, it is unclear what the two of them are discussing when Bernhardt raises her arms during moments of speech.

The man in the dark hat in *Queen Elizabeth*—who moves quickly to the right side of the screen as Essex gallantly speaks—can be identified as the Earl of Leicester, Robert Dudley, only at the point that Essex exits the scene. Were we familiar with the English history recounted, we might guess that Essex is taking over Dudley's role as commander of the English land forces during the Spanish Armada. Essex quickly returns and, following him, we see Drake, looking very much a pirate. Finally, after victory has been announced and the Queen has thanked Drake, the Queen is hoisted up in her chair by four bearers. Essex and Drake are the only two in view as they stand to exit to the left of the screen. Where Elizabeth is being transported to in this triumphant moment we do not know.

The second shot opens with an intertitle that tells us that "Essex who has become the Queen's favorite is present at a performance of the 'Merry Wives of Windsor' and presents Shakespeare to the Queen." We are not in the Richmond garden setting revealed in the photographs of the second act of the play. Further, Essex is therefore not in Ireland, away when the Queen meets Shakespeare. Instead, we are indoors and Essex is present when the trunk scene from *The Merry Wives of Windsor* is performed for the Queen and her court. This scene is not just a departure from Moreau's play, it is also cleverly self-reflexive. It prefigures and suggests Essex's romantic alliance with both the Queen and the Countess of Nottingham (Moreau's Lady Howard) since we see in this play within a play Falstaff hidden in the laundry basket by the two mistresses, Mistress Ford and Mistress Page. As Barbara Hodgdon argues, this scene "succinctly sets up a comic parallel to Essex's fate, figuring his possible escape from the jealous Nottingham through the agency of the Countess and Queen."[51]

At the completion of the *Merry Wives* scene, Essex presents Shakespeare to a gracious and smiling Queen. On film, therefore, there is no exchange as there is on stage between Elizabeth and Shakespeare. There is instead the celebration of Shakespeare's commissioned comedy (*Merry Wives*). Immediately after this, and again changing from Moreau's stage play, a fortune-teller warns Essex that he will be hanged. On film we therefore literally see the fortune-teller that is recalled in the final scene of the stage play, and much is made of the ring that Essex is given after the fortune-teller's prophecy. This is given to him by the Queen with the promise (stated clearly in the intertitles) that "should he ever be in trouble, on his returning it she will save him however great his fault may be." Just after receiving the ring, Essex is given the Irish commission. Before he goes, we see him hurry off to say farewell to his lover, the Countess of Nottingham. We then see the Earl of Nottingham jealously spying on this romantic tryst between the two.

Already, in these few scenes, we can establish two significant changes on film. In the first place, events on film occur in strict chronological order. There is, therefore, no jumping between temporally separate events as there is on the stage. Secondly, narrative is literally materialized on screen: the memory of the gypsy and the giving of the ring is enacted as part of the story we are being told. In a similar manner, the Earl of Nottingham's jealousy for his wife and her relationship with Essex is given causality and made "real" when he secretly sees the two in a romantic embrace.[52]

After witnessing his wife's liaison with Essex, Nottingham writes a letter with Francis Bacon to wrongly accuse Essex of treason. When Essex returns suddenly to court from Ireland, he is caught by the Queen as he embraces the Countess. As the intertitles state: "The Queen discovers Lord Essex is unfaithful. She then believes the anonymous letter and orders his arrest." While the actions that are described on the stage are also performed here—Bernhardt reaches onto her desk, picks up a glove, and throws it quickly at Essex, who then draws his sword—the intertitles explain Essex's treason only in terms of the false letter. We need to be very attentive to screen action to understand that the verbal exchange, the throwing of the glove, and drawing of the sword are decisive actions that determine narrative events. They come so fast, and are embedded within a scene filled with so many other characters and movements, that they can be easily missed.

Essex is then sent to trial. Through the Queen's window, we see him appear and join her in watching the procession walk by. The axe that the executioner is carrying is facing downward, indicating that Essex is about to die. A tearful Countess is then summoned to the Queen as Bacon secretly listens in. We see Bacon telling Nottingham of the Queen's intended pardon, the Countess taking the ring from Essex, and Nottingham wrestling this from his wife and throwing it into the Thames. Added to these scenes is a new one: Essex's execution, which is cut at the moment the executioner swings his axe above his head. Instead of listening for a bell to toll, on film we are shown the moment immediately prior to Essex's beheading. We then see the Queen visit the body of Essex in a dark chamber; she discovers that her ring is missing. Again, information that we discover in the fourth and final act of the play is related earlier on film. Indeed, since the Queen has seen the missing ring herself, the Countess does not confess and ask for pardon. *Queen Elizabeth* thereby replaces verbal hearsay with visual truth. It asks viewers to substitute dialogue with image and so gives Bernhardt's physical acting greater narrative agency.

In the penultimate scene on film, we are told that "The Queen forces the horrible truth from the Countess. 'May God forgive you. I never will!'" Again, it is the Queen who drives the narrative, forcing information from a recalcitrant subject rather than having it offered to her. In another departure, Elizabeth is not a bloodthirsty Queen set on vengeance, but refuses personal forgiveness. Suggesting that sins might anyway be forgiven by God, she also makes a statement about her status as a Protestant Queen: it is God only, not his titular head on earth, who pardons sin.

At the film's end, we are told that the Queen "gradually faded away." Led into her chamber and surrounded by her court, she handles (as she does on the stage) Essex's unsheathed sword. Rather than present a long and varied scene, action occurs relatively quickly: Bernhardt takes a drink from a goblet, glances into a mirror, and then flings this away. Raising her arms, Elizabeth collapses onto the cushions in front of her. As reviews noted, she "finally falls like a log on the cushions at the foot of the throne."[53] She does not die until she has had her death announced to her people. This ending recalls Queen Elizabeth's famous popularity and her allegiance to her public.

What is remarkable about this ending is its changed temporal duration. The sudden death of Elizabeth on stage is precipitated by the rage she feels at Lady Howard's confession. On film, and in a scene which lasts just over three minutes, the Queen instead experiences a lengthy and sad melancholia which (in real terms) would last from the moment of Essex's death (in 1601) to the Queen's own death (in 1603). *Queen Elizabeth* then concludes with a reflection on the transitory nature of power: "Sic transit gloria mundi," the intertitles state. "Thus passes (away) earthly glory (i.e., power)." Yet whereas earthly power might be fleeting, film was considered a salve, a way to embalm people in their place and time. As Bernhardt wrote in the *Moving Picture World*:

> It is with a feeling if gratitude that I turn to the God of genius, to offer him prayer, for that wonderful miracle he hath brought about, whereby he hath given men the power to hand down to posterity the greatest success of my career—"Queen Elizabeth." It is a great joy for me to know that my masterpiece is within the reach of all the people throughout the universe, and I hope it will be appreciated before and long after I am gone.[54]

Given these views about the durability of film, it is little surprising that Bernhardt returns one final time on film to greet us. We are her public, and it is to us she fictionally bows on the now-cleared set. She is not dying and she has not died. Film does indeed ensure that Bernhardt is still a celebrated and living figure in the world.

The Moving Pictures

While I do not know a lot about the movement of figures within scenes on the live stage, comments about Bernhardt's acting in *Queen Elizabeth* indicate how she was seen by her audience. For example, Adolphe Brisson writing in *Le Temps* speaks of her acting providing the focus of the work and keeping the improbability of Moreau's plot at bay:

> We do not understand a lot about the grievances [against Essex]. . . . But what does it matter? We watch Sarah Bernhardt. And Sarah is extraordinary. The incomplete and confused tragedy becomes instead concentrated and precise in her, in her attitudes, in her gesture, in the trembling of her hands, in her anxious eyes, in her breathless, trembling, broken voice. We are not interested in anything about Essex, about whom we know but little. But the pain of this amourous and betrayed woman, the emotion of this queen torn between the feelings of her heart and her duties as head of State stir us. In the play's denouement, Sarah Bernhardt is even more admirable. . . . Elisabeth is inconsolable, devoured by remorse. . . . Terrible, the face of the artist, her bewilderment, her dread, and in her eyes the terror of her recent hallucinations . . . [on learning of Lady Howard's betrayal] Sarah utters some marvelous cries of hatred and offers us a spectacle of sublime agony. . . . She translates with an extreme truthfulness the entire gamut of human sentiments, she expresses vehemence as much as sweetness; her acting is sincere, it is even realist on occasion.[55]

Given such a description, it is clear that Bernhardt's performance of the English Queen was a powerful and emotive one. It is hard to understand, in this context, Gerda Taranow's claim that "the play proved the most disastrous failure of the actress's career."[56] Nevertheless, Bernhardt's decision to bring the play to film was a canny one: the role exhibited a range of emotions (joy, love, jealousy, fury, pain, terror, remorse) that were expressive and intelligible through her physical acting. Developed on screen, this allowed audiences to empathetically engage with a figure (the Tudor Queen, but here also Bernhardt) who is often regarded as literally and symbolically removed from the trials of quotidian life. It was Bernhardt's expressive gesture, far more than dialogue or verbal play on the stage, that held the play together and that enabled its subsequent success as cinematized theater.

W. Stephen Bush, commenting in *Moving Picture World* on Bernhardt's capacity to make the role an emotive and compelling one, states:

> This great artist had her own conception of the character of Elizabeth. It was not the traditional Elizabeth, crafty, calculating and not at all emotional.
>
> So superb is the art of Sarah Bernhardt that she made her conception, which is that of a passionate woman, dominated wholly by her affections, seem not impossible. No student of history could pay a greater tribute to her art than to say that she successfully defied a well-known historical fact. Throughout the play, which consists of three reels, she exhibited her best powers and won from her audience such keen sympathy and compassion as the real Elizabeth could never have expected.[57]

In this context, *Queen Elizabeth*'s emphasis on the passions returns us to my earlier discussion of Bernhardt's emotive play in *Camille*. It also returns us to the ideas of gestural legibility discussed in my first chapter. Audiences could respond to Bernhardt's gesturing and emotive body, even in vocal silence. A review in *Theatre Magazine* confirms this, stating that "the artiste did not merely pose mechanically for a mechanical contrivance, but proceeded to give one of the finest performances of which this greatest living actress is capable."[58] Elaborating the character of the queen (who in Paolo Giacometti's earlier *Elisabetta Regina d'Inghilterra* was described as a woman with whom "it is hard, nay almost impossible to sympathize"[59]), Bernhardt ensured that cinematized theater adopts and maintains a focus on emotive acting. It is acting that triumphs in the cinema, or rather that joins the cinema, revealing that cinematized theater can maintain and perhaps even develop the strengths of the stage.

The Pictures Move

I have established that the plot of Bernhardt's film differs from Moreau's play. I have little knowledge, however, of how the play unwound on the live stage.

I might read that Bernhardt's acting was emotive but this does not allow me to determine precisely what *emotive* really means. I also do not know how actions were shifted or accelerated in their transcription to film. The mise-en-scène, designed by Émile Bertin, is a little easier to discuss, since this remained relatively intact. I can see on the promotional photographs of the play that the sets are far larger than those used in the film, and so I can direct attention to the way the film cropped space, making the architectural monumentality of the original mise-en-scène more intimate. I can also see how the stage production includes a painted outdoor set (the Richmond Park scene) that is not in the film. I might guess that the decision to eliminate the painted outdoors was strategic as it acknowledges that a camera might very well film outdoors. Hence, in the only scene in which we move outside in the film, we watch the fortune-teller arrive at the castle. There are no painted sets or backdrops, but instead we see a building. This indicates that the architectural space of the screen is quite different from that of the stage. As Leveratto argues, this space is "[w]ithout doubt the courtyard of the hotel occupied by Sarah Bernhardt at 56, Boulevard Pereire."[60]

Because this "real" space joins painted sets that do not appear in the play as well as the enormous stage sets of the original stage production, we might question the idea that *Queen Elizabeth* was produced in London. As Leveratto reminds us, Bernhardt's actors were resident in Paris and not London at the time of filming. It would have cost an enormous amount to ship the original set.[61] In this context, we might regard the work as a film shot largely in Paris with photographs of original documents (the 2nd Earl of Essex, Robert Devereux's original Irish commission and his death warrant) inserted later into the film.

Space might have changed on screen but other aspects of the stage play—the costumes and furniture, the first and last sets—were used in the film. Advertisements state that the film uses the "Dresses, Armor and Furniture from the Sarah Bernhardt Theatre, Paris."[62] The actors that performed on film were also those who were in Bernhardt's original theatrical production and who worked at the Théâtre Sarah Bernhardt. The few who are given screen credits are Bernhardt as Queen, Lou Tellegen as Essex, Mlle Romain as Arabella, the Countess of Nottingham, and Max Maxudian as Howard, the Earl of Nottingham. Uncredited, but nevertheless in the original production is Jean Angelo (who remained Seymour), and Albert Decoeur (who remained Drake).[63]

Far more evident to me today than the overlaps and changes between stage and screen is the use the film makes of art history. My untrained eye—that has not seen O'Neil or Ristori on the stage, has never watched *Queen*

Elizabeth as a theatrical production, has not seen Bernhardt perform live, and has difficulty in identifying actors that are uncredited on screen—finds it much easier to make visual and narrative connections between the film and the painted picture. On screen, I can identify stagings or suggestions of *Elizabeth in Procession* (ca. 1600, attributed to Robert Peake), *Queen Elizabeth viewing the Performance of The Merry Wives of Windsor at the Globe Theatre* (David Scott, 1840), *Portrait of Sarah Bernhardt* (Georges Jules Victor Clairin, 1876), *The Kiss* (Francesco Paolo Hayez, 1859), *Cromwell before the Coffin of Charles I* (Delaroche, 1849), as well as Delaroche's *The Death of Elizabeth I, Queen Elizabeth* (1828). What I can glean from this—and my list is not exhaustive—is that Bernhardt's cinematized theater included the practice of re-creating and re-presenting famous and familiar paintings to a global audience. In film, and unlike on the live stage, no pose was presented as a tableau. Because we do not have a speaking voice (and remember my comments in Chapter 3 about poses being held for 27 seconds while Bernhardt spoke), action is much faster. In this context, *Queen Elizabeth* is textually dense in a challenging way. Audiences had intertitles upon which to build the skeleton of a story, but nuances in terms of character and narrative were then compressed into a rich layering of visual detail that I must now unpack.

A screen/picture (or, rather, cinema/painting) relationship is not mentioned in any review of Bernhardt's films. While I can suggest that perhaps *Queen Elizabeth* was a success because it was visually legible as a series of reenacted paintings, I do not know if this was actually so. In other words, I do not know if Bernhardt was celebrated because she indeed enabled familiar paintings to be seen a little differently or even how conscious audience members were of the array of paintings, prints, and histories that she flashed onto the screen through her settings, actions, costume, and gesture. We know that the nineteenth-century stage "realized" paintings and prints and that Bernhardt was thus bringing a theatrical practice to film. Martin Meisel, in *Realizations*, speaks of the *tableau vivant* (the living picture) and its close relationship to the nineteenth-century theater. Arguing that the nineteenth-century stage never actually synthesized the tension between picture and motion, he states that it was only with technical resources—"in the studios, laboratories, and movie houses of the next century"—that the paradox and tension of nineteenth-century drama was resolved.[64] Does this mean, however, that the paintings, prints, and histories I will go on to discuss in relation to *Queen Elizabeth* had necessarily moved through the nineteenth-century stage? And which nineteenth-century stage? How and when? In what country and with what actor as the star attraction? I cannot answer these questions. I can only identify the images and sources that are available to me today. I am therefore footnoting Bernhardt's film, drawing connections between representations, medias, and histories that must have been so evidently a part of cinematized theater in 1912 that they warranted no discussion.

The Queen at Camp

Queen Elizabeth begins with Essex standing carefully studying a map on a table. An opened curtain with soldiers in the background indicates that we are inside a tent. The Queen enters from the left to great fanfare. When *Theatre Magazine* comments that she made her entrance "with the characteristic slow, sinuous walk,"[65] it indicates that Bernhardt's appearance on the live stage was an event in itself. Here, then, we have proof of such an appearance and of how action was changed for the film: the court busies itself, Bernhardt walks onto the screen and everyone greets her, she pauses beside her desk, and then she turns to address James VI of Scotland. Bernhardt does not walk slowly; her dress, however, does twist characteristically around her body and so her walk concludes in a sinuous art nouveau spiral.

The entrance of the Queen into the tent not only gives evidence of Bernhardt's characteristic entrance onto the live stage. It is also grounded in historic fact, recalling Elizabeth's visit to Tilbury on August 7, 1588. Bernhardt's address to the men who crowd the tent on the film—and we have in the background the long spears of infantry soldiers as well as their plumed helmets—is suggestive of the most celebrated speech of Elizabeth's reign. Famously, she said:

> I have placed my chiefest strength and safeguard in the loyal hearts and good will of my subjects; and therefore come amongst you, as you see, at this time, not for my recreation and disport, but being resolved, in the midst and heat of the battle, to live or die amongst you all, and to lay down for God, and for my kingdom and for my people, my honour and my blood, even in the dust. I know I have the body of a weak and feeble woman, but I have the heart and stomach of a king, and a king of England too.[66]

The film runs too fast for a speech of this length to be spoken. Nevertheless, Bernhardt does speak and gesture to her troops; through her physical actions she indicates an event that was recorded for posterity and that endured as recounted fact. Even the plumed hat that Bernhardt wears in this scene was famously part of Elizabeth I's costume on this visit. Ballads written at the time of Elizabeth's reign report her "tossing her plume of feathers" and Thomas Heywood, in his later *Exemplary Lives and Memorable Acts of Nine of the*

Most Worthy Women of the World, speaks of her appearing "in the head of her Troopes, and encouraging her Souldiers, habited like an Amazonian Queene, Buskind and plumed, having a golden Truncheon, Gantlet and Gorget."[67]

Although there is no truncheon, gantlet, or gorget in the film, there is reference to her having the will to fight "as a man" in the exchange we see with James VI. It is Essex, however, who encourages her and Essex who returns to announce victory just before Drake arrives. Elizabeth is thus at once a victorious Amazonian Queen, a Queen who enjoys the adoration of her subjects, and a woman who is supported by the young man she later comes to love.

Court Chivalry

When Bernhardt enters the tent and walks toward her desk, we see Lou Tellegen (playing Essex) fling a cloak at her feet. He takes a hat from his head and then lowers himself to kneel before her. Like Elizabeth's speech at Tilbury, Essex's gallant action is recorded in history. Indeed, we know from an array of sources that Sir Walter Raleigh, Elizabeth's favored courtier (who, like Essex as the favored courtier in this film, was eventually beheaded), was famous for laying his cloak before Queen Elizabeth (see figure 4.1). We can guess that Essex's character is associated with Raleigh's chivalry and acquires

Figure 4.1. Essex kneels before Elizabeth, *Queen Elizabeth*, 1912. National Film and Sound Archive of Australia.

narrative meaning because of this. As Thomas Fuller recounts in his 1662 *History of the Worthies of England I*:

> Captain Raleigh coming out of Ireland to the English Court in good habit (his cloaths being then a considerable part of his estate) found the Queen walking, till, meeting with a *plashy place*, she seemed to scruple going thereon. Presently Raleigh cast and spred his new plush cloak on the ground; whereon the Queen trod gently, rewarding him afterwards with many *suits*, for his free and seasonable tender of so fair a *foot cloath*.[68]

While Fuller's is the first description of this act, in the nineteenth century Raleigh's gesture was a popular and identifiable image. There is *Sir Walter Raleigh Laying Down His Cloak before Queen Elizabeth I* (circle of John Gilbert, 1817–1897, nd.); there also is an 1854 graphite, ink, and ink-wash image of this same scene by Peter Frederick Rothermel; and there is William Henry Charles Groome's *Sir Walter Raleigh Pulling His Cloak Out for Elizabeth I* (1880) as well as John Leech's more comical *Sir Walter Raleigh and Queen Elizabeth* (reproduced in Gilbert Abbott À'Beckett's 1864 *Comic History of England*, where Raleigh spreads his cloak over a puddle before a bemused looking Queen). Finally, there is W. M. Thackeray's woodcut of the scene in his 1848 *Book of Snobs* (see figure 4.2).[69] As Michael Dobson and

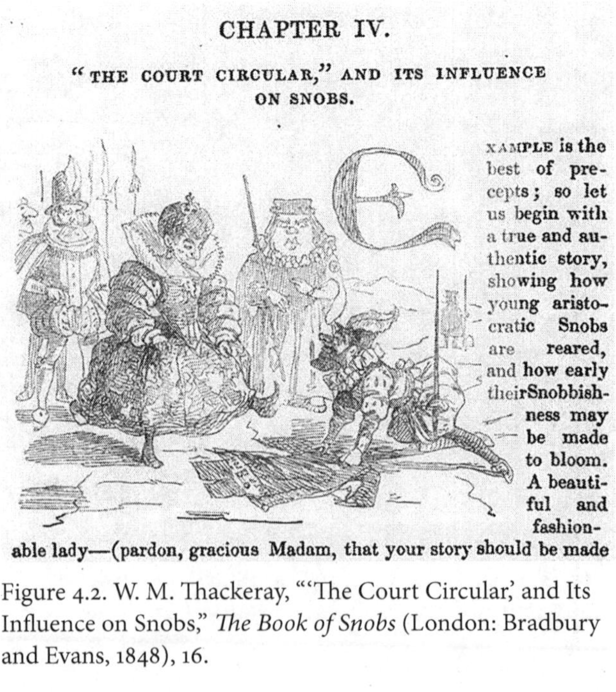

CHAPTER IV.

"THE COURT CIRCULAR," AND ITS INFLUENCE ON SNOBS.

EXAMPLE is the best of precepts; so let us begin with a true and authentic story, showing how young aristocratic Snobs are reared, and how early theirSnobbishness may be made to bloom. A beautiful and fashionable lady—(pardon, gracious Madam, that your story should be made

Figure 4.2. W. M. Thackeray, "'The Court Circular,' and Its Influence on Snobs," *The Book of Snobs* (London: Bradbury and Evans, 1848), 16.

Nicola Watson have recently observed, "Sir Walter's legendary courtesy to his queen became one of the nineteenth century's favorite images of the manly and Ruskinesque chivalry Elizabeth is supposed to have promulgated at her court: hence the popularity of such widely reproduced genre paintings as *The Gallantry of Sir Walter Raleigh* (Samuel Drummond, 1828), *Sir Walter Raleigh Spreads His Cloak as a Carpet for Queen Elizabeth* (William Theed, 1853), and *Sir Walter Raleigh Laying Down His Cloak before Queen Elizabeth* (Andrew Sheerboom, 1875)."[70]

What is interesting about these images is not just the coincidence of costume and gesture (a chivalrous young man kneels with a plumed hat as he lays a cloak) but the way in which these images are identical in terms of composition: Raleigh kneels on the right of the frame as the Queen walks toward him. In the photograph of the stage production this is inversed, so the Queen is shown walking onto the stage on the right as Essex kneels on the left with his cloak (see figure 4.3).[71] In this sense, film more closely reproduces the visual and compositional elements of the event already known to

Figure 4.3. Sarah Bernhardt in *Queen Elizabeth*, a play by Emile Moreau, Théâtre Sarah Bernhardt, April 11, 1912. Bibliothèque Nationale de France.

spectators through visual images. Further, her position on film makes her the dominant figure in the scene.

After laying his cloak, Essex stands once more and puts his hat back on. The legibility of this simple gesture and the inclusion of it in a scene that runs for just a few minutes indicates that it was not Bernhardt alone who contributed to cinematized theater as a new form of visual literature available to a popular and international audience. Indeed, the transference of Raleigh's gallant gesture onto the character of Essex signals, at the film's outset, the importance given spectators as interpreters of character and narrative action. It was the theatrical gesture itself, and not just the visual reconstruction of history through familiar costumes and sets, which gave depth and meaning to a scene.

A Procession Portrait

After Drake arrives dressed as a pirate to receive the Queen's embrace and to confirm victory, he helps Essex and two soldiers lift the Queen in a litter. They pause to receive the applause of the watching crowd. In this final moment of the film's opening scene, we are reminded of Elizabeth's triumph: arriving on foot, she is carried victoriously away (see figure 4.4). We are also reminded of one final (and famous) painting that influenced the choreography of screen action: more than any other image, this moment of triumph

Figure 4.4. Bernhardt is carried away, *Queen Elizabeth*, 1912. National Film and Sound Archive of Australia.

recalls *The Procession Portrait of Queen Elizabeth I* (after 1593, attributed to Robert Peake).[72] Horizontally disposed, Peake's painting shows Elizabeth in a canopied procession, accompanied by her court and watched by spectators who crowd behind her and lean from open windows high in the building behind her. While on film there is no canopy, no scenic hill, and no building from which spectators might watch (as though from the boxes in a theater), we can see in both pictures that the Queen is lifted above her loyal subjects as she moves, that there are women in attendance, that men with halberds crowd behind her, that four pallbearers carry her toward the left of the frame, and that all figures are shown in full length. Indeed, the film takes the same distance from its actors as the painter does from his subjects. What is cut on film—and this might explain to me the sense of crowding I have as I watch it—is the top third of the painting. Instead of a three-story building on the right and rolling hills on the left we see a moving, jostling, and cheering crowd.

Audiences at the turn of the twentieth century were familiar with Peake's image. Imitated in George Vertue's engraving *Royal Procession of Queen Elizabeth* in 1740, it was still topical at the time of Queen Victoria's accession to the throne. Agnes Strickland, in her *Lives of the Queens of England* of 1844, was critical of the *Procession Portrait*. She stated that it

> reminds us of the procession of a pagan goddess surrounded by her priests and worshippers, or the ovation of a Roman conqueror, rather than the transit of a Christian queen in civilized times. The semi-barbarous display of pomp and homage suited the theatrical taste of Elizabeth, who inherited the pride and vanity of both her parents, and understood little of the delicacy and reserve of an English gentlewoman.[73]

Written in homage to Queen Victoria, Strickland's criticism paradoxically indicates why Bernhardt might have referenced the *Procession Portrait* in *Queen Elizabeth*. It allows her to be pictured as the "Divine Sarah" surrounded by an applauding public (see figure 4.5). That a live audience in the theater was also watching her as she was raised on screen is significant: Bernhardt is not just a Queen, she is also one of global importance who travels and is seen "in carriage" abroad. This intersects with another representational strategy implicit in the original painting. Commissioned (arguably) by Edward Somerset, Earl of Worcester, who used the Elizabeth cult to commemorate his own status, the painting focuses on Elizabeth in order to explore and make evident his relationship to her. In the painting and on film there is consequently an oblique displacement. The real subject on view is Worcester and Bernhardt's relationship to the figure of the Queen, rather than the Queen herself.[74]

Figure 4.5. *The Royal Procession of Queen Elizabeth,* George Vertue, 1740. National Portrait Gallery, London.

A Home Theater

The scene that follows the procession portrait features the Queen and her court watching *The Merry Wives of Windsor*. While the composition and action of this scene is not based on a painting, there are two images relevant to depicted action. The first is David Scott's *Queen Elizabeth Viewing the Performance of The Merry Wives of Windsor at the Globe Theatre.* This painting shows Queen Elizabeth attending a public performance of Shakespeare's play surrounded by an assortment of men. As James Fowler has noted:

> Instead of restricting himself to the years 1601–1602, the then supposed date for *The Merry Wives of Windsor*, Scott adopts a broader time scheme that allows him to include leading courtiers, statesmen, and literary celebrities of the era. The figures and costumes fall mainly between c.1580 and c.1610; the former range from Sir Philip Sidney (d.1586) who wears dress of 1577, to Beaumont and Fletcher, who only established themselves as successful dramatists towards the end of the first decade of the seventeenth century. Even the Queen

> appears, though it has been well known at least since the eighteenth century that she never attended public playhouses. . . . By featuring her, Scott exploits the tradition first recorded by Scott and Rowe early in the eighteenth century that Shakespeare wrote *The Merry Wives of Windsor* to satisfy Elizabeth's desire to see Falstaff "in Love." This singular acknowledgement of Shakespeare's art fuelled the avid interest taken in his life by the nineteenth century, which would surely have invented the legend had it not already existed.[75]

In Bernhardt's film we have a similar sense of historic spectacle ("history-painting on the grand scale," as Fowler characterizes it) and a similar joining of Shakespeare and Elizabeth in celebration of Tudor theater. This celebration of both patron and playwright explains the renaissance of the theater in Elizabethan England. We also have *The Merry Wives of Windsor* performed with little view to historical exactitude. Fowler notes that Scott's painting is based on a thirty-year window of time and also includes within it the Earl of Essex (who stands at the front of the royal box) (see figure 4.6). In *Queen Elizabeth* we have Essex with the Queen attending a performance of a play that was published after his death in February 1601 (the play was published in 1602).

In the film, again with this same use of temporal flexibility, Essex is handed his Irish commission only after the time period depicted in the film. In fact, he had already left for Ireland in 1599. The film is a little more precise than the painting in the staging of this event: we are not inside the Globe Theatre

Figure 4.6. The Queen greets Shakespeare, *Queen Elizabeth*, 1912. National Film and Sound Archive of Australia.

but instead at a private performance before the Queen. On this occasion, we see the Queen wearing rows of pearls that reach almost to her waist. We know that the pearl was Elizabeth's "signature jewel and a conventional symbol of chastity."[76] While these are not featured in Scott's painting they are featured prominently in the famous *"Armada" Portrait of Queen Elizabeth* (artist unknown). We might guess that Bernhardt has taken the pearl, its symbolic meaning, and the way in which it was worn, from this image. Pictorial history, used creatively and loosely as a resource in *Queen Elizabeth*, informs cinematized theater. It prompts us to explore the visual density of film.

Celebrating Shakespeare

In 1840, at the time that Scott was painting *Queen Elizabeth Viewing the Performance of The Merry Wives of Windsor at the Globe Theatre*, the joining of Shakespeare with Elizabeth was common. As Fowler has demonstrated, novelists, playwrights, and artists together elevated Shakespeare in the Queen's favor.[77] In America, Shakespeare and Elizabeth were also popularly paired well into the late nineteenth century. An 1889 report on the opening of the Harlem Opera House in New York described, for example, the drop curtains in the theater (painted by E. T. Harvey) representing Shakespeare reading a play to Queen Elizabeth.[78] Even the fact that Bernhardt commissioned plays—I have mentioned Marcel Schwob and Eugène Morand in relation to *Hamlet*, but there is also Victorien Sardou on the live stage—overlaps with Elizabeth's relationship with Shakespeare, suggesting yet another coincidence between Bernhardt and Elizabeth in this scene. Patron and player, Queen and performer, Bernhardt cleverly multiplies the ways in which she is seen.

In making a clear link between Elizabeth and Shakespeare, *Queen Elizabeth* also presents itself as film that animates history. As W. Stephen Bush states in *Moving Picture World*, "What has been so often urged in these columns, the cooperation of the scholar and historian in the preparation of historic feature films, has been most literally carried out here."[79] As the *New York Times* explains, Frohman engaged Bernhardt to perform *Queen Elizabeth* in order to engage the working classes with film. Linking this to the effort of Charles Lamb, the English essayist who had published *Tales from Shakespeare* in 1807 with his sister Mary in an effort to bring Shakespeare to children, it explains:

> Mr Frohman made his start in motion pictures, fittingly enough with the most celebrated living player, Sarah Bernhardt, in Emile Moreau's "Queen Elizabeth." . . . He expects by means of it to so familiarize the class of theatre goers to whom the motion pictures particularly appeal with the beauties of the Shakespearian

drama that they will seize every opportunity to hear its oral productions. He considers his project analogous, to a certain extent, with the "Tales from Shakespeare" by Charles and Mary Lamb, which provide for children their first and sometimes only really palatable taste of the bard.[80]

Queen Elizabeth is a work that presents Shakespeare to us, making him not only accessible to children but available to a global audience. More importantly, it combines theater and history, adopting the role of historian and educator. The silence of film does not compound Shakespeare's inaccessibility or even the theater's absence, but instead provides a conduit for the ongoing celebration of cultural learning.

A *Portrait of Sarah Bernhardt*

In this "Shakespeare" scene, we not only have recourse to Shakespeare and his representation in nineteenth-century painting, but can see Georges Clairin's 1876 *Portrait of Sarah Bernhardt* reenacted by Bernhardt as a physical tableau (see Chapter 1, figure 1.2) In Clairin's work we see Bernhardt seated on a plush red couch with a dress swirling round her into a semicircular fan with a wolfhound at her feet. White fur lines the hem, sleeves, and neck of the white dress she has on, making her collar look like a softened version of the sharp ruffle of Elizabethan times. Depicting the famous actress alone, it invited a peek into a personal space audiences could not enter. Bernhardt is lounging in an intimate interior: no one else is present, and she gazes back at us in a languid, seductive way. A sensation at the Paris Salon of 1876, the picture infuriated Emile Zola, who railed against its shocking color and the fact that Bernhardt's "sinuous body is so serpentine that it is impossible to guess the outline of her body."[81] Later reproduced in other paintings and photographs—it is painted into Walford Graham Robertson's painting *The Actress Sarah Bernhardt in Her Salon* (1889), is included in Paul Nadar's photograph "Studio of Sarah Bernhardt on the Boulevard Péreire" (ca. 1889), and is the compositional model for Dornac's photograph "Sarah Bernhardt chez elle," 1896—Clairin's image was mediated and adapted in a variety of different ways.

In *Queen Elizabeth*'s "Shakespeare" scene, Clairin's painting is again reenacted. We see Bernhardt from the side; she is not facing us as she is in Clairin's work. We therefore have Clairin's pose repeated differently. There are now also two wolfhounds at her feet; the one closest to us on the screen replicates exactly the position of the dog in Clairin's portrait (and even shares the same patched coloring). Bernhardt still has a soft white ruffle around her neck. Now, however, there is also a sharp Elizabethan collar, standing stiff and starched around this. In both pictures Bernhardt has her hair cropped in dark curls around her face. Although Bernhardt's Elizabeth is not sexually alluring in the way that her portrait certainly is, I would note that this scene in the film ends with Elizabeth giving her ring to Essex alone in a room now cleared of courtiers. It is Elizabeth's most intimate moment with Essex and resonates, in this way, with the suggested intimacy of Clairin's portrait. That a seated pose can be part of a film narrative while also being related to a history of portraiture and media exchange should remind us of the interdisciplinary breadth and range of different epochs brought together by cinematized theater.

The Kiss

The scene that follows Essex receiving his Irish commission shows Essex telling the Countess of Nottingham of his imminent departure. The two lovers embrace in a room that is furnished in a minimal way (see figure 4.7). They are surrounded by walls of large stone and stand on a floor patterned by simple rectangular tiles. Behind the two lovers is a flight of three steps leading up to a doorway. To the left of the screen is the curtained entrance through which the Countess's husband will jealously spy. It is the lovers themselves that we focus upon: Essex leans over the Countess as she sits on the chair, she then stands, and they embrace. We see, behind them, the Count

Figure 4.7. The Kiss, *Queen Elizabeth*, 1912. National Film and Sound Archive of Australia.

of Nottingham appear and express his anger. He retreats. We are therefore the only witnesses to their eventual kiss.

The mise-en-scène and composition of this scene is based loosely on Francesco Hayez's famous painting, *The Kiss* (1859). We have the same somber interior with large stone walls and three steps stretching behind the lovers. We also have a doorway or entrance behind the lovers that, in both instances, makes an apparently private affair one that is nevertheless witnessed by another. Hence, in the film the watching Earl hides behind the curtain; in the painting there is the shadow of an unidentified maid whose head is turned away from the couple. Further, both pictures describe a common moment: although on film Essex does not have his foot impatiently resting on the staircase (as the male figure does in the painting), we know that action is anyway hurried. As Essex leans down to kiss the Countess, Hayez's painting is again suggested, at least for the short duration of the kiss (see figure 4.8). The

Figure 4.8. Francesco Hayez, *The Kiss*, 1859. Pinacoteca di Brera, Italy.

Countess, like the female figure in Hayez's portrait, stands closest to us, the back of her gown exposed as Essex steps forward to kiss her. Essex's hands, like the hands of the lover in *The Kiss*, clasp her face as she embraces him. In this way, a painting that was made by the most famous Italian romantic painter of the nineteenth century was used to help describe a furtive love affair in *Queen Elizabeth*.

What is interesting about this intermedial layering of theatrical action on screen is not just the easy way we can recognize the painting that has inspired the scene. It is also the fact that Hayez's painting returns us to a past that is narratively commensurate with the tale that Bernhardt was telling about Elizabethan England. On film, Essex is a young man about to go off and fight the Irish; his love for his Queen and country is stronger than this personal affair. Similarly, *The Kiss* can be identified as an emblem of Italian youth leaving their loved ones to participate in the Risorgimento.[82] Hayez's paintings are also philologically correct. Like Bernhardt including a close-up of Essex's Irish commission and death warrant and keeping her costume and décor true to the Tudor period, Hayez was famous for studying the architecture, setting, and costume of Renaissance Italy. As Fernando Mazzoca states, "In his sumptuous canvases Hayez resumed the 'narrative' tradition of the great Venetian painting of the *Cinquecento*; just as he pursued, with the philological precision now customary in the international language of history painting (of which the leading representative was the Frenchman Delaroche, whose fame was secured by the engravings of his works), the faithful rendering of costumes—the strong suit in his repertoire—and of architectural and environmental details."[83]

While it is relatively easy to identify the gestural similarities of both "kisses," it is more difficult for me to determine whether Hayez's painting was indeed important to Bernhardt or whether there was a history of his work informing performance on the live stage. I know, however, that Hayez was involved in the theater. There are accounts of Verdi asking for Hayez's advice in the staging of his operas, the two were involved in Milan in the Salon of Andrea and Clarina Maffei, and they drew upon the same repertory of themes in their work.[84] There are also records at La Scala that show that Hayez painted works for the theater.[85] Was Hayez's painting enacted as visual tableau in the live stage production of *Queen Elizabeth*? Was it consciously included in the film? I do not know. What I can attest is that I recall Hayez's painting, however briefly and however imperfectly, when I watch this scene. Cinematized theater again elaborates physical action, making a hasty kiss much more than a simple narrative event on screen.

Discussing Delaroche

Paul Delaroche was a French painter of the nineteenth century who, like Hayez, worked in a spectacular historical manner. In my opinion it is Delaroche, more than any other artist I have discussed, who is closest in spirit and practice to Bernhardt. Like Bernhardt, he was a canny publicist since he was not just one of the most widely known and acclaimed painters in the Western world in the mid-nineteenth century but also the most extensively reproduced artist of his age.[86] He used the very techniques—lithography and photography—that would make Bernhardt identifiable in the later half of the nineteenth century to expand the public for his own images. Delaroche was not only materially available to the public, he was also similar to Bernhardt in choosing subject matter that provided him with a lingua franca accessible to all.[87] Like the *Ciné-Journal* indicating that Bernhardt's film had a long and popular history, so too did contemporaries of Delaroche mention that the subject of his portrait was popular. Hence, the *Ciné-Journal*'s comment: "Everyone knows the tragic history of Queen Elizabeth of England and about her relationship with the valiant Earl of Essex"[88] is met by the statement in the English *Art Journal* of 1849 that "Perhaps no modern historical painter has achieved a wider or more deserving popularity than Paul Delaroche, arising not less from his high attainments as an artist, than from his choice of subjects, which generally have been selected from some well-known passages of history, to which all men lay a prescriptive claim on the score of knowledge."[89]

Although we have no record of Bernhardt mentioning Delaroche and his working methods, there is also overlap in the way the two visually reconstructed history. Stephen Bann, citing Eugène de Mirecourt's description of Delaroche's artistic process, explains how "Before throwing an idea onto the canvas, he would bring it to maturity by lengthy studies, rummage through public and private libraries, and research old collections, folios of old engravings, histories of deeds, furnishings, and costumes."[90] Bann also cites an *Illustrated London News* article of 1848 where it is explained that the costume and the bedstead for Delaroche's famous *Princes in the Tower* (1830) were carved and made in England and that the artist went "expressly to London to visit the scene of his picture."[91] Here, we can note that Bernhardt included details of costume and décor that confirm her own historic rummaging, and incorporated shots of material history (again, the Irish commission and death warrant) in her film.[92] The *Ciné-Journal* accordingly boasts that the film was "Executed with great concern for historical truth and at the cost of considerable sacrifices, with the permission of the English government."[93] W. Stephen Bush, reviewing *Queen Elizabeth*, extends the issue of historic accuracy to that of stage action, stating that "The most remarkable part of this play is its accuracy to historical detail. The procession to and from the court was a masterpiece of historical cinematography. . . . The mournful pageant itself was true to recorded history."[94]

What, however, was this recorded history? And how much of this was already prefigured in Moreau's theatrical production? I am not sure. I have already mentioned that some of the play's costume and décor was carried into film. In the scenes where I have no photographs that I can use to establish overlap between the play and film and where I can recognize no painting as a pictorial source, I believe that printed historical sources were consulted to inform action. For example, action in the beheading scene—where Essex addresses men near the scaffold, is flanked by a chaplain, and exchanges pardons with his executioner—is in my opinion informed by historical sources since eye-witness accounts of the 2nd Earl of Essex's execution describe this same detail.[95] In this way, Bernhardt brings to film the same practices and processes that Delaroche had earlier brought to history painting. She joins historical research with engaging narrative events, using theatricized cinema as a way to educate us about history.

Developing Delaroche's Deaths

The first Delaroche painting that we see referenced in *Queen Elizabeth* is *Cromwell before the Coffin of Charles I*. This work is suggested rather than reenacted in the scene where Elizabeth visits Essex in his coffin. In other words, we do not see the painting as a tableau re-created on screen. Compositional and narrative differences exist: Bernhardt is a woman, she does not open a casket as Cromwell does in the Delaroche image, and she stands on the left (rather than the right) of the image. In another departure, Elizabeth is accompanied by a maid who crumples to the floor, and there is a guard behind her. What is similar in the two images, however, is the physiognomy and costume of the dead men, the somber interiority of the room, and the fact that we see the head of a decapitated man who was killed in the seventeenth century for high treason.

Cromwell and Charles I was hugely popular with audiences of its day, yet widely criticized for failing to express any discernible feeling on Cromwell's face. "Is it joy, disdain, scorn, remorse, fear for the future, regret for the past, a sudden understanding of the nothingness of grandeur? hope or repentance? I see no trait in his face which reveals to me a single of these sentiments," stated Gustave Planche in response to Delaroche's work at the *Salon* of 1831. Patricia Smyth has recently argued that such indeterminacy explains Delaroche's popularity, since it inspired emotional response in an untutored and emerging nonexpert viewer of art. In her view, it was precisely because the artist guarded "against manner" that he "signified real emotion allowing it to spread throughout the audience like contagion."[96] In *Queen Elizabeth* there is no such indeterminacy: Bernhardt registers her shock at finding the ring missing from Essex's hand and brings obvious despair to the scene. Bernhardt thereby makes performed emotions our visual currency: we empathize with emotional distress at injustice and sadness at the loss of a loved one.

In the final death scene, we see another reference to Delaroche. Here, Delaroche's *Death of Queen Elizabeth* is the loose model for the costume, characters, and choreography of the scene (see figure 4.9). Indeed, the Queen

Figure 4.9. *Mort d'Elisabeth, reine d'Angleterre, en 1603*, Paul Delaroche. RMN-Grand Palais (museé du Louvre)/Gérard Blot.

wears a similar costume with a high ruff and ermine cloak, there are cushions strewn on the floor, a trio of genuflecting maids in front and to the left of the image, a backdrop with royal insignia on its surface, and members of the court in attendance. These details are true to recorded history: we know, for instance, that ermine is an emblem of chastity and was considered appropriate to the depiction of the Virgin Queen. Elizabeth was painted, for example, with an ermine on her arm in 1585 (*The "Ermine" Portrait*, attributed to William Segar).[97] We also know that during her final hours Elizabeth was surrounded by her closest female maids, that she lay on cushions, and that she did not name her successor until shortly before her death (see figure 4.10). As David Hume wrote in the *History of England* (published in 1800): "Ten days and nights she lay upon the carpet, leaning on cushions which her maids brought her; and the physicians could not persuade her to allow herself to be put to bed, much less to make trial of any remedies they prescribed to her."[98] This source was included in the 1828 *livret* that accompanied the painting's exhibition at the Salon and in the catalog for Delaroche's posthumous exhibition in 1857.[99]

In returning to depict this famous account of Queen Elizabeth's death, Delaroche anticipates what Roland Barthes would call the "intense immobility" of the photographic image.[100] That is, although his work is novel in that it renders a moment of a death that is unavailable to us for contemplation, this does not transform the image or change its ascribed meaning. Although

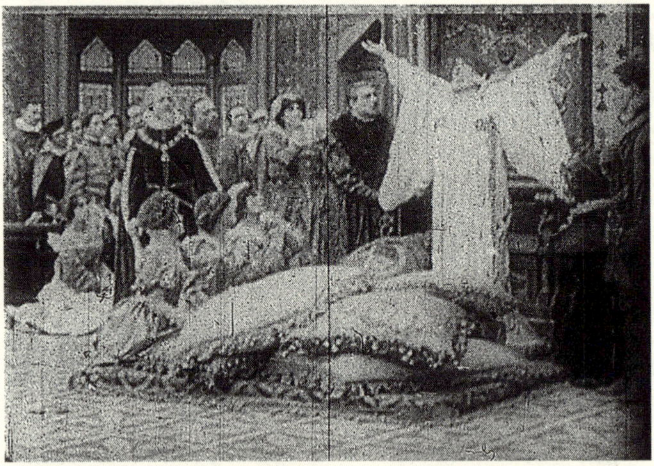

Figure 4.10. Queen Elizabeth dies on film, *Queen Elizabeth*, 1912. National Film and Sound Archive of Australia.

the androgyny of Delaroche's Queen might provide me with the *punctum* of the image (the profile of her masculine face emerges from a bed of female opulence), Delaroche's painting is nevertheless prescriptive: the Queen will name her successor after ten days of writhing on the cushions and die a slow death.

On film we have, instead, fast physical action. Where Delaroche depicts the Queen twisted into a serpentine form as she lies on her ermine cloak (and where descriptions of Moreau's play speak of a scene that clearly took time), on film Bernhardt dies quickly. She walks into the room, is offered Essex's sword, discards this, stands before the pile of cushions and calls for a goblet from which she drinks. She then holds a mirror to her face. Discarding the mirror (which alludes to her awareness that her court had misrepresented her enduring beauty),[101] she refuses support. Pulling herself straight, as though driven by a final burst of energy, she calls for the Earl of Nottingham. She speaks, raises both arms upward, and then falls frontally onto the cushions.

May Agate, a former student of the actress, describes Bernhardt's stage performance of this scene. She argues that the flop to her death indicates Bernhardt's reinterpretation of Hume's and Delaroche's description of the Queen's character. She states:

> [Bernhardt's] performance was one of a soul-seared woman who still loves the man she has put to death. She was regal, immensely dignified, terrible, and as a picture of remorse I can think of nothing more haunting. What is more, you felt here was a woman capable of putting people to death, for she was hard, inexorable, terrifying. Even in her last throes of suffering she made no appeal to pity. There was no truck with the pendants; she died standing up, falling forward on to a mass of cushions, not writhing, senile amongst them as is recorded historically.[102]

There is evidence that Delaroche's painting had been used as a tableau on the stage. As early as 1829, we have record of François Ancelot basing a tragedy upon Elizabeth's life and concluding it with a deathbed scene similar to that depicted in Delaroche's work.[103] In 1867, when the playwrights Eugène Nus and Alphonse Brot opened their play *Testament de la Reine Elisabeth* at the Théâtre de la Gaité in Paris, a review in *Le Temps* would confirm this, stating: "Since the painting of Paul Delaroche, the dramaturgical painter who concerns himself much more with historical mise-en-scene than with philosophy, one can not but represent Elisabeth, old and dying, unless lying on cushions and railing through the golden lace of her bristling ruffles."[104] Their play specifically called for such staging: the opening to the fourth tableau asks that Delaroche's *Queen Elizabeth* be re-created (see figure 4.11).[105] Viewed in

Figure 4.11. Sarah Bernhardt in Act IV, *Queen Elizabeth*, a play by Emile Moreau, Théâtre Sarah Bernhardt, April 11, 1912. Bibliothèque Nationale de France.

this context, Bernhardt's return to Delaroche takes an added significance. She actively changes the character and meaning of the history depicted. In this way, an event was figuratively *and* rhetorically freed from what Barthes would call its "intense immobility."

There is one final reading of Bernhardt's death flop in *Queen Elizabeth* that has yet to be included in this discussion of painting, pose, and movement. This is the humor of the scene. An aged actress spectacularly reenacts the death of a famous English Queen. As one exhibitor cautions: "If you run *Queen Elizabeth*, stop with the scene before the last, cutting out that absurd death flop into the pile of cushions placed before the throne for no other reason than to save the Bernhardt bones. It gives a comedy finish that is hurtful."[106] While we might ask who or what might have been hurt by a comedy finish (Bernhardt? film? Queen Elizabeth? an audience?) we cannot deny that Delaroche was relevant to public discussion of the film. In this sense, we might speak of cinematized theater as a process of rhetorical expansion: even in her most famous film and in her most famous death scene, Bernhardt multiplies performative meanings.

Sic Transit Gloria Mundi

Bernhardt's elaboration of how we might think about and understand Elizabeth I was part of a celebration of "Gloriana" in the early twentieth century. As Leonée Ormond explains, by the 1880s the Elizabethans were no longer considered barbarians but were instead celebrated across the arts for their contribution to English history. The three hundredth anniversary of the Armada saw public festivities as well as new poems, paintings, sculptures, and edifices.[107] Whereas Victorian England had initially characterized Elizabeth as a vain and cruel Queen, a pagan and uncivilized goddess, by the time Bernhardt appeared on film, public sentiment had changed. What Bernhardt thus portrays is not just a Queen who loves Essex, but a woman who can herself be loved as an empathetic, historical subject. The enduring irony of this is that the change that Bernhardt brought to the history of art—to Peake, Scott, Hayez, and Delaroche, and even to Nance O'Neil, Mrs F. W. Landers, and Ristori—has long been forgotten by film scholars: "Sic Transit Gloria Mundi." It is paradoxically Bernhardt's richly complex integration of theater, cinema, and painting, rather than the nitrate print, that has in this instance proved fleeting.

5. *Sarah Bernhardt at Home*

Cinema and the Home, ca. 1915

In my previous chapters, I have argued that Bernhardt's films were cinematized theater. I have yet to demonstrate that cinematized theater involved anything but narrative film. Not only does Bernhardt's *Sarah Bernhardt à Belle Isle* (*Sarah Bernhardt at Home*, Louis Mercanton, Hecla) allow me to ask what documentary film might tell us about cinematized theater in the teen years, it also forces new questions about Bernhardt. The most obvious question begins with the subject of the film itself. Why did Bernhardt make a film that had little or nothing to do with her famous theatrical roles? Why didn't she take another of her famous theatrical roles—*Phedre*, *Cleopatra*, *Theodora*, or *Jeanne d'Arc*, for instance—and bring it to film? If Bernhardt was using film for publicity alone, why not take us backstage in the theater, introduce us to her cast, give us a glimpse of her famous wardrobes and jewelry, or a tour of her atelier in Paris? Why bring us to Belle Isle, an island in Brittany and a holiday retreat for herself, and show us pictures of her walking around windy landscapes collecting flowers? Why not focus on the urban home or why not, again, return us to her famous salon in Paris? Why all of this movement, this roaming from place to place, particularly since Bernhardt found it difficult to walk?

These are some questions that can be asked of the film. Rather than directing discussion toward the issue of theatrical celebrity or self-promotion, I want to ask what it is we are seeing when we watch *Sarah Bernhardt at Home*. It is obvious that Bernhardt was famous and that the film promotes her internationally. It is not obvious, however, why the film was shot on Belle Isle, why certain activities are performed there, and why there is constant change in terms of the roles and spaces that constitute Bernhardt's home. In this sense, my interest lies in what we can see on the film today: the different places, activities, and people that constitute Bernhardt "at home."

Hecla Films, ca. 1912–1915

In America in July 1915, it was announced that the Photoplay Releasing Company of Chicago had acquired the American and Canadian rights to the two-reel feature film, *Sarah Bernhardt at Home.*[1] Although the film's release was predicted as early as February 1913 by the "All Star" Film Supply Company of America,[2] there is no evidence in the trade press of the film's emergence or circulation until 1915. The film was probably shot, however, sometime in late 1912, shortly after the success of *Queen Elizabeth.* Indeed, I believe that *Sarah Bernhardt at Home* was filmed sometime in 1912 because the festivities it shows on the island of Belle Isle look very similar to those reproduced on the cover of the *Excelsior* on August 21, 1912. The explorative, often playful mood of the film is also at odds with the patriotism and fervor that Bernhardt expresses during the war years.[3] Because of this apparent contradiction, comments about the film being shot just "two months prior to the amputation of her limb" (and therefore in December 1914, since her right leg was amputated in February 1915) are less factual than they are marketing efforts that make the film relevant to the war.[4] Indeed, the suggestion that Bernhardt's "halting walk gives outward and visible evidence of the impending ordeal which followed on the surgeon's table" is less a description of what we see on the film than an effort to link what we see on the film with contemporary affairs, namely the injured war veteran.[5]

While the date of the film's production can be contested, we know that the film circulated globally on its release in 1915. The American and Canadian rights noted earlier indicate this. So, too, do the German intertitles that we see on the restored print that the Filmarchiv Austria presented at *Cinema Ritrovato* in 2006. Further, the fact that "HECLA FILMS" is on each intertitle of this print indicates that the film is made by Hecla, the English film company. This company was formed in 1912 with the aim of producing "sensational films with fashionable actors such as Sarah Bernhardt."[6] In addition, with Louis Mercanton serving as its head and as Bernhardt's personal manager,[7] we know that *Sarah Bernhardt at Home* is a transnational production. Publicity for films made by the company reach beyond national borders, stating that the "world renowned Hecla features" were "of Paris and London."[8] Articles describing the company state that it is "one of the largest European manufacturers of pictures, with establishments in London and Paris."[9] Although the company seems to have folded in 1916, at the time of *Sarah Bernhardt at*

Home's showing Hecla had offices in the United States and Canada and had already released Bernhardt's *Adrienne Lecouvreur* (*The Romance of an Actress*, 1913) and Mounet Sully's *Oedipus Rex* two years earlier.[10] In this context, *Sarah Bernhardt at Home* is part of an ongoing effort to promote Bernhardt's global visibility in a new technology. However, rather than see the film only in terms of Bernhardt's business acumen, I want to explore the function of the film. As *Moving Picture World* states, *Sarah Bernhardt at Home* is "two reels of a most unusual and unique film."[11] How is the film unusual? Why is it unique? In my opinion, the film must be one of the first of an actor at home to circulate commercially.

The Art Nouveau Home

Sarah Bernhardt at Home provides a significant insight into the way that art nouveau entered and shaped the home at the opening of the twentieth century. Mobile in a global market, the film exposed Bernhardt's home to international viewership and scrutiny. What impact did this exposure have on viewers and the modeling of their own homes? I would suggest that Bernhardt was something of a pioneer when she invited the film camera into her home and made this a setting for her social life and creative work. In the teen years, magazines document women who work in the film industry in their homes. For example, Lois Weber is featured "At work on a script in her study" in an article in *Photoplay Magazine*,[12] Geraldine Farrar is depicted in a "specially posed home picture" leaning on her piano in *Motion Picture Magazine*,[13] and Ann Murdock ("the Mutual star" launched by Charles Frohman) is pictured knitting at her home with a caption that explains: "She is not darning socks for the soldiers, she is knitting a muffler for herself."[14] What Bernhardt reveals in this film, however, is not a single photographic image of creative activity but the ongoing and consuming importance of the home to creative work and production. Art nouveau emerges from within the home; it is a creative style that shapes all aspects of life. Indeed, we see art nouveau in the floral interiors of Bernhardt's rooms, in the range of creative activities she undertakes, in the sea and landscapes she traverses, as well as in the making of a film that shows global celebrity (Bernhardt) alongside local craft industries and folk communities.

Advertisements for the film emphasize its art nouveau style. In one, we see Bernhardt photographed with her dogs relaxing alone on a couch. This image is flanked by ornate shields that feature "PRP Co." (the Photo Releasing Company) and that remind us of Bernhardt's own use of the decorative *SB*. The title of the film is below this, its ornate type ("SARAH Bernhardt /

AT HOME") reinforcing the art nouveau framing of the film. Sandwiched between this title is a description of the film, its emphasis on change and flexibility making Bernhardt a prototype of a modern art nouveau woman. It states:

> The Divine Sarah is pictured in every detail of her home life, showing her in her various moods and her many foibles. . . . The picture itself is a marvel of photography. She is reflected in the act of a highly interesting game of tennis—she is seen climbing from rock to rock to escape the oncoming tide—she is seen in the floral jungles which abound on Belle Isle . . . and finally the Divine Sarah is pictured in her den overlooking the sea. In all, it shows Bernhardt as Bernhardt in the flesh. It evinces the flow of soul which is within her.[15]

The actress and her home emerge not in terms of a fixed identity and space but as fluid and shifting categories. Filling domestic environments with flowers, curved furniture, and oriental screens as well as with newly forged links across the arts, Bernhardt is an active and changing figure. She exposes an art nouveau we are familiar with (nature, including flowers, water, animals, women) just as she reveals the home to be a site that brings the arts and various media together. What is new is the affirmation of the home as a creative space where things can happen and communities and cultures can mix. We see a home but we see a film and also see "a marvel of photography." Famous paintings are invoked in the composition of shots, folk dances are enacted by local villagers, and local customs are represented. We see a telegraph arrive and watch Bernhardt respond to this. Bernhardt also fishes, plays tennis, and camps. Bernhardt is successively and perhaps even simultaneously an artist, host, patron, mother, friend, sportswoman, actress, sculptor, and writer. From this collection of arts, scenes, materials, and activities we understand that art nouveau is more than a visual style or a physical way of materializing gesture on stage. It is a way of inhabiting the home in a creative and expansive way; it is a way of affirming that traditional female culture is part of the new world and the new century.

Playing at Home

I argue that in exploring the different spaces that together represent "the home," Bernhardt reveals her home's expansive horizons. In developing this idea I follow the recent work of Heide Schlüpmann in her article, "An Alliance between History and Theory." Here, Schlüpmann argues that the cinema in the teen years materialized women's perceptual realities, particularly their capacity for perceptual play.[16] Schlüpmann makes the argument that the bourgeois home in Wilhelminian Germany is not necessarily a space of entrapment. It is instead a space that allows us to understand the developing cinema. Following Georg Simmel and his concept of the "Haus," she argues that women's emancipation from the bourgeois home is coincidental with the emergence of the cinema. Intimately tied to their capacity for perceptual play, these two spaces see the housewife and the actress become cultural and social figures who negotiate and realize perceptual play across both public and private spheres.[17]

In Bernhardt's film, the actress is a female "player" who negotiates not just a range of spaces but also a range of roles within the home. She is creative as a mother, artist, patron of the local village, sportswoman, explorer, and general host. The home is perceptually and politically female in Bernhardt's capacity to shift between these roles; she asserts the myriad of different relationships that constitute her artistic and social reality. Bernhardt does this, we must remember, through film. A global medium, film is publicly intimate, engaging us in the very play that is unfolding in Bernhardt's home. As spectators, we become part of this community, accepting the perceptual shifts that the film reveals. Schlüpmann's formulation of the relationship between the Haus and the actress resonates here, revealing the way that film frees the home from the private. She states:

> [T]he play in which the woman on screen engages is something that the women in the cinema are deeply familiar with: it is part of their actual world. This is suddenly realized in the perception of the female audience. The actress breaks through the spell of spectatorship and places the reality of play in a public space. Thanks to her, a life sphere, a form of communal life, that the women formed in and with the home is freed from the walls of the private.[18]

The idea that *Sarah Bernhardt at Home* is a film that documents perceptual play in the home makes Bernhardt less a theatrical intruder in film than an actress who early engages the cinema in a "cinematic" way. In this context, I argue that Bernhardt does not lose theatrical agency on film; she instead makes play in and with "the home," making the home the paradigmatic subject of her film.

This play in and with the home coincided with the popularity of women's home journals (for example, *Woman's Home Companion*, *Ladies' World*, *Ladies' Home Journal*, and *American Sunday Monthly Magazine* in America, *Je sais tout* and *Femina* in France, and *Woman at Home* and *Lady's Realm* in Britain). The home, even in its most traditional and domestic form, was publicized, promoted, and performed in and through such public forums that give proof of its new frontiers. Emerging discussions about the cinema were part of this development. As an editorial in *Ladies' Home Journal* explains to its readers in 1921, "Feminine patrons of the movies are very largely in the majority. In most families the women lead the way. Primarily the pictures are made for her."[19] *Sarah Bernhardt at Home* is a film that was made with this female audience in mind. Above all, it begins with the premise that the home is publicly interesting, creatively enlightening (it joins traditional and folk arts to film) as well as a site of performance and play. As though to emphasize this focus, the advertisement for *Sarah Bernhardt at Home* declares that the film is "IN TWO ACTS" and can be booked "simultaneously with Bernhardt's personal appearance in your city."[20] Presented in terms of a theatrical play, the home becomes a public site of intrigue.

An Island Landing

How does the film begin? The film's establishing shot shows Bernhardt rowed to shore from a steamship, *L'Union*. This was a steamship hired by Bernhardt to take her to Belle Isle en Mer, an island in Brittany where she kept a home. Bernhardt would also use a similar steamship, *Emile Solacroup*, to arrive at the island. This was a famous passenger ship that took people from mainland France on trips to Belle Isle. The steamship indicates both a growing trade in tourism and the expanding reach of steam and rail travel. Indeed, we can associate the steamship that regularly serviced Bernhardt's island with Solacroup, the famous nineteenth-century director of the Paris-Orleans railway. Victor Laloux had completed the Parisian Gare d'Orsay in 1900 on the eve of the Exposition Universelle and in a record two years. This was the terminus for the Paris-Orleans line. As the first electrified railway terminal in the world, the Gare d'Orsay was a masterpiece of industrial architecture. As the starting point of her journey, we are returned to a modern Paris that Bernhardt helped to shape. We are also reminded that the home is linked to modern travel.

Bernhardt arrives home by modern modes of transport but is then rowed ashore. This is not a landing at the Port de Palais, the "actual" port of Belle Isle where Bernhardt would later be photographed amid crowds of people. Nor, too, does this image duplicate the images that circulated on postcards of Bernhardt's arrival at this beach (the remote "Plage de Poulains") since we cannot see a waiting crowd watching her disembark from the rowboat.[21] Instead, ours is a solitary regard held on an otherwise empty beach. This suggestion of privacy, of a secluded and privileged spectatorship, helps to confirm the idea that the film is an intimate and revealing document of the actress returning "home."

In this same opening scene, we can see a small boat to the far left. This is a fishing boat, identifiable through its distinct sails. These recall the boats and landscapes in the paintings that Maxime Maufra had recently completed a few years earlier on Belle Isle: *Entrée du Port de Palais, Belle-Isle-en-Mer* and *Port Castle of Belle Isle* (both 1910). Establishing the presence of local community, we then see three small rowboats head from the steamship to shore. Figures wave and although we cannot see precisely who these are, the introductory title has already told us that Bernhardt is traveling with her son, Maurice. We can assume, then, that we have been included in Bernhardt's group of close intimate friends and that the actress is signaling her awareness of our presence even if she cannot really see us. In the same manner, we cannot really see Bernhardt, since she is both too far away and, anyway, a film. In this sense, the waving figures realize our presence even as they signal our distance from them. This is not an instance in which as viewers we imagine ourselves part of a crowd (the beach is empty, unlike the beach featured on the postcard mentioned earlier). It is instead an instance in which we can enjoy the fiction of our own uniqueness, our undisturbed importance upon an unnamed beach. Moreover, everything we see—the steamship, the fisherman's boat, the newsreel-type footage of Bernhardt's arrival—is shot, grouped, and framed entirely for us. Hence, in the second shot, the steam stops pouring from the funnel, the fisherman's boat disappears from sight, and yet Bernhardt smoothly continues her approach toward us. As Bernhardt approaches us in her rowboat, visual meanings therefore multiply. We have a collage of respective boats (the steamship, the rowboats, and the fishing boat), a range of media with which we might associate them (the postcard, the painting, and film) as well as a range of different viewing positions (we are on shore and Bernhardt waves to us, we are not in her boating party, we are spectators to a film).

We later have one final shot of Bernhardt in a boat when she returns to sea to fish for lobsters (see figure 5.1). Departing from the same shore but this time alone with two men who row, this shot of her single boat moving mid-distance at sea suggests the composition and style of Manet's *Escape of Rochefort* (1881) (see figure 5.2). Manet's painting depicts an indistinct grouping of four people on a rowboat, moving on bobbing water. Yet, whereas Manet was reconstructing the escape that had occurred six years earlier (Henri Rochefort escaped from the Isle des Pins, Noumea, by stopping a ship on an excursion in 1874),[22] Bernhardt's trip depicts a holiday activity as it unfolds. Although painted some years before Bernhardt made her film, Rochefort had been included in a 1897 waxwork display of her Salon in America and was part of her intimate social circle.[23] Absent on film yet emerging through visual

Figure 5.1. Bernhardt departs from shore, *Sarah Bernhardt at Home*, 1915. Filmarchiv Austria.

Figure 5.2. Édouard Manet, *L'évasion de Rochefort, 1880–1881*, photo © RMN-Grand Palais. Musée d'Orsay/Hervé Lewandowski.

suggestion and similarity, Bernhardt's film actively engages us as viewers. Her home emerges less an island retreat than an inclusive space of artistic, social, and intergenerational exchange.

Doing Things Differently

The stylistic intersections between Bernhardt's boats at sea and Manet's and Maufra's paintings can be linked to the fact that film, like Impressionist painting, was made in plein air, depicted outdoor seabound excursions, and made physical movement a focus. Although film therefore intersects with painting, it does not re-create painting as a frozen tableau on film. This approach is clear in the opening scene when Bernhardt's boat arrives at shore, she is carried to the sand, and her greyhound rushes forward to meet her. As I have noted in my chapter on *Queen Elizabeth*, this greyhound features in Georges Clairin's famous 1876 portrait of Bernhardt. On film, however, the dog is free to move. No longer curled at the foot of a chair, Bernhardt's dog is freed into movement. In other words, film moves an indoor portrait outside, and it changes a dog that had served to describe the art nouveau tendril into a dog that now depicts movement. Thus, the dog rushes to join Bernhardt just as she too moves and waves, actively acknowledging her watching audience (see figure 5.3). Gone, therefore, is the relationship of the actress to a

Figure 5.3. Bernhardt's greyhound meets the boat, *Sarah Bernhardt at Home*, 1915. Filmarchiv Austria.

solitary and seductive interior. Still dressed in white and still the subject of the "portrait," Bernhardt now actively inhabits the world and waves to her unknown audience.

This renegotiation of Bernhardt's image says much about the possibilities that film enables in depicting and describing the actress; it also says much about changing gender relations and dynamics. For in this same scene—and later in others that I will discuss—we have Bernhardt carried by anonymous men to the shore, we have her luggage boxes carried by men uphill, and we have her feted in a manner that is quite different from her representation in late-nineteenth-century portraiture. Indeed, we need only realize the extent to which gendered roles are being reversed (or at least significantly revised) in order to appreciate the extent to which the actress is newly defined.

Bernhardt does not just return home, she arrives a celebrity at home: she is carried off the boat and given flowers. The house we see in opening shots of the film confirms her status as owner of her own house. But this house is a fort. It sits like a castle on the rocks, emerging in a long pan of the camera. No longer removed from the traditional bourgeois woman's space of the home, the actress is a queen who returns to her castle. In this sense, Bernhardt refuses the actress' traditional association with prostitution or loose morals (she has a home, she is feted like a queen). Bernhardt also makes the home the subject of her film. This interpretation challenges ideas about reclusive Victorian domesticity, the power of men to rule over and define traditional women's culture, and the hidden private life of the nineteenth-century stage actress.

The people who surround Bernhardt are both men and women. In particular, we see a supportive band of women who reappear in many scenes. When Bernhardt arrives on shore, there are six women in her party and only a couple of male companions (one of whom is the painter Georges Clairin). We later see evidence of female companionship when Bernhardt is attended by a woman while she sculpts and again later when she writes. A large group of women also collect flowers with her in the fields. Men eat meals with her and play tennis with her, but they also row her to shore, carry her luggage, pull her cart, applaud her speeches, and help her fish: they provide the physical labor that supports her various activities (see figure 5.4). What are the implications here? In one of the opening scenes we see men with caps on their heads, bowing beneath the weight of Bernhardt's luggage as they carry it from shore to the fort. Millet's painting *Peasant Women with Brushwood* (1858) is suggested in this scene, since it is visually similar in terms of formal composition: anonymous workers are burdened by loads, their heads bowed, as they walk along a path heading left to right of the frame (see figure 5.5).

Figure 5.4. Men carry Bernhardt's luggage, *Sarah Bernhardt at Home*, 1915. Filmarchiv Austria.

Figure 5.5. Jean-François Millet, *Peasant women with Brushwood*, ca. 1858.

Figure 5.6. Bernhardt's female companion takes a photograph, *Sarah Bernhardt at Home*, 1915. Filmarchiv Austria.

On film, men bend over their loads and work for a female proprietor. Noticeably, it is a young female companion who later takes a quick photograph of Bernhardt being pulled along the beach on a donkey-drawn cart (see figure 5.6). Walking alongside Bernhardt and joined by three men who help push the cart (Clairin is part of this team), this young lady rushes ahead, turns and takes a picture, and then resumes her place beside Bernhardt. Clearly, it is women who take their own pictures, make their own portraits, and who might document the anonymous labor of men.

The Artist's Atelier

Perhaps because of the difficulty in lighting indoor spaces, *Sarah Bernhardt at Home* features few indoor scenes. Those that are shown focus on Bernhardt in an atelier (see figure 5.7). Her atelier is an organized space filled with sculptures that reveal the amount and quality of the work she has done. We can guess from the figurative works that surround her that Bernhardt is an artist who sculpts many people in different materials. Bernhardt is also clearly active: she physically moves, tools in hand, in the scene. Dressed in a work apron that covers a long skirt and white top, attention is less on her dress and pose than on her work. Further, Bernhardt's audience in this scene is a female companion who is seated beside her, leafing through a book. Occasionally, comments are passed between the two, and her companion looks

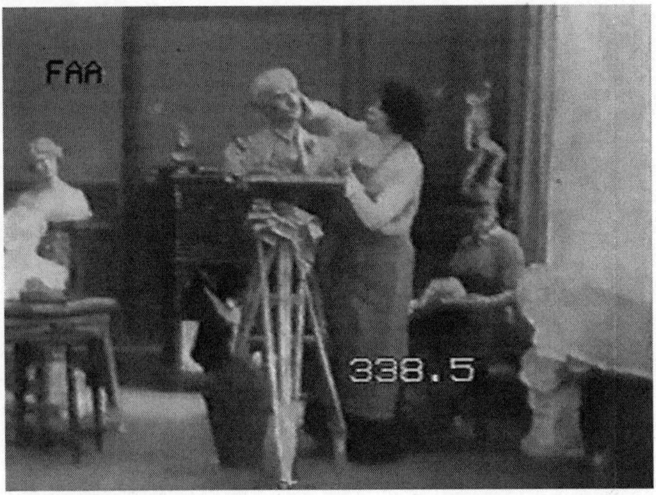

Figure 5.7. Bernhardt in her atelier, *Sarah Bernhardt at Home*, 1915. Filmarchiv Austria.

up and leans to see the bust on which she is working. The atelier is a space of comfortable female companionship and creativity. The intertitles inform us that the bust Bernhardt is shaping is Edmond Rostand, the playwright whose *L'Aiglon* she had made famous on the stage a decade earlier. Bernhardt is therefore a professional artist capable not only of bringing Rostand's verse to the stage but of sculpting his physical form. Women make and shape their own impressions of the world.

This scene is a development of earlier depictions of Bernhardt as a sculptor. In Melandri's famous photograph of the actress from ca. 1875, for example, she stands alone with just one work in sight. She is dressed in a white silk pantsuit designed by the couturier Charles Frederick Worth. With one foot resting in a provocative way on a block of wood (we can see her ankle) and her head turned coolly toward us, Bernhardt leans an elbow on a stand that features her sculpted self portrait. As Janice Bergman-Carton notes in her discussion of the photograph, in this image Bernhardt plays a variety of roles:

> The composition and cropping . . . showcases Bernhardt's self-aware play—her identity as actress, artist, and work of art. She poses, in the decorative and androgynous costume of "the artist," adjacent to her own sculpted self-representation. The sculpture, seen in profile, and slightly elevated to the right of her actual head, is compositionally implied to be the mirrored reflection of the actress, whose pose and gesture further substantiate that relationship.[24]

Figure 5.8. Bernhardt writing in her domestic space, *Sarah Bernhardt at Home*, 1915. Filmarchiv Austria.

In Bernhardt's film we see her making new work that foregrounds her ongoing creativity. Filmed in a space that is female and private but also communal and public, Bernhardt makes the home a locus for artistic production.

The shot that follows shows Bernhardt in a different room, pen in hand, seated at a desk with another female companion beside her (see figure 5.8). She has two dogs resting in front of her: the greyhound that we saw in the opening shot of the film rests at her feet, and a smaller dog is curled on a decorative stool in front of her desk. The room is far more decorative than the Spartan surrounds of the atelier in which she sculpts. Here, art nouveau becomes a domestic style: the floor is carpeted in intricate patterns, there is a decorative screen to one side that is ornately oriental, the desk and the stool have been carved so that their legs curve and turn, there are palms and flowers surrounding the women. The space might be domestic but it is also productive: as the intertitles tell us, Bernhardt is writing to the American press. This point would not surprise an American public since in the teens Bernhardt wrote syndicated columns for the U.S. press. For example, the *Boston Globe* ran a series in October in 1912 that for a week was signed by Madame Sarah Bernhardt.[25] Articles such as "Will Power as Beauty's Aid," "Bernhardt and Suffragettes," and "Don't Be Fashion's Slave" were published in her name, preceded by publicity that announced that "Mme Sarah Bernhardt, the acknowledged Empress of the Stage, will begin a series of articles of absorbing interest to the women of New England. . . . [The] list of subjects for the current week gives but a faint idea of the variety of topics over which the keen intellect of this remarkable woman ranges."[26] What we see on film, therefore, is the image of an educated woman actively engaged in modern media and the "new" world (the newspaper, America). It is significant that Bernhardt joins her female companion in consulting the heavy books resting on the table; Bernhardt is not just an author but has the knowledge and learning to support this intellectual role.

Together with this focus on female companionship, productivity, and intelligence, there is also a suggestion of the famous writing scene in *La Dame aux Camélias* where Marguerite (at the behest of Armand's father) tearfully writes her farewell letter to her lover. Indeed, the overlap between the two scenes lies in the similarity of costume (the white high-collared dress), the mise-en-scène (a similar table, palms and flowers behind the actress, a feathered writing quill) and the setting (a country retreat, an attendant female companion). What we have on film, however, is a changed play. No longer performing the role of a kept woman in a script written by a famous playwright, Bernhardt is writing her own play within her own home. She is also writing to an audience who is dear to her: the American public. We see her pluck a flower, pause to think, and continue writing. This is a leisurely and enjoyable moment, one that reinforces the privately public nature of Bernhardt's newspaper columns (they are written at home to be read globally in other homes; we see this intimate moment together in a cinema theater). Seated beside a folded oriental screen, Bernhardt is also tastefully modern. This is not Marguerite's emotive and personal note of farewell, which has been forced upon her by Armand's father and by the moral imperatives of the bourgeois family in the mid-nineteenth century, but evidence of Bernhardt's calm engagement in contemporary affairs.

Woman as sculptor, woman as writer: as early as 1901, it was explained how "one of the phenomena of the present day is the number of female artists now practising sculpture and the allied arts, practising them steadily." By 1903, *Femina* magazine featured images of female artists in their respective studios.[27] At the same time, women wrote columns for newspapers in order to inform readers about the cinema. As Richard Abel argued recently, women writers were crucial to the development and expansion of early cinema.[28] In *Sarah Bernhardt at Home*, Bernhardt plays the role of the creative artist in the home in order to depict what she (and other women) did in the home. No longer associated with reclusive entrapment or with domestic chores, Bernhardt made works that circulated abroad. Ideas about what constitutes "woman's work" are accordingly challenged and revised.

Painting and Presence

In the same manner as those paintings suggested in key scenes in *Queen Elizabeth*, the visual composition of many scenes in *Sarah Bernhardt at Home* draw upon pictorial works that are familiar to us. Previously I argued that Bernhardt uses Impressionist paintings of the 1880s to compose the opening shots of the film. Bernhardt employs this approach throughout the film, recontextualizing familiar paintings in order to fashion new visual meanings for us. The paintings that are re-created are not presented as *tableaux vivants* inside the house but are mapped onto the landscape itself. This movement out of the home into an abundant and often wild nature indicates a desire for exploration and a passion for untamed, wild environments. Bernhardt invokes famous paintings of landscapes and seascapes, revealing an expanded geography of the home. She confirms that the home can be wild, untamed, and nondomestic.

The most obvious instance of the untamed home is revealed in the shot where Bernhardt inserts herself as a protagonist at the sea's edge. She gestures to the sea that beats against rocks and defines a wild, windswept coastline (see figure 5.9). Like Gustave Courbet in the 1870s painting a wave in terms of its sensory impact or like Claude Monet or John Russell (both in 1890) painting the effect of water hitting rock on Belle Isle, Bernhardt defines nature in

Figure 5.9. Bernhardt gestures to sea, *Sarah Bernhardt at Home*, 1915. Filmarchiv Austria.

terms of sensory impact and physical freedom. However, where Bernhardt departs from these paintings is in the inclusion of herself in the frame: she and her companions are part of this rugged nature, not merely spectators to it. They intrude upon it, introduce us to it, gesture to it, inhabit it. In this way, they are part of a savage and bountiful nature that unfolds, that cannot be contained, and that challenges the image of woman and the home as a safe, domestic interior.

Not all the shots in the film show a savage landscape. There are shots of Bernhardt outdoors, in fields, directing a collection of ten women who gather flowers into huge bundles that are then piled into waiting carts. Monet's and Vincent van Gogh's fields of poppies are points of comparison for us here. Only occasionally populated by people, these paintings make women blend into the landscape and, if defined in terms of social activity, women are ascribed a maternal role. Hence, Monet's wife and son stroll indistinctly through his 1873 canvas, *Poppy Field near Argenteuil*. These two—and there are another two figures behind them again—might be any mother and son. Bernhardt, however, is at the front of the screen in her field of flowers, telling the women what to do. She is more proprietorial than maternal. The poppies are roses and camellias, flowers that we associate with Bernhardt's plays (*La Dame aux Camélias*) or with the floral arrangements that border Mucha's art nouveau posters of her plays. It is women who pick and collect the flowers. Defined by physical activity, the women work cooperatively together.

In another scene in the film, Bernhardt hosts an outdoor picnic (see figure 5.10). The camera pans across a group of men that recalls Édouard Manet's *Le déjeneur sur l'herbe* (1863): three men lounge on the grass with a fourth cooking behind them. With no naked woman in the group and no woman bathing in the background, there is the suggestion that men can be objects and themselves objectified in a landscape. The camera continues to pan away from this group and we see the striped sides of a tent that opens on Bernhardt seated at a table surrounded by six companions. They are enjoying a relaxed lunch. While the sexual and social transgressions of Manet's painting have been removed, they have not been completely elided. There remains the playful reminder that the home is not a fixed physical structure, and there remains the suggestion that men might act on the behest of women. Hence, Bernhardt's male companions cook the food, they lean forward into Bernhardt's conversation, and a man stands to pour tea into her outstretched cup.

The setting of this tent, with its striped canopy, casual collection of bottles, glasses and cups, table with white table cloth, wooden chairs, and relaxed grouping of people chatting among themselves is also reminiscent of Pierre-Auguste Renoir's *Luncheon of the Boating Party* (1881) (see figure 5.11). Renoir's image opens out, however, onto a group of friends with no clear

Figure 5.10. Bernhardt's luncheon on the grass, *Sarah Bernhardt at Home*, 1915. Filmarchiv Austria.

Figure 5.11. Pierre-Auguste Renoir, *Luncheon of the Boating Party*, between 1880 and 1881, oil on canvas, 51-¼ x 69-⅛ in., 130.2 x 175.6 cm. Acquired 1923, The Phillips Collection, Washington, D.C.

Figure 5.12. Bernhardt's lunch, *Sarah Bernhardt at Home*, 1915. Filmarchiv Austria.

centralized focus (the symbolist poet Jules Laforgue, pictured in the distance talking to art collector and critic Charles Ephrussi, triangularly tops the image in compositional terms but he is clearly not the "subject" of the painting). In Bernhardt's luncheon, activity is instead focused around herself and the table opens onto her (see figure 5.12). Indeed, hers is the one face and figure we continually and clearly see. She directs conversation and choreographs action. In this way, the home, and the reasons for women's centrality within it, is redefined.

Posing as Patron

The similarities and differences between Bernhardt's film and famous identifiable paintings is best illustrated in the penultimate scene. Here, Bernhardt is finally placed within a public group (the local Breton community on Belle Isle) and celebrated as their patron. As a discussion of the film in *Moving Picture World* tells us, Bernhardt's interest in and sympathy for the welfare of the "natives" saw her become for them "something in the nature of a divinity."[29] We see her celebrated upon her arrival at festivities held by her local fishing village in her honor: bouquets of flowers are offered by girls in white dresses and hats, attending men remove and raise their caps, a speech is given by Albert Craissac, the municipal official. After speeches, a Breton dance is performed by locals (see figure 5.13). Bernhardt is in the

Figure 5.13. Local Bretons dance, *Sarah Bernhardt at Home*, 1915. Filmarchiv Austria.

far distance on a podium signing autographs; it is unclear whether she is aware of the performance. In the foreground, however, a group of men and women dance around two seated musicians, one of whom plays a traditional Breton bagpipe. The women are dressed in the familiar white conical hats of the peasant community, and many wear a dark, covering apron; the men instead wear jackets, coats, and dark Breton sailor caps.

The obvious source for this image is Paul Gauguin's *Breton Girls Dancing* (1888), in which three girls have flowers pinned to their chest and hold hands, their figures describing a similar circular movement (see figure 5.14). Behind this trio is a village, with its church spire and small cluster of houses set against the backdrop of farmed hillside. In Gauguin's image, the Breton community is imagined as a spiritually pure peasant community isolated from the corruption of the modern world. It is also uniquely feminine: the peasant girls dance, spontaneously. We might sense that Gauguin alone witnesses this act, and that it was his task as an artist to document the joining of traditional dance with folk community in the rural landscape of the Pont-Aven region.

In *Sarah Bernhardt at Home*, Belle Isle and its peasant community is instead documented and brought forth as a vibrant part of the modern world, dependent upon outside patronage for its sustenance and new technology for its

Figure 5.14. Paul Gauguin, *Breton Girls Dancing, Pont-Aven*, 1888. Collection of Mr. and Mrs. Paul Mellon, National Gallery of Art, Washington D.C.

visibility. Indeed, we see Bernhardt support local activities (fishing, farming), and we are told in the intertitle that introduces the local festivities of her importance as patron to the community. Her role as benefactor of the local cooperative bakery was common knowledge in the teen years. Publicized on the cover of the journal *Excelsior* in August 1912, Bernhardt had previously responded to the storms that destroyed the island's fishing fleet in 1911 by staging a "'Matinée de Gala." A benefit performance of the play *Pain d'hiver des pêcheurs de Belle-Ile-en-Mer* (*Winter Bread for the Fishermen of Belle-Ile-en-Mer*), it was accompanied by a program illustrated by Georges Clairin.[30] While we cannot surmise all of this information from the film, it does make us aware of the change from Gauguin's untouched peasant retreat to an island where locals (both men and women) celebrate the presence of an outsider. The notion of an original primitive innocence, untouched and separate from the modern world, is implicitly eroded in the film.

Belle Isle is an island traditionally celebrated for its cultural and geographic isolation. It was regarded by the French as a frontier against the Dutch and English. This location is where Alexandre Dumas set his novel *The Man in the Iron Mask* (1850) and where his king explains that he wants the fortifications to remain intact upon the Island, but that it is not these that draw him to the place. He explains: "You would not guess what I want to see at Belle Isle, Monsieur Fouquet; it is the pretty peasants and women of the lands on the sea-shore, who dance so well, and are so seducing with their scarlet petticoats!"[31] It is also on Belle Isle that Porthos, one of his characters in the *Three Musketeers*, dies. In *Mademoiselle de Belle Isle* (1839), a work that marks the beginning of his historic dramas, Dumas focuses on Gabrielle, an attractive youth from Belle Isle. Gabrielle is a role that Bernhardt played in November 1872 on her return to the Comédie Française. *Mademoiselle de Belle Isle* was also one of the few works by Dumas that remained in the repertory of the Théâtre Française in the twentieth century. In this context, the film's reference to folk culture brings a new relevance and new visibility to a community that had long been featured in the performing, literary, and visual arts.

"Most Aggressively Young"

It would be misleading to suggest that *Sarah Bernhardt at Home* develops only figures and activities familiar to the traditional arts. Indeed, Bernhardt's involvement in the local community (dancing, farming, fishing), shows her constantly physically active. As a review of the film in *Moving Picture World* notes:

> She is a tireless worker and player at the same time and we see her start out at the hour of a. m. to look after her lobster pots. She fishes in the pools of her own fine estate and varies it with fishing excursions on the deep sea. Whatever the calendars may say, this woman in the films is most aggressively young.[32]

Those shots of Bernhardt lunching, or gesturing to a windswept seascape, or even being rowed in a boat out to sea might therefore be seen as a renegotiation of trends in art *and* as evidence of Bernhardt's outgoing and exploratory nature. She is a woman in a rugged environment who celebrates the home as a space in which to move, walk, create, and climb. Rather than sit passively and contemplate a landscape, or have it described to her, she actively participates in its unfolding, directing when and how it is to be seen.

This focus upon physical engagement—the touching, as it were, of the scene—is most obvious when Bernhardt and her companions help local fishermen with their dragnet fishing. Pulling on a cord, Bernhardt and her friends stand on rocky terrain, wind sweeping their hats and coats as three of their male companions stand watching. They are smiling, talking among themselves; for a moment Bernhardt pauses and lets go of the rope. This makes no difference to the fishing. Burly fisherman with Breton fisherman's caps head the line and pull the nets from the water. The women and their companions rush to cluster around and pull at the nets, waving fish in the air. In this scene, they not only participate in a local activity but demonstrate that they know how to fish and have a good rapport with the locals. While their smiles and gestures are at odds with the modesty and anonymity of the fishermen, they happily describe their capacity to gather not just flowers in fields but food for their tables.

Bernhardt leaves the fishermen folding the nets and heads back home again on a donkey-drawn cart. In the following shot, this cart is replaced by a large horse-drawn carriage that takes her to a farm. Accompanied again by a group of female companions, she feeds chickens. A local woman, with the white cap, clogs, and long dark dress of the Breton, holds a pan and throws seeds into the air. Bernhardt, with her small pointed shoes, gloves, and tall supporting staff, looks out of place in this setting. She reaches to throw some seed down to the animals. The woman beside her throws her seeds instead high into the air. Bernhardt, gleefully copying her, begins to scatter the feed, calling to her female companions to join her. It is obvious that none of them have ever fed chickens. The point, however, is that Bernhardt enters the yard and makes it her own: she is not a patron who rules from afar but makes a play of knowing where and how people work.

Tennis, Tea, and Technology

These local activities contrast with the tennis that is later shown. As the intertitle tells us, "Sarah Bernhardt adores sports." This commentary is followed by a shot of Bernhardt playing doubles tennis on a windswept lawn court with her friends. She is dressed—appropriately—in white, the color that was the established color of the game. As William T. Tilden reminds novices in his 1922 book, *The Art of Lawn Tennis*, "Do not appear on the courts in dark clothes, as they are apt to be heavy and hinder your speed of movement, and also they are a violation of the unwritten ethics of the game."[33] Bernhardt is dressed properly for this role, but she demonstrates little facility for the game. She serves, is handed balls from waiting aides, serves again, and participates in no rallies. She also barely moves: apart from her serves, she does not move or make any effort to engage play. As her friend Reynaldo Hahn explains in his book *Sarah Bernhardt: Impressions* (he is describing a match in 1904), Bernhardt was famously immobile on court:

> Tennis. It is not easy to play tennis with Sarah. She serves well and returns energetically, but as she refuses to budge, the balls have to be placed exactly where she can return them without shifting. Maurice, a fine player, is a past

master at this. [Émile] Geoffrey and [Georges] Clairin manage fairly well, but with frequent failures, which rouse great rage. . . . Suddenly a laugh, Sarah's own laugh, bursts out. What's happening?

"I have just realized that we three—Geoffrey, Clairin, and I—are more than two hundred years old between us. Invalid tennis," she says gaily. And this idea she elaborates in all its comic aspects. She laughs, specifying the age of the protagonists.[34]

May Agate, Bernhardt's student, similarly speaks of how

> Always at four o'clock there was the tennis. . . . The tennis was fantastic. It always reminded me of "Alice through the Looking-glass"; everything was topsy-turvy like in a mad dream. . . . Sarah had quite a brisk service, but as the poor darling could not run, and ought not to have played at all, her balls had to be returned gently so as to come down where she could reach them easily; otherwise they had to be left to her partner, and that she did not like at all.[35]

Other accounts published in the press endorse this vision of the actress insistently playing afternoon tennis. As Miss Ray Rockman, a young American actress who accompanied Bernhardt to Belle Isle in 1901, recounts in the *New York Times*: "At 4 o'clock lawn tennis begins and lasts until the dinner bell rings at 7:30. It is marvellous to watch Mme. Bernhardt play with such agility for over three hours each day, no matter how windy it may be. Through it all her cheery temperament pervades everything and everybody."[36]

Film, in this context, reinforces the information that readers of newspapers across the globe were already privy to. It is also a clear statement of Bernhardt's engagement in modern sporting activities. We see her demonstrate her skill at fencing in *Hamlet* in 1900; here, we have evidence of her engagement in the sport of tennis, which was becoming the "distraction préférée" among fashionable women in Paris. Indeed, in the early 1900's women's presses such as *Femina* published articles explaining how "tennis has now become one of the most characteristic past times, one of the most distinctive pleasures."[37] One article published in 1903 presented a photographic description of this "summer sport" now so popular with "strong, elegant, female Parisian players." A young woman, racquet in hand, is featured in various athletic poses. Beneath an image of her jumping, it is explained that "A player is sometimes obliged to jump in order to hit a ball too high."[38] With her leg injured and soon to be removed, this is a leap that Bernhardt never makes. It is important that no attempt is made in *Sarah at Home* to argue otherwise: this is not Bernhardt, racquet in hand, standing still before an empty court, her physical immobility representing a material handicap. Instead, on film, we see Bernhardt at age sixty-eight playing tennis, her restricted mobility revealing a woman who *quand même* is part of the modern world.

In Hahn's account, Bernhardt's tennis game is interrupted by a servant carrying food, in Miss Ray Rockman's account they stop for dinner, on film the game is instead interrupted by tea. We have already seen a brief pause for tea after Bernhardt's arrival, when she and her guests stand on a terrace and are served by a maid. Here, her dog joins her, and a large oriental birdcage is perched conspicuously in the foreground. In this new tea scene there are, however, many more people and many more maids: at least two are bustling about with a pot of tea, a jug for milk, sugar, and cups while another comes to give Bernhardt a telegram. What is interesting about this tea break is its inclusion in the film as a ceremonial interlude, where everyone crowds together to rest after a bout of physical activity. Kakuzo Okakura, writing his *Book of Tea* for an occidental readership in 1906, terms tea "the queen of the Camellias," explaining how it was a substance and ritual that facilitated *chanoyu*, a kind of aesthetic and moral awareness of the world. Speaking about the Western use of tea, he states:

> Strangely enough humanity has so far met in the teacup. It is the only Asiatic ceremonial which commands universal esteem. The white man has scoffed at our religion and our morals, but he has accepted the brown beverage without hesitation. The afternoon tea is now an important function in Western society. In the delicate clatter of trays and saucers, in the soft rustle of feminine hospitality, in the common catechism about cream and sugar, we know that the Worship of Tea is established beyond question. The philosophic resignation of the guest to the fate awaiting him in the dubious decoction proclaims that in this single instance the Oriental spirit reigns supreme.[39]

This Asiatic break is the one activity that ceremoniously repeats itself in the film. In this instance, however, tea also serves as pretext for the arrival of news. Indeed, the shot opens with a maid rushing forward, carrying a telegram that Bernhardt opens and reads. The maid returns with a pen and waits for Bernhardt's written reply. Her rushing forward and backward and the pace of Bernhardt's own scribbled reply—there are no pauses or consultations here as there were with her writing to the American press—indicates that we are dealing with wireless communication as a matter of speed and urgency. The telegram also represents Bernhardt's familiarity with new and modern technology. As the *New York Times* explains to its readers in an article that reflects on the sinking of the Titanic, "Few New Yorkers realize that all through the roar of the big city there are constantly speeding messages between people separated by vast distances, and that over housetops and even through the walls of buildings and in the very air one breathes are words written by electricity."[40] Evidently, Belle Isle formed part of this same global mapping, where Bernhardt could send wireless messages across the seas as she paused from tennis and sipped tea. Her home might be geographically distant but it was culturally, socially, and technologically very close to watching audiences.

Conclusion: The Woman at the Window

When Bernhardt made *Sarah Bernhardt at Home* in 1912 she showed audiences what she enjoyed most about the island. As she explains, she loved its "savagery, fishermen, sea, and sky." She also noted that the island was "little and immense," and we may infer from this comment that for Bernhardt her home expanded to the frontiers of the New World. As the telegram or even the images of Bernhardt writing or gesturing to sea indicate, we are in Brittany but we are also part of an invisible but very present America. This is a very different tale of the wrangling between capital and province, Paris and Brittany, described by Dumas in *The Man in the Iron Mask*. As Bernhardt explains in an article written in 1904, "Yes, it is small, Belle Isle; but it is savage and it is immense, because Belle Isle is one of the points of the old world, the point where Europe plunges into the Ocean, and this Ocean, with its black rocks and transparent green waves hurls itself infinitely ahead, where I imagine America, and still more worlds!"[41]

The film concludes with a portrait of Bernhardt. She is indoors, with three dogs, seated comfortably as she turns and looks through a window. This moment is the closest we have been to her; we never otherwise see her in medium shot in the film. This final image is therefore an intimate one, exposing a quiet interlude alone. It is telling that it is at this moment and through this image that we finally see Bernhardt seated calmly alone within her home. There are no waiting maids and no female companions. Gone, too, is the bonnet that covers her head for most of the film. She turns and looks out from the window (see figure 5.15). She smiles and gestures to someone we cannot see. We might say that Bernhardt is old, that the camera is still, that she represents an image of Europe's decay. But we can, alternatively, compare this image to the portrait painted by Clairin forty years earlier and argue that we must evaluate the film for the changes it represents. *Sarah Bernhardt at Home* shows Bernhardt arriving by steamship and by rowboat. It shows her sculpting, writing, and transforming the visual and narrative meaning of her home. Finally, it shows her at home looking out onto America, the New World, a modern world where she plays an ongoing and central role. In other words, this film is not about the decorative arts constructing a safe sanctuary in a confining home. It is about the home opening outward, becoming a

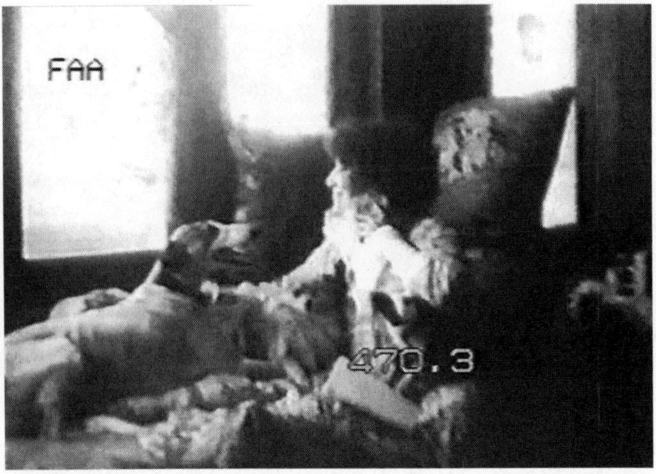

Figure 5.15. Bernhardt at the window, *Sarah Bernhardt at Home*, 1915. Filmarchiv Austria.

changing and expansive site of female play. Brought to the cinema by a famous actress, it is a paradigmatic example of Schlüpmann's "Haus": an enduring reminder of our need to reevaluate the historical and theoretical limitations of our ideas about the cinema, the theatrical actress, and the home in the crucial teen years.

6. *Mothers of France*

World War I, Film, and Propaganda

Mothers of France enables us to move from the domestic home to war and the international home front. In this film, we explore new interconnections between private and public life, the provincial home and the global stage. *Mothers of France* is a patriotic film that was made to encourage American participation in the First World War. When the film was released in America in February 1917, France was engaged in a war that the United States had not yet joined. Indeed, the U.S. Congress did not declare war on Germany until April 6, 1917. Bernhardt's film was released eight weeks earlier and gave impetus to American engagement in the war. Bernhardt was not, however, merely a familiar face arguing the need for united military action; she was also a female figurehead who could reach and engage female audience members. As the title of the film reminds us, this is a film about French mothers. In this chapter, we therefore move from the art nouveau style and inclusive autobiography of *Sarah Bernhardt at Home* to a film that documents the war, engaging all homes and motivating all people—particularly women—to participate in it. We also address an event that brings new meanings to the notion of "the home front." Now engaging ideas about nation and nationhood in explicitly combative ways, the film's narrative begins in the bourgeois home but very quickly moves into a provincial village and then into the trenches of the First World War. We follow Bernhardt as a mother in the home, then see her as a patriot in the town, and finally as a nurse on the home front. Presenting new perceptual realities, Bernhardt documents the brutal impact that war has on familiar spaces. Husbands die, sons and lovers are injured and blinded, buildings are bombed, daily tasks are violently interrupted. War denies the opportunity for carefree play, dividing the world into unbridgeable binaries: friend and foe, life and death, peacetime and mobilization.

Because we no longer watch Bernhardt in a role we can associate with the late-nineteenth-century stage, we know that the world has radically changed. The theater of war is now Bernhardt's focus; it is war that explains her film, that impacts upon her life, and that justifies the film's production. Jean Richepin was the playwright who wrote the screenplay for *Mothers of France* and whose *Nana-Sahib* and *Pierrot Assassin* Bernhardt had brought to the stage in 1883. As he explains, Bernhardt's film is important because it can engage the empathy of viewers. Bernhardt was physically legible on screen: Richepin states this point with a new urgency, with a new awareness of what it means to say that acting has agency and emotional power on screen. At the film's debut in France in January 1917 he explains:

> It is not me, a poet, who would speak badly of the word, the verb, of written text which is marked so solemnly in our spirit. However, there is something more expressive than the word, and this is the look, the gesture, the pose. One does not only speak with the voice, with the words one uses; one expresses with one's entire body, with one's entire soul, and that is why a comedian ["*un comédien*"] is called an actor. He is a man who acts. One must touch the spirit, the heart of the public. And so! Nothing will be more active in this than the new form of art that one calls cinema.[1]

Mothers of France is a work that opens new discussions about Bernhardt and her engagement with film. This discussion must now include Bernhardt's capacity to respond to contemporary global events as they unfold, her ability to join narrative to nonscripted realism, and her status as an actress who uses film strategically, to influence the emotions of her viewers and, with this, the political, social, and cultural allegiances of the public.

The Filmic Front

Mothers of France was sponsored by the French Ministry of War. As an article in *Le Comœdia* explains, in 1916 the four major French firms—Pathé, Gaumont, Éclair, and Éclipse—were asked by the Ministry of War to propose ideas to the Service cinématographique de l'armée (the SCA) for a series of propaganda films destined to circulate in France and abroad. Louis Mercanton (who had directed Bernhardt in *Queen Elizabeth*, *Jeanne Doré*, and *Sarah Bernhardt at Home*) and the *Comœdia*'s own Jean-Louis Croze (who was the head of the SCA), proposed that the playwright and member of the French Academy, Jean Richepin, write a screenplay for Bernhardt. Bernhardt and Richepin accepted the idea; Mercanton and René Hervil, both working for Éclipse, were then enlisted to direct the work.[2] Bernhardt's involvement in *Mothers of France* was therefore framed by the SCA; her purpose was to promote the French cause abroad.

Jean Richepin made the aim of manipulating and securing the emotions and allegiances of the American public clear in his address to the Union des Arts at the debut of the film in Paris, 1917. As he states, *Mothers of France* speaks to a neutral America. It reveals to the American public not what they read in newspapers, but the true horror of war. The film's aim was to reveal physical suffering so that the ideas and ideals for which the French were fighting were clear. Richepin explains:

> One must have seen massacres, buildings in ruins, blood still streaming, as I have seen in a burnt church where people were crushed underfoot, where slabs of stone were still sticky with human fat and blood. One must have seen that, and for those who are fighting there, to have engaged in a bayonet charge. . . . When they [the American public] will see what the horrors of the war are, even a war which is just and fair as the one which we are undertaking, then they will understand the symbols which it evokes; why we have undertaken it, why we have been obliged to undertake it, not only with the aim to defend ourselves . . . but to defend the ideas that are dear to us, that are sacred, that are the health of France and at the same time of Europe itself.[3]

Clearly, the importance of *Mothers of France* lies in what it can show of the war to audiences abroad. As *Moving Picture World* explains, *Mothers of France* is epochal not because it features Bernhardt and engages Richepin, but because these two were engaged in a film that "was photographed in the trenches by the arrangement with and the assistance of the [French] government, which retains ownership in the war scenes and thus [became] a partner in the picture."[4] I will discuss this indexical use of film later; for now, it is important to note that the film was an organized attempt, on behalf of the French military and theatrical establishments, to sway American audiences to the Allied cause.

Witness to the (Great) War

A recent issue of *Film History*, dedicated to cinema during the Great War, makes an important case for the ongoing need to explore the film industry during the 1914–1918 period. As Stephen Bottomore notes in his introduction, film history has long emphasized British or American aspects of the war. Explaining the need to look at other case studies and to revise received ideas, Bottomore states that "one is struck by how much is still being discovered about the relationship between film and the War."[5] Indeed, in this issue, scholars such as Richard Abel, Laurent Véray, and Sabine Lenk demonstrate the need to expand the confines of our traditional knowledge about cinema during the Great War and, with this, the need to revise presumptions about the exhibition, circulation, and production of films during this period. For example, Abel explains in his article "'Documentary' War Pictures in the USA, 1914–1916" that the war pictures advertised in American newspapers did not refer to newsreels but to feature-length nonfiction films. Even more remarkably, a high number of these popular pictures were pro-German, even well into the summer of 1916.[6] It is in this context of rereading the European film industry's engagement with the American public at a particularly sensitive historical moment that *Mothers of France* might be understood. While *Mothers of France* reveals Bernhardt's capacity to now represent and even incarnate France, it also more broadly reveals the propaganda efforts that were made by French dignitaries, the film industry, and the government to secure the allegiance of neutral Americans "at home."

Laurent Véray explains in his article entitled "1914–1918, the First Media War of the Twentieth Century. The Example of French Newsreels" that when the SCA made films for neutral countries, "the emphasis was to create an effective counterpart to enemy propaganda."[7] It was the background to the war that was shown in newsreels—parades, organized troops, as well as bombing and explosions from afar. Significantly, these are the same kinds of scenes we see in *Mothers of France*: men are mobilized in the town, lines of trucks head up an open road, there are shots of men clambering out of trenches and running ahead into anonymous, smoking landscapes (see figure 6.1). There is also the picture of barbed-wire fences in desolate, flattened fields. In this sense, we see both the effective organization of the French troops in towns and the intimate horrors of the war at the front.

When Bernhardt arrives at the front in *Mothers of France*, desperate to see her dying son, we are told that she and her military companion are "lost under the bombardment." Explosions of missiles cloud our view. Bernhardt is in a trench covering her ears and ducking her head as men suddenly appear and rush past her carrying grenades on their shoulders. In another shot, Bernhardt is in the foreground as men behind her do nothing in particular. They lean against the sides of the trench, their heads ducking to avoid the billowing smoke. The horror of such standing and waiting in these anonymous warrens is a reminder of the changed tactics of modern warfare. In this sequence there are two further shots that are empty of people. In these shots we peer up, out of the trenches: the screen divides into wall and sky,

Figure 6.1. Men clamber out of trenches, *Mothers of France*, 1917. Lobster Films, Paris.

and then the black smoke of a bomb repetitively rises against the white sky. As viewers of the film, we metonymically inhabit the trenches of the French ourselves.

Other scenes further expose the war on the front: a group of soldiers zigzag their way through trenches as smoke clouds around them. Bernhardt is not, therefore, presenting only the narrative that drives action in *Mothers of France* (that is, the pain that a wife and mother of France might feel at the loss of husband and son) but enables us to realize the shock and vulnerability of having the enemy appear invisibly from nowhere as one stands in trenches. As Robert H. Zinger explains in *America's Great War: World War I and the American Experience*, of all the horrors of modern warfare,

> it was artillery bombardment, with unseen enemy guns hurling high explosives at men crouched in dugouts and trembling in trenches, that many soldiers described as the worst ordeal of all. The victim, after all, was not only defenceless—his survival was purely a matter of chance. A direct hit several yards away turned comrades instantly from men into pulverized chunks of flesh. "I want to scream and run and throw myself," recorded Corporal Harold W. Pierce. "When I hear the whistle of an approaching shell I dig my toes into the ground and push on the walls of the dugout."[8]

In his article on French newsreels produced during the War, Véray discusses scenes of ruins, destruction, and battlefields. He argues that these are porous images that give testimony to the pervasiveness of death. Film visually relays the horror of war, revealing to viewers the randomness and brutality that Zinger describes. Shots of warfare—the ruins, trenches, and battlefields—are, he states, "captured moments of time, bearing the irreducible imprint of what preceded." Arguing that the shots leave autonomy to the spectator, Véray explains:

> [D]espite the apparent banality of the scenes filmed, there is almost always something troubling that remains. Such discovered allusions are ways of subverting the invisibility of the real war. The duration of shots, their size, the signs and lack of signs, leave many openings for the viewer, offering him[/her] the opportunity to imagine and to supplement the deficient images, thus leaving open a field of meanings.[9]

It is in this context of leaving open a field of meanings that we can understand the impact that *Mothers of France* might once have had. Further, reviews focus on the access viewers are given to war and on the multitude of images available to them. For example, the *New York Times* begins an article about the film with the phrase: "Camera Shows [Bernhardt] in Hospitals, Camps, and the Very Trenches with the Poilus." Focusing on the variety of the images available, it then states that "the French Government offered every facility for enacting its scenes before a truly martial background." It continues:

> *Mothers of France* atones for most of the sins of the movies; to see it is to recompense for having sat through a series of atrocious and banal war films. . . . [Bernhardt] stands before the statue of Joan of Arc in front of the war-scarred Cathedral of Reims, its shattered windows and bag-protected buttresses plainly visible. Real chateaux, real peasant women toiling in the fields, and real munitions smoke give a flavour that no amount of paint and plaster villages and trenches filled with tin soldiers hired at a dollar a day could ever hope to approximate.[10]

The publicity booklet for the film similarly focuses on the indexical quality of the film and on the multitude of the images available to viewers. Arguing that it is the documentary nature of the work that distinguishes it from other films about the war the booklet states:

> MM. Mercanton and [René] Hervil, who assumed the task of filming this work, have held that it cannot be, in any way, confused with all the other war films. They were committed, above all, to be truthful. Thanks to special authorisation the scenes of the front, some of which were taken at Reims before the cathedral, were taken on the spot. The different places where the action unwinds are of a perfect exactitude and make this cinematographic work nearly a documentary about a corner of France during the war.[11]

The Ruins of Reims

Shellfire damaged and destroyed important parts of Reims cathedral during the German bombing of French territory on September 19, 1914. The wooden roof over the nave was burned, statuary on the façade of the building was ruined, stained-glass windows were shattered, and pews, choir stalls, and furnishings were burnt. In February 1915 and again in April 1917 and early 1918, the cathedral withstood further bombardment. As Nicola Lambourne argues in "Production versus Destruction: Art, World War I and Art History," Reims cathedral stands as "the most notorious example of cathedral bombardment."[12] Images of the cathedral in ruins were used during the war as propaganda images by both the French and the Germans. Although I concern myself with the French version of events here, it is important to recognize that the cause for the shelling of the cathedral was contested. While the French argue that the Germans bombarded the cathedral "for the simple pleasure of destruction . . . [in a] revolting act of vandalism,"[13] the Germans argue that the bombardment was necessary because the French put the cathedral to military use. By making it an illegitimate military base, they made it a legitimate target. As a cartoon in the satirical journal *Kladderadatsch* explains: "The cunning French have used the Reims Cathedral as a shooting platform—next they'll be building trenches with the contents of the Louvre."[14]

Images of Reims cathedral burning were circulated on French postcards and posters. These painted, sketched, and photographed images of the cathedral were put to different propaganda uses. In 1916, a lithograph of this image provided, for example, the backdrop to an exhibition in the town Fontenay-aux-Roses entitled "The Crime of Reims." In Montreal, the image of the burning cathedral was instead used to exhort countrymen to enlist into the 178th French-Canadian battalion (see figure 6.2). Such images of a damaged cathedral expressed an emotive appeal to audiences. Indeed, by avoiding the censorship law of August 5, 1914 (that greatly restricted comment on military activities), the damage wrought by the Germans nevertheless became a potent tool of propaganda. As Lambourne states, "At a time when precise figures on the human damage caused by the war were not released to the public, bombarded cathedrals and damaged statues acted as metaphors for the other, censored destructions of war."[15]

Although Véray makes no indication whether Reims was a central image in film as it was in reproduced prints and pictures during the war, he nevertheless mentions Reims when he states:

> Images on national and foreign screens showing damage sustained by France were seen throughout the conflict. The shots of shattered landscapes, of ruins,

Figure 6.2. Canadian poster, WW1. Gift of Sir John Eliot, 1982, Imperial War Museum, London.

including churches, constituted solid evidence of the suffering endured by France, and were highlighted to demonstrate the "savagery of German aggression." . . . The best example of this genre is undoubtedly *Les monuments historiques d'Arras victims de la barbarie allemande* [*Historic Monuments of Arras, Victims of German Barbarity*] (Pathé, June 1915). But one could also cite an Éclipse film about the symbolic case of Reims Cathedral: the martyred city of Reims was regularly bombarded by artillery from the air, and its silhouette appears in a locket as the last image of the film with the caption: "They shall not take it!"[16]

In a full-page advertisement in *Le Cinéma*, the image of Bernhardt before the cathedral is flanked by the statement: "Filmed at the FRONT notably in front of the cathedral at REIMS thanks to special authorisation."[17] Clearly, this filming of the desecrated cathedral at the front and the use of this as a key image in publicity was a calculated attempt to emotively engage viewers. The symbolism of the image was legible not just to French and Canadian viewers but to the American audiences. Marion Howard's response to this scene in *Moving Picture World* indicates just how closely American viewers identified with what they saw in this scene. She remarks:

> Will you ever forget her [Bernhardt] standing in front of the Joan of Arc statue at Rheims, the only object around that desecrated cathedral to escape shot and shell. How significant it all looked to us, Joan's hand held high bearing the French flag in motion, and the eminent French actress praying for divine strength, her face transfigured. I saw many about me weeping at the sight of it, for here we had it all brought home to us straight from the front.[18]

The suggestion that audiences could join Bernhardt in witnessing the theater of war gives cinematized theater a changed imperative. Film engaged spectators and gave them the illusory experience of being there.[19] Further, cinematized theater now adapts itself to contemporary circumstance. Rather than re-creating or changing stage action in a familiar tale or play, film indexically transmits the physical impact and emotional shock of war. The emotional and symbolic impact of Bernhardt now standing outside the bombed cathedral cogently expresses the values—cultural, human, political—that were under seige.

A French Ambassador

In *Mothers of France*, Bernhardt is a unifying symbol of France. Caricatured and often criticized in the late nineteenth century for her Judaism and for capitalizing on her commercial appeal to foreign audiences, Bernhardt now embodies the values of France and is used to promote the Allied cause. Twenty years earlier, on the occasion of the "Journée Sarah Bernhardt" in 1896, Bernhardt accepted the accolades of her colleagues and friends with a speech that explains how she had fought for French visibility in the world:

> I have journeyed across the ocean, carrying with me my ideal of art and the genius of my nation has triumphed. I have planted the French language in the heart of foreign literature, and this is my proudest achievement. My art has been the missionary whose efforts have made French the common speech of the younger generation.[20]

She styles herself as a global ambassador for France. After the turn of the century, comments in the French press endorse this image. In 1910, for example, the author and literary critic Georges Pioch describes her as "a glory, herself a national institution. Her renown contributes to the prestige, the politics, the negotiations of France. One must admit that Mme Sarah Bernhardt has made France penetrate the Americas, all of Oceania."[21] In 1914, when Bernhardt was awarded the Chevalier of the Legion of Honour as France's foremost actress, M. René Viviani (the Minister for Public Instruction and soon to be France's prime minister for the first year of the war) reiterates these sentiments, stating that Bernhardt's pilgrimages across the world ensured the global spread of French and were a success and "moral profit" for the nation.[22]

At the debut of *Mothers of France*, in America (in February 1917), discussion in the press indicates that Bernhardt indeed represents "La France." As the *New York Times* explains:

> A nation at war provided the mise-en-scene for this universal drama of France, and that nation's greatest actress gave her services so that the world might weep with the mothers of France and rejoice at their courage of the spirit, a courage that passes all understanding. Mme Bernhardt acted the role of the central figure of the story, a choice that was ideal both because of her art and because more than any other living person she typifies to America the joy, the warmth, the strength, the capacity to drink to the full of life that is France.[23]

With *Mothers of France*, Bernhardt brought the spirit and suffering of a nation at war to foreign audiences. She embodied France, becoming a symbol of national courage and fortitude. This role was not new to her. It was an identity that Bernhardt had long claimed but that only now was put to strategic political and military use. The success that Bernhardt enjoyed on the filmic front is indicated by a report in the *Courrier Cinématographique*. As the report explained to readers in France, at the film's premiere in America:

> One no longer remembered that one was in a theatre: everyone wanted to join the combatants and march with them to the tune of the *Marseillaise*. Frenetic applause covered the sound of the orchestra, and the attendees, rising together in a single movement, waved their programmes in frenzy to endlessly repeated cries of "Long live France!"[24]

Joining Joan

Toward the end of *Mothers of France*, there is a scene that shows Guinot, the school teacher, failing to hide Georges d'Urbex's death from Bernhardt (Bernhardt plays the wife of Georges, Jeanne d'Urbex). Guinot returns blind from the war. Because of this, Bernhardt is able, in his company, to find what he is trying to hide: her husband's wallet, her portrait photograph, and the associated proof of her husband's death. Immediately after this scene, Bernhardt leans sadly across Guinot's hospital bed. Here, there is a cut to the statue of Joan of Arc on a horse that stands outside the cathedral at Reims. We then return to the hospital bedside where a vision of Joan of Arc appears before Bernhardt (see figure 6.3). As I mention later, this vision of Joan of Arc was an excerpt from Geraldine Farrar's film *Joan the Woman* (Cecil B. DeMille, 1916) that Samuel 'Roxy' Rothapfel inserted into the film when it arrived in America through a special process of double projection.[25] Not only does this image of Joan appear in Bernhardt's moment of need, offering solace and explanation for her loss, it also creates a slippage between the two figures. Just as Joan of Arc was famous for being a visionary, so too is Bernhardt able to see the greater good for which she is suffering; just as Joan of Arc was a *porte-parole*, urging her countrymen on to fight, so too does Bernhardt act on the advice of the saint and spread her message of collective action. Explaining in an intertitle to the grieving mother of Guinot that the public is united in their fight against a common enemy in their suffering, she states: "Think of the other mothers who cry like you . . . think of those mutilated, of the orphans. Everybody has the need to be consoled."

The use of Joan of Arc as Bernhardt's patron saint in the film emphasizes the film's patriotism. Whereas once Bernhardt acted Joan of Arc on the live

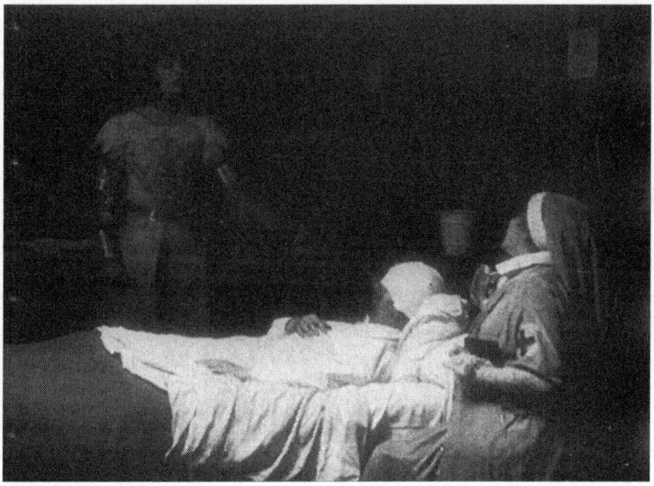

Figure 6.3. A vision of Joan appears, *Mothers of France*, 1917. Lobster Films, Paris.

stage in a revival performance of Jules Barbier and Charles Gounod's *Jeanne d'Arc* (in 1890) and in Émile Moreau's 1909 *Le Procès de Jeanne d'Arc*—and was famously depicted by Eugène Grasset in a poster advertising this last work—on film she does not reincarnate the Maid in a theatrical interpretation of her life but instead turns to her for inspiration. Hence, before Bernhardt leaves her house with her husband and son as they head off to the front, she addresses a statue she has of Joan of Arc in her salon, stating: "Oh Jeanne my patron and that of France, protect our soldiers and give them Victory." Later, when she is outside Reims cathedral in front of Paul Dubois' equestrian statue of Joan of Arc (1889–1895), she again beseeches her, "Oh Jeanne, patron saint of France and my own, come to the help of a mother who wants to see her son who is dying for the country." Both this public statue and Bernhardt's private one at home depict Joan as a bold warrior and a courageous patriot. This image is not the enfeebled and praying Joan of Arc portrayed in Delaroche's painting *Jeanne d'Arc, Sick, Interrogated in Prison by the Cardinal of Winchester* (1824), nor is it the Joan who is depicted standing inside Reims cathedral in her armor, with long golden hair and a halo rimming her head, in the 1854 portrait by Jean Auguste Dominque Ingres (*Joan of Arc at the Coronation of Charles VII*).[26] Instead, it is Joan of Arc going valiantly into battle: in the small sculpture shown in Bernhardt's home, Joan of Arc raises a flag in both hands as she walks forward; in the large equestrian sculpture outside the cathedral she has a sword raised in her right arm as she rides, armored and defiant, into battle.

The decision to use statuary models rather than pictorial sources for Bernhardt's Joan of Arc is significant since it focuses attention on objects in the material world, on how they inhabit the space they occupy. Rather than return us—as Ingres does—to an idealized and timeless moment in which Joan of Arc stands composed and reflective in Reims cathedral watching the moment of the King's coronation, Bernhardt positions Joan of Arc in the domestic drama of a husband and son's departure from the home and in a city square where German bombings and war pose the threat of death and destruction. Hence, in the scenes where Bernhardt stands before Dubois' statue in the Reims square, we plainly see the sandbags and fortifications used to buttress the cathedral and can newly appreciate the relevance of Joan of Arc's charge (see figure 6.4). As my discussion earlier indicates, audiences were aware of the significance of the view: the Cathedral was under fire from the Germans and had sustained substantial damage. There was another statue of Joan of Arc at the Reims cathedral that could feasibly have been used in the film. Why does Bernhardt use the Dubois work instead of the other sculpture available to her that was housed inside the cathedral, Prosper d'Épinay's

Figure 6.4. Bernhardt beseeching Paul Dubois' Joan before the cathedral at Reims, *Mothers of France*, 1917. Lobster Films, Paris.

1900 work? This work had been donated to the cathedral on the occasion of Joan of Arc's beautification in 1909. Instead of moving inside to witness Joan of Arc standing sacred and reflective in the cathedral, Bernhardt leaves us outside the cathedral watching Joan of Arc's charge against the backdrop of a damaged yet consecrated site.

The use of Geraldine Farrar to represent Bernhardt's vision of Joan of Arc in the hospital scene reinforces the contemporary relevance of Joan of Arc. This is not just France turning to the Maid of Orleans, but France employing a figure who is also dear to America and its own cultural heritage. While Farrar's film was, in its turn, edited and changed for a French audience,[27] in *Mothers of France* Farrar and Bernhardt are two divas of the stage who unite around the one figure. Significantly, an American is given the space, in a French film, to incarnate Joan of Arc. Here, the idea of an Allied female culture fighting for shared ideals against the brute force of a common invader is reinforced. In an article written in 1916 (*The Book of the Homeless*, ed. Edith Wharton), Bernhardt reiterates this image of allied motherhood: "Children of Flanders, dry your tears! . . . to those homes made desolate, we, the women of France, of England, of Russia, and of Italy, will bring happiness and sunlight."[28]

By the midteens, American women had already begun to employ Joan of Arc as their symbol of female fortitude and as a rallying point in the fight against a common enemy. For example, Anna Hyatt Huntington's bronze equestrian statue, *Joan of Arc*, was erected in New York City in 1915. Publicity such as Haskell Coffin's 1918 lithograph for War Saving Stamps also featured an attractive and armored Joan of Arc raising her sword, headed by the title "Joan of Arc Saved France." Beneath this image, and in capital letters, was added: "WOMEN OF AMERICA SAVE YOUR COUNTRY *Buy* WAR SAVINGS STAMPS." The film press also saw Joan of Arc as a unifying symbol. An article published in *Le Cinéma* shortly after the release of *Mothers of France* translated an article from *Moving Picture World* entitled "The Celluloid Link. How America and France Are Joined." Referring to "the celluloid chain that solidly joins the country of Washington to the gentle country of Joan of Arc," it positions Bernhardt as France's representative and confirms the respect that Pearl White and Bernhardt share.[29] In this context, Farrar's appearance on the screen of *Mothers of France* materializes the link between two film cultures.

The relevance of Joan of Arc lies not simply in her status as a shared reference, but in the fact that she gives a new, spiritual face to Bernhardt. Again, Bernhardt does not incarnate Joan of Arc on film but instead beseeches her: she prays to her as her patron saint. This emphasis on the spiritual resourcefulness of Bernhardt, as a French woman playing the role of mother and wife, had enormous impact in the early years of war when the American public needed to be convinced of the moral virtue of military action and of their need to join with France in this spirit of sacrifice. Jules Bois (famous for his *L'Ève nouvelle*, 1896) was a representative of the French government in America during the war and included, on a trip to America in 1915, the task of describing a "new France" to American audiences. As he states in an interview entitled "War Is Making France Religious":

> The France that prays. I want Americans to know this France, so different from the one that most of them imagine. Do you think that I can make them realize that this other France, the France of the great war, exists? . . . The France that prays! It is the whole nation, everybody, rich and poor, high and low, united in a new religion. In the French Revolution we Frenchmen fought and died for the religion of liberty. Now we fight and die for the liberty of religion. . . . Religion is sacrifice. The Virgin Mary sacrificed her Son and ever since the idea of sacrifice has entered into religion. Now, in France, thousands upon thousands of mothers are sending their sons into battle, sacrificing them as did Mary, and, just as religion formerly gave the idea of sacrifice, this nation-wide sacrifice which France is making is breeding the idea of religion.
>
> It is not a matter of creed. . . . That is our new France. I want Americans to know about it—Americans who think of us as a nation without faith, a land of frivolity and gaiety and cynicism and scepticism. . . . America and France are the two great nations destined to hold aloft over the Old and the New World the inextinguishable torch of the world-civilization.[30]

In another related attempt to describe the "changed" French woman to the American public, Mme Mendès (wife of Catulle Mendès who wrote *Médée*, performed by Bernhardt in 1898) explains that French women were not "creatures of light, vain, shallow, easily flattered, fond only of dress, of pretty speeches, selfish as some have held" but were instead "brave, resourceful, ready to do and to suffer for the sake of 'La Patrie.'" Continuing with the explanation that it is not surprising such strength and courage is found in "women of the higher classes in society," Mendès speaks of the "extraordinary grandeur of soul shown by the women of the people, in Paris as well as in the unfortunate provinces that have been invaded."[31] The inclusivity of DuBois' religious sacrifice is now joined to patriotic classlessness. Bernhardt's film plays out this vision, depicting a provincial, wealthy mother sacrificing her husband and son, hand in hand with the sacrifices made by local working women. After the death of her husband and son, Bernhardt adopts another son, Nonet, an orphaned youth who has gone to war to fight for France, "the only mother he has." Bernhardt, whose appeal once lay in her capacity to bring Parisian theater and fashion to foreign audiences, now represents a provincial, spiritual, and egalitarian France.

Talking, Teaching

While Joan of Arc provides *Mothers of France* with a spiritual reference, it is the historian Jules Michelet who is used to articulate a broader message about the role of the French in the war. France was a pacifist country, fighting for liberty on behalf of all mankind. Literally written into the film through a series of shots that feature Guinot (the schoolmaster and village official) teaching a class of schoolboys, we read Michelet's words on a school blackboard: "In the twentieth century France will declare peace to the world—Michelet" (see figure 6.5). The children write, a boy at the back of the class leans forward and throws pellets of paper, another tickles his companion. Guinot raps his pointer. We cut to a shot of Bernhardt in her car in the village and then return to Guinot in the classroom. This time, Bernhardt's husband enters (he is the village major), and the children stand up. Turning to read the same blackboard—and with Guinot in medium close-up, clearly marking the words again with his pointer—Georges d'Urbex nods his head in agreement. D'Urbex then pulls out a newspaper article that announces diplomatic hostilities. The two converse and class is dismissed: France will declare peace to the world but she must go to war to achieve this.

At this point, Guinot himself goes to war. When he finally returns to the village and reenters the classroom, he is blind and led by Bernhardt. Deeply

Figure 6.5. Guinot teaches Michelet to the children, *Mothers of France*, 1917. Lobster Films, Paris.

distressed by both his physical disability and by the fact that he is alone after freeing Marie (a village girl) to marry Nonet (the orphan), this return to school provides him with reprieve. When he enters the room, the students crowd around him, offering flowers. Then the children sit down in quiet rows: solemnity replaces the joviality that we see in the opening of the film. Bernhardt takes the pointer in her hand and, with Guinot attentive beside her, reads one final phrase: "So that mothers do not have to suffer any longer, France must still go to war: it must face war with war, so that French bayonets light the dawn of the future paradise to come." The film concludes on this last shot of the blackboard. The pacifism of Michelet's opening quote is modified to include a phrase that Richepin also cites in his address to the Union des Arts. As Richepin explains, the film realizes "the prophecy of Michelet who said: 'One sees the gleam of the door of paradise where humanity will enter, because France in the twentieth century, will declare peace to the world.'"[32] War, in other words, is justifiable; it is the only means through which we can achieve peace in the twentieth century.

Here, the use of Michelet is significant. Not only was he France's most noted modern historian who imagined the nation as a collective with roots in republicanism and in Christ's moral teachings, but he also imagined Joan of Arc as a secular martyr who selflessly redeemed France. As he states: "She who had saved the people, and whom the people deserted, gave voice to no other sentiment when dying than that of compassion for them."[33] In other words, the very compassion that Bernhardt shows others and encourages others to exhibit in *Mothers of France* returns us to the Joan of Arc whom Michelet describes in his 1846 book, *Le Peuple.* As spectators, we are also encouraged to be compassionate champions of war. Like students, we read Michelet's text on the blackboard and link Christian morality to passionate patriotism. War is just and necessary; it is the only way we will achieve a future.

Arriving in America

Mothers of France enjoyed a sensational reception at the Rialto Theatre, New York, when it opened the week of March 11.[34] We know little about this opening; there is indication that it was a gala event. It was reported, for example, that the manager of the theater (Rothapfel) personally conducted the orchestra for the screening and arranged "a distinctive musical program for the occasion and has devised lighting and scenic effects to heighten the effect."[35] As I noted earlier, these scenic effects involved superimposing sections of *Joan the Woman* featuring Geraldine Farrar into a scene so that Joan appears as a vision to Bernhardt. In another scene, Napoleon was superimposed, and in yet another, Rothapfel superimposed "the French legions of today" (described in another report as "the steel wall of France.")[36] The origin of these images is not clear; one report states that the Napoleon scenes were from a film that had yet to be released.[37] The impact that these special effects had on audiences was tremendous. As *Motography* explains, "it brought the people in the audience to their feet time and time again, cheering, waving their programs, an applauding with fervour perhaps never before heard at a motion picture entertainment."[38]

Rothapfel's efforts indicate how important Bernhardt's film was to his theater and to the New York public. Indeed, the film was advertised as being "Selected by Rialto Theatre for New York First Run" and as "The Greatest Special Ever Released."[39] Rothapfel stated that the film was one of the most profitable engagements he had enjoyed in his career.[40] Further, there is indication that the film—and not only the superimposed special effects—were watched in an unusually emotive and empathetic way. As *Motography* explains, "Spectators at the big motion picture theater as a rule do not applaud, but the crowds at the Rialto Theatre, afternoon and night, received 'Mothers of France' with great bursts of hand clapping."[41]

The public was so enthusiastic about this film that "frequently during the afternoon and night the box office line stretched along Seventh Avenue for three-fourths of a block. So great was the rush that the management arranged to open the doors at 10 A.M. through the week."[42] Soon after the Rialto's success in screening *Mothers of France*, the World Film Corporation secured American distribution rights for the film. In its first official announcement about this deal, the World Film Corporation explains that "Against the determined competition of leading special feature producers, spurred by the knowledge that this was and is the most powerful and distinguished feature ever filmed, we have bought 'Mothers of France.' This extremely important transaction was closed so late that we have not been able to prepare an announcement."[43]

Difficulties in negotiating the film's American release were not due to commercial competition alone. As notices about the film make clear, the French government was "part owner of this wonderful seven reel SPECIAL."[44] This meant that it retained permanent ownership of all scenes taken in military zones (in trenches, military hospitals, and sites of military operations).[45] Mercanton negotiated the release of a film that was listed as a "military drama" in the trade presses but one that was also considered "part of the official record of the present European war" carrying to the world "that provincial France of which the outside world knows little or nothing."[46] The differences between the Breton folk community featured in *Sarah Bernhardt at Home* and the provincialism of the small town of Meurcey represented in *Mothers of France* here come into sharp relief. In the former, we observe a community whose traditions and crafts help to shape an art nouveau whose reach is global; in the latter we see a community pulled brutally onto the global stage and realize the invasive and pervasive spread of war.

Mothers of France was in circulation in America throughout 1917. Often shown at benefit screenings for war causes, it remained a rallying point for American participation and support for the war. For example, Red Cross benefits screened the film at the Wayne Opera House in Philadelphia (paired with *The Zepplin Attack on New York* (Mutual, 1917)),[47] it was screened again in Philadelphia by the American Ambulance Field Service for a benefit drive at the Metropolitan Opera House on April 12, 13, and 14,[48] it was shown at the Capitol Theater in Pekin, Illinois,[49] and on a large screen that was suspended on the lawn of the state capitol in Madison, Wisconsin.[50] *Mothers of France* was also used in a benefit drive in Cincinnati, Ohio, to aid the National Association of the Orphans of the War.[51] As a review in *Moving Picture World* explains, *Mothers of France* "fans the fire of patriotism in a white heat. It is a call to duty that will not be denied."[52] Months after the film had been replaced in the theaters, it was still strategically circulating in special benefit screenings, raising money and gaining supporters for the Allied cause in America.

Documenting Details

In the discussion of and publicity surrounding *Mothers of France*, particularly in the focus given the reality of the scenes and landscapes depicted, film emerges as a media that documents events that cannot be put into words. Bernhardt's presence is, in this sense, the pretext for a dramatically real mise-en-scène; she enables and guarantees the truth of what we see on screen. Hence, when she arrives at the small village center of Meurcey in her car and is surrounded by villagers, her husband reads the mobilization for war. When Bernhardt returns (again in her car) to bid her son and husband farewell as they head off to fight, we see further scenes of mobilization. We see open cars full of waving men, with tearful women saluting them goodbye. At this point, and after the intertitle "Mères Françaises," Bernhardt is joined by two other bereaved women under a poster ordering the "Ordre de Mobilisation Général." It is significant that this poster is a mobilization order tacked to the wall of a public building: it reminds viewers that it is in the villages of France that the war is being fought. The women stand in front of the order, their bereavement marking the sacrifices that all mothers of all classes share.

Immediately after the mobilization, Bernhardt is shown as a head nurse in a hospital in Reims, caring for injured men. After hearing of her son's injury in battle, we see her waiting before the cathedral in Reims, on her way to the front. She is then transported in the back of an army truck and arrives at a makeshift hospital where things are very different from the scene in the hospital at Reims. There are no quietly administering nurses, only military men and doctors, and the once orderly rows of beds are now replaced by a haphazard arrangement where stretchers litter the floor. While Bernhardt's Jewishness is elided in this effort to make her an integral part of village life and the French war effort, there is nevertheless a Jewish physician (his black hat and long pointed dark beard marking him "apart" from his colleagues) notably present in this scene.

Joining this focus of narrative action around the military front is the way in which Guinot, the village school teacher, returns to Meurcey blinded from war. Clearly, changing tactics of modern warfare are evident in the way his disability references the gas warfare then underway. This chemical attack was an aspect of the war that was difficult to film but which is also suggested, perhaps, in the focus given the billowing fumes on the barren battlefields. Given that the use of poison gas on a large scale was initiated just a year earlier by the Germans with the use of chlorine gas at the Second Battle of Ypres, Guinot's injury is certainly topical. Later photographs and paintings diffused the image of the blinded soldier, and it became increasingly common to viewers: both Eric Kennington's *Gassed and Wounded* (1918) and John Singer Sargent's *Gassed* (1918) resonate with these scenes. These paintings depict (respectively) men lying on stretches with their eyes bandaged and two desolate lines of soldiers being blindly led across a field of similarly bandaged men. In 1916 and early 1917, however, images such as these were not an iconic part of war. *Mothers of France* therefore documents both an unseen and disembodied enemy (we never see a German in the film) and the emergence of an invisible weapon that was only beginning to make its physical presence felt.

That the film ends with Giunot again in front of his class, once more recalling the words of Michelet, is significant. The wounded soldier can return to a "normal life"; the destroyed body can be rehabilitated with the support and love of a community. What we sense, however, is that the wounded body on screen also recalls what Véray calls the "never seen" of the images of the wounded in war.[53] Although Guinot is only acting blind, his blindfolded eyes stand in for the awful spectacles that we have missed and will never see on screen.

The Motion Pictures

The physical movement that we see in *Mothers of France* is different from the physical movement that we have seen in Bernhardt's earlier films. The question is no longer how Bernhardt adapts theatrical gesture to film, but how she is newly mobilized for war. We might speak, for example, of the way in which the earlier marketing of Bernhardt's global appeal is now restricted to an Allied audience, or how the importance of reading gesture is now focused on the possibilities for developing military messages and propaganda. We can also note that Bernhardt is now billed alongside Richepin, with the related implication that the film is primarily important for what it says.[54] More significant, however, is what the film does, what it enables. Bernhardt enjoys a degree of action that she has never before exhibited on film. She moves, literally, from a village in central France to the front line. This is particularly significant because Bernhardt's right leg was amputated in 1915. A disability that recalls and suggests the disabled body of the returning solider, *Mothers of France* rehabilitates Bernhardt, making her both a moving and mobile protagonist in the war effort.

Jeanne Doré, a film released in 1916, also shows the actress moving around contemporary France. She is at home, in a news agency, at the post office, in court, visiting her son in jail, and so on. I will not recount the details of this film: it is evident that *Mothers of France* and *Jeanne Doré* create the impression of physical movement. As the *New York Times* relays in an article entitled "Bernhardt IN PHOTO PLAY: Her Lameness Hidden in 'Jeanne Dore,' Shown Privately":

> The first acting done by Sarah Bernhardt since the loss of one of her legs by amputation last summer was shown in motion pictures exhibited privately yesterday. . . . The film was so arranged before it was sent to the country that all evidence of the actress' lameness because of her artificial leg have been deleted. So the film, as it reached America, never shows the actress walking. In every scene in which she appears she is shown either seated or standing, and whenever she starts to walk the scene is immediately changed through the devices of the switchback, the cut-in, or the printed legend. Thus, if Madame rises from a chair and starts to walk across the room to a window, she is seen to rise, the picture is snuffed out for an instant, and when it again covers the screen the actress is shown at her destination.
>
> The effect is no more confusing than in the average picture, which often baffles and irritates all but the most incorrigible movie fan. The picture is so focused that the feet of the actress do not show, or if they do only for short intervals, so there is nothing in the many scenes of the melodrama, which is melodramatic in the extreme, which would inform the uninformed of her misfortune. . . . The picture shown yesterday, after further excisions and rearrangement, will be exhibited publicly within the month.[55]

Although the *New York Times* suggests that there are audience members "uninformed" about Bernhardt's operation, it is likely that most knew of the event. Undertaken by the fashionable Dr. Samuel Pozzi (who was famously painted by John Singer Sargent in his *Dr. Pozzi at Home*, 1881), it received much press.[56] Clearly, Pozzi's role as one of the leading doctors in the military health service[57] is relevant to Bernhardt's disability: it resounds with the image of the wounded soldier returning home from war. This connection was picked up by the actress herself and by discussions in the press.[58] Further, in 1915, Edmond Rostand describes Bernhardt's amputation in a poem in the following way: "Remorse is not for thee; for thou hast aimed / To make thyself like those our martyrs maimed."[59] In this context, public knowledge of the operation indicates that film was indeed seen in terms of its instrumentality: it enables Bernhardt to circulate and move (through the narrative, on the international film market) notwithstanding the fact that she was physically incapacitated. As *Moving Picture World* explains in its review of *Jeanne Doré*: "Here we have once more a striking illustration of the amazing development of the motion picture art which has enabled the great Frenchwoman to take just the precaution which will permit the millions of playgoers all over the world to pay her homage even if she never in the flesh faces the public again."[60]

Bernhardt did, of course, face the public again "in the flesh." The shock of seeing her perform in 1916 is recounted by Béatrix Dussane of the Comédie Française who organized performers in the Théâtre aux Armées to travel to the French front and perform for soldiers. Expecting Bernhardt on film, she instead appeared before the soldiers "old, handicapped, fragile, immobile"; she was an actress who now used "the magic of her words" to perform for her compatriots.[61] The photographs of Bernhardt visiting the Maison des Moines (used as a hospital) at Dieulouard in Bois-le-Prêtre in 1916 illustrate this visit, revealing her French patriotism and commitment to the War. In one image, Bernhardt is shown carried in a sedan chair surrounded by military servicemen (see figure 6.6). Reproduced in the popular press, the picture reiterates the fact that Bernhardt is a patriotic celebrity visiting troops at the Front.[62] Moreover, Bernhardt is visiting a site that is symbolically rich. Bois-le-Prêtre was where the first Battle of the Marne took place in September 1914, when French and British forces successfully prevented the German Imperial Army's advance on Paris. The fact that Bernhardt's leg was newly amputated and that she would travel *quand même* to the Front in this condition reiterates her commitment to the war and suggests a similarity between her disabled body and the war wounded. A January 1916 cover of the journal *Excelsior*, showing photographs of Bernhardt performing the play *Du théâtre au champ*

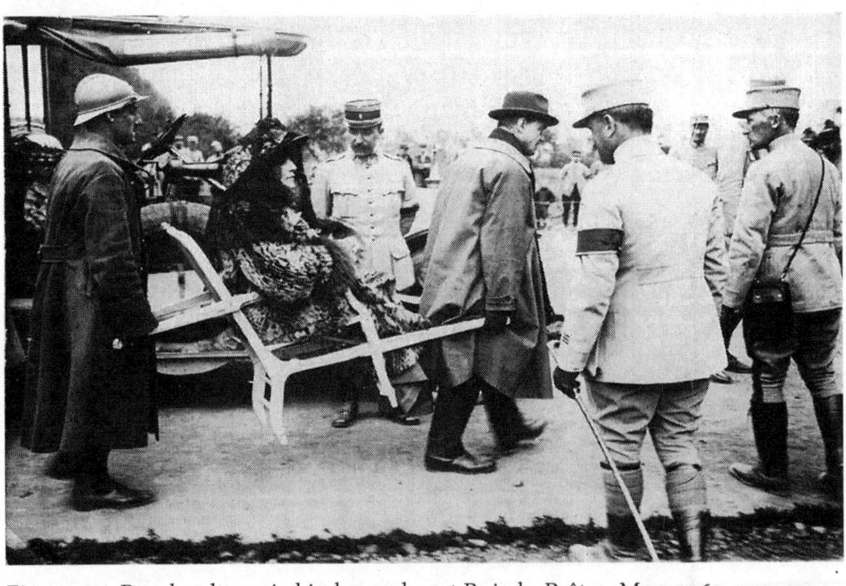

Figure 6.6. Bernhardt carried in her sedan at Bois-le-Prêtre, May 1916.

d'honneur at the Coliseum in London, confirms that Bernhardt adopted, performed, and was known to play the role of a wounded (and dying) soldier, valiantly defending France from the Germans.[63] During the war, Bernhardt also sponsored matinee galas for the National Disabled Servicemen Association at her Théâtre Sarah Bernhardt.[64] When the *New York Times* reviewed *Mothers of France*, it worked this (now familiar) knowledge of Bernhardt's disability into the discussion. Explaining that Bernhardt's transition from one scene to the next, from one space to another, was enabled by film itself, it states: "The power of the movies to obliterate space removes the handicap of [Bernhardt's] inability to walk freely."[65]

Conclusion: Telling the Time

Film overcame not just Bernhardt's physical handicap but our incapacity to otherwise witness the war. This aspect of the film resonates with the instructive capacity of film. As I mentioned earlier, *Mothers of France* shows "real chateaux, real peasant women toiling in the fields, and real munitions smoke." More importantly, the film shows the cathedral at Reims. The symbol of the religious values and moral virtues under attack in the war, the cathedral is also testament to a changing sense of temporality. Indeed, it is here that Bernhardt waits to be taken to the front. She is in a hurry, and she wants to see her son before he dies. Guinot, who will escort her to the front, walks to meet her; we see Bernhardt in the distance before the statue of Joan of Arc and in front of the sandbagged cathedral. Guinot looks at his watch and then hurries to Bernhardt. This sense of urgency is different from acceleration of gestural action and the cutting of scenes that I have described in my previous chapters. Indeed, time in *Mothers of France* is not a question of theatrical adaptation as a play moves onto film, but a matter of urgency, a question of life or death. It is also specific to the narrative: Guinot's watch explains action itself. In the same way, the large round clock that is above the blackboard in the school room reminds us that time involves the issue of personal and public accountability.

More significant than this use of the watch or clock to mark time is the way in which the façade of the cathedral also marks time. No longer does the façade of a cathedral represent—as it did some twenty years earlier in Claude Monet's famous *Rouen Cathedral* series—the ability to make a building visually decorative.[66] And no longer can spectators speak of the poetic passing of a day or suggest that it is light itself bringing stone to life. Nor, too, can spectators marvel at natural light and shade (as artist Mme. Morisot does, when she states: "Before one of Monet's pictures, I always know which way to incline my umbrella").[67] Even the idea that a building remains physically intact is refused in the film's image of a scarred and bombed façade. Indeed, against the urgency of Guinot's and Bernhardt's departure (and knowing that bombs had actually fallen upon the cathedral at Reims), we can compare the comparatively luxurious three years Monet took to study the cathedral at Rouen. And against Monet's unstable and changing universe—a world still imagined very much in terms of the retina and its sensitivity to light—we might compare a universe that has been truly transformed and changed through war (see figure 6.7). Daylight alone no longer gives testimony to the passing of time.

The angle in which the cathedral has been shot in *Mothers of France* is visually very similar to the Monet canvases. The camera pans to include Guinot in the frame. When it fixes on the cathedral we are standing slightly to the left of its main entrance. This is the same angle from which we see Monet's cathedral, which was painted from the view he had of the structure from the rooms he rented in its vicinity (23 place de la Cathédrale and 81 rue Grand-Pont in 1892 and 1893, respectively). Our distance from the cathedral is, however, a little different: whereas Monet has the cathedral fill his canvas, in *Mothers of France* we see only two flanking portals buttressed by structural reinforcements. We see the small rose window in the middle but only indistinctly; it is a circular shape crowning the reinforcements below. There are no Gothic towers and, accordingly, there is no vertical sweep to match

Figure 6.7. Reframing Monet's cathedral, *Mothers of France*, 1917. Lobster Films, Paris.

the attention paid to the cathedral's lateral surface. Indeed, whereas Monet allows an opening of sky at the top of his frame and suggests that the flanking towers rise up endlessly into this expanse (the towers do not fit his frame), in *Mothers of France* we are at ground level, have no indication of the towers, and see the changes brought to the building through the intervention of war alone. Our vision is momentary; it lasts the 20 seconds or so it takes Guinot to reach Bernhardt at the statue. We are not told when the bombs fell or when the reinforcements were built. Clearly, the time that has been marked here is not one that unfolds poetically or spontaneously across a building that then transforms itself into an object of decorative grandeur. Time is instead marked by bombardment, and this has ruined the object itself. We can no longer speak about visual recomposition through phenomenological impression; *Mothers of France* requires us to accept that gaps and holes are intrinsic to what we see.[68]

It is here, on this image of an iconic gothic cathedral newly presented on film, that I want to end. This is an incomplete image, one that does not allow us to compare film to painting in the same manner that we have in previous chapters. Then again, even Monet's use of seriality is different from the work of painters such as Delaroche since Monet forces us to speak of painting in terms of a collection rather than of a singular and original art object. From many images to the unwinding film frames, from a play upon retinal impression to the impression of actual movement, from the transience of nature to the transience of life itself: there is clearly an argument that can be made about the particular relevance of Monet's paintings to *Mothers of France.* What it tells us about two separate epochs, or about two different and separable art forms, or even about the role of the painter as compared to that of the cameraman, is valuable. As Walter Benjamin explains, the painter is akin to a magician healing through touch, the cameraman to a surgeon moving mechanically into a patient's body. What the surgeon/cameraman thereby achieves is "an aspect of reality which is free of all equipment."[69] We might, however, go one step further and compare film to film. If one of Bernhardt's earlier, more "theatrical" films, were compared to *Mothers of France*, we would have to acknowledge that *Mothers of France* has an element of randomness written into it. We do not know how the war will end, when it will end, or even if this cathedral will stay standing. The surgeon, in other words, no longer knows his subject. It is instead an aged and disabled Bernhardt who grounds this image and who provides us with a shared focus. Her mobile and moving body is the film's necessary fiction, assurance that reality might still be arranged, penetrated, and fixed.

Conclusion

A Little Too Much Is Enough for Me

Can we recuperate a cinema that has been lost to us, not materially (because the films I discuss are available in archives), but perceptually? I think we can. By questioning what Bernhardt brings to the cinema, I expand what we can learn from her films beyond the simple—but nevertheless extraordinary—fact that Bernhardt was active in the film industry during the opening decades of the twentieth century. In exploring her films, I enlarged not only what we know of her biography, her performance on the live stage, and her engagement with film but also our understanding of what we can achieve through the practice of film history today. Armed with the tools of the contemporary film historian—with the Internet, its resources, and archives—I have explored advertisements, newspaper and trade press articles, photographs of original stage plays, and Bernhardt's films themselves. I demonstrate how together these materials helped me unpack films that have been criticized and marginalized for roughly a century, sidelined from film history for being too theatrical and from theater history for not being theatrical enough. In my view—and this is a view shared by my colleagues researching women's work in early film[1]—the teen years were a rich period in film's development. Women participated in the industry as makers, performers, editors, writers, reviewers, and spectators. They were not sidelined and surpassed by the new technology and the development of a new industry but were active in its development and promotion. Indeed, until the First World War changed the political imperative of filmmaking in France, an actress of Bernhardt's stature had no qualms in adapting her performances to film, in presuming that she could creatively engage with the cinema, and in attending screenings in cinema theaters themselves. Bernhardt similarly understood that the cinema was a way to bring her performances to ever-new audiences. As I demonstrate, the First World War changed this perception. It saw Bernhardt's art nouveau aesthetic give way to somber propaganda. It saw her transform from a popular performer who traveled in great luxury to America into a serious and mature *porte parole* for the French government. This shift is not subtle: *Mothers of France* concludes my exploration precisely because the agency Bernhardt enjoyed as an actress changed.

Cinematizing Theater

Bernhardt's films tell us much about the early relationship between theater and film, particularly in the teen years. Engaging fluidly with film, changing roles and functions in each work, Bernhardt understood that film did not merely record live physical action but was an evolving media that encouraged creative experimentation. As I have demonstrated, the creative art nouveau spirit that Bernhardt embodied on the late-nineteenth-century stage was brought to her involvement in film. This art form is key to understanding Bernhardt's films. My work argues that Bernhardt's films demonstrate the cinema's capacity to engage with art nouveau, to collaborate and re-present art nouveau performance and mise-en-scène to new audiences, publics, and cultures. Rather than regard Bernhardt's films as evidence of commercial opportunism, I therefore approach them as textually dense examples of a style of cinema that is unfamiliar to us today. Indeed, while we are used to speaking of art nouveau in the context of interior design, art objects, and poster art, we have yet to examine the extent to which art nouveau implicated itself in film.

I have been careful, however, to speak of Bernhardt in terms of cinematizing theater rather than speaking of her creating a distinctive art nouveau style on film. I believe cinematizing theater keeps us better focused on the actress and her agency in the new media. Rather than periodize film in relation to an aesthetic style, I want to keep a focus on the theater and its productive relationship to film. "Cinematizing theater" carries, I hope, no presumption that any art is superior to another. Unlike the traditional term *filmed theater* used in film studies, it suggests that the theater and the cinema can engage each other in a malleable and productive way. Cinematizing theater also indicates that Bernhardt's films brought disparate audiences together, facilitating cultural, generational, and even class exchange on a scale that was previously unimaginable. I hope to bring a similarly diverse public to her work once more.

What Were They Watching?

My interest lies in what we can learn from looking at Bernhardt's films today. I am consequently aware that I have not provided evidence of Bernhardt's historical reception. Many questions therefore still remain. How did audiences around the world look at and interpret Bernhardt on film? Did audiences see the same fashions and tastes that I identify or were they so familiar with these that they went unnoted? Did each country, if not each city, have different ways of understanding and appreciating her films? Even within a given city, there were different theaters, with different programs, music, publicity, timetables, and so on, that engaged different audiences. Was the publicity for her films the same in Australia and New Zealand as it was in Canada and North America? How did England differ from France? I know that photographs of key scenes were reproduced in the trade press. I am therefore confident that my discussion of *Queen Elizabeth* and the way its publicity promoted "the moving pictures" is accurate, at least in the context of France and America.[2] I have not established, however, advertising differences between cities and do not explore Bernhardt's global promotion of film. I need to emphasize, in this context, that this book is not a reception study. How can we today establish and then reconcile these differences?

The recently published collection, *Importing Asta Nielsen: The International Film Star in the Making, 1910–1914*, systematically scrutinizes Asta Nielsen's appearance and interpretation in local newspapers across the world. It is an exemplary model of scholarship, providing a conceptual and methodological example of the historical research that still needs to be conducted in relation to Bernhardt's own distribution, exhibition, and marketing. As Uli Jung and Martin Loiperdinger explain in their introduction to the volume, the proficiencies of Asta Nielsen as an actress have been explored by commentators and scholars. Their volume departs from this traditional analysis of the actress and instead develops a systematic examination of the early international film trade. As they explain, in this changed context we discover not just "an overview of the various strategies applied in different countries to establish Asta Nielsen as a film star within an environment of film marketing" but the emergence of the exclusive feature-length film as "a new film commodity requiring new modes of film trading and film exhibition . . . [that] profoundly and subsequently [changed] also the habit of cinema-going."[3]

Because my focus is on screen content, my conclusions are speculative. Indeed, while I locate pictorial sources to explain scenes in Bernhardt's films, I can only speculate that these were identified by audiences at the turn of the twentieth century. Were Bernhardt's references to Peake, Hayez, Delaroche,

Clairin, Maufra, van Gogh, Renoir, Monet, and so on isolated and identified? Were these artists as relevant historically to the viewing experience as I find them today? I do not know. Further, although I identify visual overlap between film and paintings, I have not established whether the pictures I isolate were realized as *tableaux vivants* on the live stage. This relationship remains a substantial absence in my work: the role that the live theater played in establishing the visual composition of what we see on screen.[4] I have not yet ascertained when or even if the majority of the paintings I discuss were re-presented on the live stage. The question remains as to whether or not audiences were familiar with the works, if they had previously seen the paintings in reproductions, or even if they were watching for the visual cues I identify.

Questions of Authorship

Bernhardt was the most celebrated actress of her generation; she is arguably the most renowned actress that has ever lived. As my research indicates, we are still evaluating what she achieved in the twentieth century, at the point at which she was a mature woman with the money and power to direct her own projects. I believe that just as she managed her theaters in Paris and directed people such as Mucha and Lalique to create publicity and stage jewelry for her, she managed her exposure in film. We know, for example, that if a discussion of Bernhardt's narrative films were to begin in strict chronological order, it would be *Tosca* that initiates discussion. Made in 1908, this film was not released until 1912. The reason for this delay is attributable to Bernhardt herself: unhappy with her appearance in the film, she refused to have the work released.[5] What this indicates is the extent to which Bernhardt monitored and controlled her appearance on film. It also suggests that the business savvy she brought to the stage was applied to film: even if she was unhappy with *Tosca*, it was released one year after *Camille* had established her popularity on film and the same year that *Queen Elizabeth* was drawing audiences to the longer-playing multiple-reel film. Advertisements for *Tosca* consequently reiterate the idea that Bernhardt was a bankable commodity and make no note of the film's production date.[6]

While I might surmise that Bernhardt largely controlled when a film was made or released, I would like to know more about the practicalities of Bernhardt's filmmaking. I have not discussed the directors of Bernhardt's films, and because of this suggest that Bernhardt was as proactive in the setting up and staging of her films as she was in the organization of her live stage productions. Was this so? Did Bernhardt direct each shot, knowing how, where, and when she would be filmed? If so, what was her relationship with her directors, with men such as Calmettes, Pouctal, Desfontaines, and Mercanton? Further, who wrote or adapted her screenplays? I have mentioned Jean Richepin in relation to *Mothers of France*, but I do not know if Bernhardt chose her single shot for *Hamlet*, if she adapted the narrative of *Camille* to the screen, who decided to change the narrative of *Queen Elizabeth*, and so on. These questions of agency—of filmmaking itself—still need to be explored.

I began my book with a discussion of gesture on silent film. Although I was able to demonstrate that gesture made Bernhardt's films legible and "sound," I have not explored in any depth the issue of what people heard when they watched Bernhardt's films. Again, questions of agency are relevant. What music accompanied her work? Even if accompanists were generally pianists, what scores did they use? Was Breil's score universally applied to *Queen Elizabeth*? Were music and film marketed together? And in the absence of any ongoing mention of music—apart from the "Marseillaise" with *Mothers of France*—what was heard? Why would such evident care be given to the picturing of Bernhardt—why all this attention to gesture, costume, sets—if care was not also given to sound? Again, these questions call for further research.

Concerning Camp

It is hard to argue for an appreciation of Bernhardt's films when they require such time and effort to unpack and when so many questions remain unanswered. In my introduction I explain how art historians such as Stephen Bann and Alex Kidson have newly introduced figures such as Delaroche and George Romney to us and how this indicates a growing awareness of the need to contextualize and explain visual taste. It is one thing, however, to stage art exhibitions with explanatory catalogs; it is quite another to invite the public to watch silent films they do not know featuring an actress they associate with the nineteenth-century stage and to then ask them to read my research in order to "see." I worry, therefore, that the work I undertake is accessible to just a handful of scholars. Indeed, even though I have chosen films that are either available to purchase online or that can generally also be seen on YouTube, the problem is not physical access but visual style and taste. Seeing Bernhardt's films can change the way they are interpreted only if we are willing to review film history.

In the 1960s, Susan Sontag famously included Bernhardt's films in her "Notes on Camp." In this influential article, Sontag joins Bernhardt's *Queen Elizabeth* to a host of other art nouveau artefacts and links these to other, more urbane expressions of American popular culture: "Tiffany lamps/Scopitone films/The Brown Derby restaurant on Sunset Boulevard in LA/The Enquirer, headlines and stories/Aubrey Beardsley drawings."[7] Sontag identifies Bernhardt's film as an object that can be recuperated and redeemed from the margins of history; she is making Bernhardt's film relevant to a contemporary 1960s audience by suggesting that *Queen Elizabeth* is cinematized camp. Prior to Sontag, critics and commentators indicate that Bernhardt's films are indeed funny. Erwin Panofsky suggests that Bernhardt's films are ridiculous when he speaks of *Queen Elizabeth* as an "unbelievably funny film tragedy."[8] Salvador Dali's abridged history of the cinema, published as preface to his book *Babaouo* in 1932, describes the early teens—the period that my own research focuses upon—as the golden age of film. Focusing on the Italian divas who were trained in the legitimate theater (Francesca Bertini, Gustavo Serena, Tullio Carminati, and Pina Menichelli), Dali celebrates their films for being "marvelously, correctly close to theatre." Characterizing the teens as the "grandiose period of hysterical cinema," Dali argues that film subsequently separates itself from the theater, preoccupies itself with film language, and so enters rapidly in decline.[9] Dali's celebration is, unlike Panofsky's comment, proto-camp. Even Bernhardt's contemporaries found humor in her film. Maurice Lefèvre explains in his article "Sur le Cinéma" (cited in my introduction) that Bernhardt reduces herself "to the level of the histrionic, to amuse the crowd."[10] I believe that Sontag's camp and Dali's proto-camp humor is therefore just one available response to films that are nuanced and layered with meaning.

The sheer volume of information we can obtain today through newspapers, films, and ephemera allows us to understand film history in new and interesting ways. In many ways, it is not lack that we are dealing with as we navigate the net, but excess. Where and when should we stop our research? In 1935, Jean Cocteau was dealing with a different kind of excess when he reflected on the art nouveau period, stating "A little too much is just enough for me." Explaining that this is "the response an Indian chief gave when he was reproached for eating a little too much at the White House table,"[11] Cocteau celebrates margins and intentional excess. He celebrates the visibility of excess, presenting excess as a pioneering visual language that can be enjoyed and consumed by all. "Hail to Isadora Duncan! Hail to [Jean] Mounet-Sully! Hail to Sarah Bernhardt! Hail to [Édouard] de Max!" he enthuses. As we research and write film history of the teens, we would do well to remember that Bernhardt's excess was not a lone expression of theatrical anachronism but intrinsic to a vision that embraces the margins of performance. As Cocteau reminds us, Duncan, Mounet-Sully, Bernhardt, and de Max were French actors that go hand in hand with the emerging century and the New World.[12]

Today, we are beginning to reconsider and understand what Cocteau was suggesting in his celebration of physical melodrama. I have argued that art nouveau and the Belle Époque contextualize and help to explain Bernhardt's pioneering work. Central to my argument is the idea that Bernhardt's excess is a strength, a craft that was learned and then applied to film in order to engage global audiences. Like Cocteau's Indian chief at the White House, Bernhardt was aware that she made choices when she performed, particularly in foreign environments. Choosing excess over restraint, melodrama over naturalism, Bernhardt makes the margin a powerful place from which to speak. For generations, however, we have demonized excess, giving support to the idea that naturalism is the sine qua non of twentieth-century performance.[13] If we accept, however, that Bernhardt's physical language consciously prioritizes gesture, then we might reevaluate her relevance to the silent cinema. She does not compete with or challenge naturalism. Bernhardt instead demonstrates that there is a different language, one of gestural emotion, that speaks to us and that exists and functions alongside (and sometimes even inside) other gestural forms and styles. I think Bernhardt is film history's Indian Chief: a visible reminder that excess was an available, potent, and performative choice in the silent cinema.

Notes

Introduction

1. Carlo Ginzburg, Introduction, *Threads and Traces: True, False, Fictive*, trans. Anne C. Tedeschi and John Tedeschi (Berkeley: University of California Press, 2012), 3.

2. "Sarah Bernhardt et le cinéma," *Le Théâtre et Comœdia Illustré*, 18 (June 1923), np.

3. René Clair, *Cinema Yesterday and Today*, trans. Stanley Appelbaum (New York: Dover Publications, 1972), 35.

4. Richard Abel, *The Ciné Goes to Town: French Cinema 1896–1914* (Berkeley: University of California Press, 1994). Among other relevant books on national cinema is also Abel's *The Red Rooster Scare: Making Cinema American, 1900–1910* (Berkeley: University of California Press, 1999). This is particularly relevant in its focus on French-American relations. My focus is the teens, but for cinema's very early years, see Charles Musser, "Nationalism and the Beginnings of the Cinema: The Lumière Cinematographe in the US, 1896–1897," *Historical Journal of Film, Radio and Television*, Vol. 19, No. 2 (1999), 149–176, for a nuanced discussion of how this nationalism instead impacted the nascent cinema. Note also that my focus is Anglo-American scholarship: Heide Schlüpmann's *The Uncanny Gaze: The Drama of Early German Cinema*, trans. Inga Pollmann (Urbana: University of Illinois Press, 2010) is relevant here but was not translated until two decades later. Because of this I discuss it under feminist historiography.

5. Abel, *The Ciné Goes to Town*, xiv.

6. Debora Silverman, *Art Nouveau in Fin-de-Siècle France: Politics, Psychology, and Style* (Berkeley: University of California Press, 1989).

7. See, in particular, the work of Elena Mosconi in relation to this: "Lyda Borelli as Liberty Icon" in *Not So Silent: Women in Cinema before Sound*, eds. Sofia Bull and Astrid Söderbergh Widding (Stockholm: Stockholm University Press, 2010), 137–148.

See also, more generally, Angela Dalle Vacche, *Diva: Defiance and Passion in Early Italian Cinema* (Austin: University of Texas Press, 2008).

8. See the images in Carol Ockman and Kenneth E. Silver, eds., *Sarah Bernhardt: The Art of High Drama* (New Haven: Yale University Press, 2005), for the cutlery, plate, and standing mirror (8 and 113). See also the chair and objects featured in the photograph "Sarah Bernhardt contemplating a statuette in her home on the boulevard Péreire," fig. 12, 109.

9. See, in contrast, the discussion in Gabriel P. Weisberg, "S. Bing's Craftsmen Workshops: A Location and Importance Revealed," *Source: Notes in the History of Art*, Vol. 3, No. 1 (Fall 1983), 45, where it is argued that Bing's workshop was close to his shop in 22 rue de Provence in Paris because "Bing did not want to transport furniture an excessive distance (from manufactory to showroom)."

10. André Gaudreault, "The Culture Broth and the Froth of Cultures of So-called Early Cinema," *A Companion to Early Cinema*, eds. André Gaudreault, Nicholas Dulac, and Santiago Hidalgo (Chichester: John Wiley and Sons, 2012), 16, 17, 20.

11. Ibid., 24.

12. Ibid., 28.

13. Charles Musser, "Towards a History of Theatrical Culture: Imagining an Integrated History of Stage and Screen," *Screen Culture: History and Textuality*, ed. John Fullerton (Eastleigh, U.K.: John Libbey, 2004), 3–19.

14. See John Stokes and his discussion of Bernhardt as manager in John Stokes, Michael R. Booth, and Susan Bassnett, "Sarah Bernhardt," *Bernhardt, Terry, Duse: The Actress in Her Time* (Cambridge: Cambridge University Press, 1988), 13–64, especially 16–30.

15. Ibid., 24.

16. Ibid., 26.

17. Ginzburg, *Threads and Traces*, 3.

18. See Carlo Ginzburg, "Details, Early Plans, Microanalysis: Thoughts on a Book by Siegfried Kracauer," *Threads and Traces*, 180–192.

19. Ginzburg, *Threads and Traces*, 185. For the quote from Proust that Kracauer returns to in his book, see 184–185. For the quote in Kracauer, see Siegfried Kracauer, *History: The Last Things before the Last*, completed posthumously, by Paul Oskar Kristellar (Princeton, N.J.: Wiener, 1995), 84.

20. M. M. Bakhtin, *Speech Genres and Other Late Essays*, trans. Vern W. McGee, eds. Caryl Emerson and Michael Holquist (Austin: University of Texas Press, 1986), 7.

21. Kracauer, *History*, 6.

22. Bakhtin, *Speech Genres*, 2.

23. Jean Levèque, "En éncoutant 'Sarah' Parler du Cinéma," *Le Journal*, April 17, 1914, 7; Andrew Broan, trans., "'Sarah' Talks to Us about the Cinema," in *Red Velvet Seat: Women's Writing on the First Fifty Years of Cinema*, eds. Antonia Lant with Ingrid Periz (London: Verso, 2006), 597.

24. Translation my own. Lefèvre continues: "It is no more than an empirical process that is irremediably inferior to speech. It has, by consequence, between itself and

the truth beauty; this is the same difference that lies between a work of art painted by a master and a vulgar photograph. This difference is further accentuated by the gesticulation of perfectly ridiculous marionettes. A magisterial portrait is more living, more vivid, more moving, in its apparent immobility than all the agitations procured by the cinema." "Sur le Cinéma," *Le Film*, June 19, 1914, 1.

25. Vachel Lindsay, *The Art of the Moving Picture*, ed. Martin Scorsese (New York: The Modern Library, 2000), 108.

26. David Mayer, "Learning to See in the Dark," *Nineteenth Century Theatre*, Vol. 25, No. 2 (Winter 1997), 94, 95.

27. Ibid., 96–97.

28. David Mayer, *Stagestruck Filmmaker: D. W. Griffith and the American Theatre* (Iowa City: University of Iowa Press, 2009), 27, 29.

29. Christine Gledhill, *Reframing British Cinema 1918–1928: Between Restraint and Passion* (London: BFI, 2003), especially Chapter 1, "Theatricalising British Cinema."

30. Matthew Solomon, *Disappearing Tricks: Silent Film, Houdini, and the New Magic of the Twentieth Century* (Urbana: University of Illinois Press, 2010), 7–8.

31. Tom Gunning, "The Cinema of Attractions: Early Film, Its Spectator and the Avant-Garde" in Wanda Strauven, *The Cinema of Attractions Reloaded* (Amsterdam: Amsterdam University Press, 2006), 382. See also Gunning, "'Now You See It, Now You Don't': The Temporality of the Cinema of Attractions" in *Silent Film*, ed. Richard Abel (New Brunswick, N.J.: Rutgers University Press, 1996), 71–84.

32. Jon Burrows, *Legitimate Cinema: Theatre Stars in Silent British Films, 1908–1918* (Exeter, U.K.: University of Exeter Press, 2003), 17.

33. Ibid., 18.

34. Ibid., 14.

35. Mayer, *Stagestruck Filmmaker*, 29.

36. Stephen Bann, *Paul Delaroche: History Painted* (London: Reaktion, 1997), especially 22.

37. Claude Allemand-Cosneau and Isabelle Julia, *Paul Delaroche: Un peintre dans l'histoire* (*Paul Delaroche: A Painter in History*) (Paris: Éditions de la Réunion des musées nationaux, 1999).

38. T. J. Clark, *Farewell to an Idea: Episodes from a History of Modernism* (New Haven: Yale University Press, 1999), 1.

39. Ibid., 407.

40. See particularly pages xiv–xx in *The Cheese and the Worms: The Cosmos of a Sixteenth-Century Miller*, trans. John Tedeschi and Anne Tedeschi (Baltimore: The Johns Hopkins University Press, 1992).

41. Susan A. Glenn, *Female Spectacle: The Theatrical Roots of Modern Feminism* (Cambridge: Harvard University Press, 2000), 39.

42. Ibid., 218–219.

43. Gerda Taranow, *Sarah Bernhardt: The Art within the Legend* (Princeton: Princeton University Press, 1972). See, for example, page 95 where she states: "Like all

experimental films, that of *La Dame* is more theatrical than cinematic and is therefore basic to the reconstruction of the death scene."

44. Robert Gottlieb, *Sarah: The Life of Sarah Bernhardt* (New Haven: Yale University Press, 2010), 204.

45. See the accompanying catalog, Ockman and Silver, *Sarah Bernhardt*. Note that there is no discussion of the films in this catalog, and only brief mention made of them.

46. See Giuliana Bruno, *Streetwalking on a Ruined Map: Cultural Theory and the City Films of Elvira Notari* (Princeton: Princeton University Press, 1993); Schlüpmann, *The Uncanny Gaze*; Miriam Hansen, *Babel and Babylon: Spectatorship in American Silent Film* (Cambridge: Harvard University Press, 1994).

47. Jennifer Bean and Diane Negra, eds., *A Feminist Reader in Early Cinema* (Durham: Duke University Press, 2002); Vicki Callahan, ed., *Reclaiming the Archive: Feminist Film History* (Detroit: Wayne State University Press, 2010); Shelley Stamp, *Movie-Struck Girls: Women and Motion Picture Culture after the Nickelodeon* (Princeton: Princeton University Press, 2000).

48. See also Jane Gaines, "Film History and the Two Presents of Feminist Film Theory," *Cinema Journal*, 44.1 (2004), 113–119, for a discussion that explicitly acknowledges the belated arrival of feminist film history. Mention must also be made of Gledhill's work with the Women's Film History Network–U.K./Ireland and with the organization of the ongoing "Doing Women's Film History" conference.

49. Schlüpmann, *Uncanny Gaze*, 12.

50. Ibid., 15.

51. Ibid., 20.

52. Ibid., 22.

Chapter 1. *Nullius in Verba*

1. See Sarah Bernhardt, *My Double Life* (rep., London: Zenith, 1984 [1907]), 68; Suze Rueff, *I Knew Sarah Bernhardt* (London: Frederick Muller Ltd., 1951), 48, as well as Taranow, *Sarah Bernhardt*, Chapter One ("Voice"), and Ernest Pronier, *Une Vie au théâtre: Sarah Bernhardt* (Geneva: A. Jullien, 1942), 158, 181, 182, 196.

2. David Mayer, "Acting in Silent Cinema: Which Legacy of the Theatre?" in *Screen Acting*, eds. Alan Lovell and Peter Krämer (London: Routledge, 1999), 10.

3. "Daniel Frohman Gets Big Stars to Act for Movies," *New York Times*, December 22, 1912, SM7.

4. Broan, "'Sarah' Talks to Us about the Cinema," 597.

5. See John Stokes, "Aspects of Bernhardt," *The Yearbook of English Studies*, Vol. 11, 1981, 143–160, especially 156–160, where Stokes explores Bernhardt's relationship to the "mechanical." He argues that Bernhardt's "mechanical" reproduction on the stage (in the sense of internationally commodifying her acting by the 1880s and 1890s) undermined her aura. He concludes, however, with the suggestion that her career foreshadowed and then paralleled the cinema (Stokes makes no indication of whether or not he is aware that Bernhardt engaged with film). See page 160.

6. Georges Michel, "Sarah-Bernhard [*sic*] au Cinématographe," *Ciné-Journal*, March 16, 1912, 13.

7. Translation my own. G. Dureau, "Madame Sarah Bernhardt sur l'écran," *Ciné-Journal*, February 24, 1912, 3–4.

8. "Bernhardt Conquers New World," *Moving Picture World*, March 9, 1912, 875.

9. Francisque Sarcey, "Chronique Théâtrale," *Le Temps*, January 18, 1869, 1.

10. Richard Kendall, *Degas and the Little Dancer* (New Haven: Yale University Press, 1998), 29.

11. Sarcey, "Chronique Théatrale" [*sic*]. All entries in *Le Temps* are spelled this way.

12. Ibid., 2.

13. Rueff, *I Knew Sarah Bernhardt*, 48–49. See also Bernhardt's comments about this "'band of students,' called the 'Saradoteurs'" in Paris, in Sarah Bernhardt, *Ma double vie: mémoires de Sarah Bernhardt* (Paris: Eugène Fasquelle, 1923), 290.

14. Sarah Bernhardt, *L'art du théâtre* (Paris, 1923, repr. Paris: L'Harmattan, 1993), 121.

15. Fracisque Sarcey, "Chronique Théatrale," *Le Temps*, June 20, 1881, 1. Sarcey is here discussing the debut of the play, *La Dame aux Camélias*, by Bernhardt in London and the response in terms of cultural censorship.

16. Full-page advertisement, *Ciné-Journal*, March 9, 1912, np.

17. Double-page advertisement, *Ciné-Journal*, February 3, 1912, np.

18. See Albert W. Halsall, *Victor Hugo and the Romantic Drama* (Toronto: University of Toronto Press, 1998), Chapter 7 ("Social Justice as Erotic Aspiration; 'An Earthworm in Love with a Star': *Ruy Blas*"), especially 160.

19. Sarcey, "Chronique Théatrale," *Le Temps*, February 19, 1872, 2.

20. Sarcey, "Chronique Théatrale," *Le Temps*, February 26, 1872, 2. It is "yearning and tender, and well arranged; her diction is so perfect that you do not lose a syllable, although her words touch her lips like a caress."

21. Sarcey, "Chronique Théatrale," 2.

22. Louis Ganderax, "Revue Dramatique," *Revue des Deux Mondes* (LXVII), 1885, 226.

23. See the booklet for "Représentations de Mme Sarah Bernhardt et de sa Troupe du Théâtre Sarah Bernhardt de Paris, 1908," Théâtre Sarah Bernhardt, np. I thank David Mayer for finding and giving me this source.

24. Ibid.

25. Cited in Jan Thompson, "The Role of Woman in the Iconography of Art Nouveau," *Art Journal*, Vol. 31, No. 2 (Winter 1971–72), 162.

26. See Paul Mantz, "Le Salon," *Le Temps*, May 21, 1876, 2.

27. See the cover of *Too Thin or Skeletal Sarah* (New York: Evans and Kelly, 1880).

28. See William Hogarth, *The Analysis of Beauty* (London: W. Strahan, 1653, repr. Cosimo, 2009), 102, 106, 193. On the association of bright color with Hogarth and popular tastes, see E. H. Gombrich, "Dark Varnishes: Variations on a Theme by Pliny," *Burlington Magazine*, Vol. 104, No. 707 (February 1962), 51, 53, 55. On the relationship between Hogarth and art in the late nineteenth century, see Lynn Federle Orr

and Stephen Calloway, *The Cult of Beauty: The Victorian Avante-Garde, 1860–1900* (London: V and A Publishing, 2011).

29. David Mayer, *Henry Irving and the Bells* (Manchester: Manchester University Press, 1980), 1.

30. Mayer, "Learning to See," 22.

31. W. Stephen Bush, "Bernhardt and Rejane in Pictures," *Moving Picture World*, March 2, 1912, 760. See also the note made in *Moving Picture World*, "Facts and Comments," about the way film will enable Bernhardt to be preserved for future generations and how this will see not only her spirit but her "embodiment" living after her death (October 14, 1911, 104). See also comments in *Motion Picture Story Magazine*, which state that "Bernhardt . . . has already posed for the 'little pictures.' She is perfecting her title to immortality, so that when, for the last time, she ennobles her art in life, it will live for ages after her." "Letters to the Editor," Vol III, No. 5, June 1912, 166.

32. See the poster reproduced in Charles Musser, "Conversions and Convergences: Sarah Bernhardt in the Era of Technological Reproducibility, 1910–1913," *Film History*, Vol. 25, No. 1–2, 2013, 162.

33. See the journal *1895*, with its special issue No. 56 (in 2008) dedicated to the Film d'Art (*Le Film d'Art et les films d'art en Europe, 1908–1911*), for a discussion of the many forms that Film d'Art adopted.

34. Joseph R. Roach, *The Player's Passion: Studies in the Science of Acting* (Newark: University of Delaware Press, 1985), 60. See in general Chapter 2, "Nature Still, but Nature Mechanized."

35. Ibid., 60.

36. Ibid., 70.

37. See Gustave Garcia, *The Actor's Art: A Practical Treatise on Stage Declamation, Public Speaking and Deportment* (London: Simpkin, Marshall and Co., 1888), repr. Milton Keynes (U.K.: BiblioBazaar, 2010), 86–97, especially 86.

38. "Letters to the Editor," *Motion Picture Story Magazine*, 168.

39. *Moving Picture World*, December 31, 1909, 961.

40. "Bernhardt Conquers," 874.

41. See Lance Bertelsen, "David Garrick and English Painting," *Eighteenth-Century Studies*, Vol. 11, No. 3 (Spring 1978), 308–324.

42. See Georges Banu, *Sarah Bernhardt, sculptures de l'éphémère* (Paris: Caisse nationale des monuments historiques et des sites, 1995), especially page 18, where he speaks of Bernhardt's poses and postures. He differentiates these, stating that the poses place her within a continuum of the present and function as a form of myth-making (these are the portrait photographs) while the postures drawn from theatrical plays recall the historicity of theatrical ethnography.

43. Martin Meisel, *Realizations: Narrative, Pictorial, and Theatrical Arts in Nineteenth-Century England* (Princeton: Princeton University Press, 1983), 93.

44. Roach, *The Player's Passion*, 145.

45. *New York Dramatic Mirror*, April 10, 1912, 27, repr. in George C. Pratt, *Spellbound in Darkness: A History of the Silent Film* (Greenwich, Conn.: New York Graphic Society, 1973), 115–116.

46. Adolphe Brisson, "Chronique Théatrale," *Le Temps*, April 15, 1912, 1.

47. "Mme. Sarah Bernhardt as Queen Elizabeth," (London) *Times*, April 13, 1912, 5.

48. In *Bernard Shaw, Collected Letters, 1898–1910*, ed. D. H. Lawrence (London: Max Reinhardt Ltd., 1972), 283.

49. "The Eloquence of Gesture," *Moving Picture World*, November 4, 1911, 357–358.

50. See Gledhill, *Reframing British Cinema 1918–1928*, 32–33, and Lynda Nead's discussion of the *tableau vivant* in *The Haunted Gallery: Painting, Photography, Film, c. 1900* (New Haven: Yale University Press, 2007), 69–82, for a related discussion of pictorial tableau and its relationship to early film.

51. Bernhardt, *L'art du théâtre*, 76–77.

52. Ibid., 202.

53. Ibid., 203.

54. "Echi di cronaca," *La Stampa*, April 22, 1912, 5; Advertisement from *Saint John Globe*, March 23, 1912, reproduced in David Menefee, *The First Female Stars: Women of the Silent Era* (Westport, Conn.: Praeger, 1994), 32.

55. Bush, "Bernhardt and Rejane," 760.

56. Mayer, "Acting in Silent Cinema," 18, 20.

57. "Sarah Bernhardt's Rehearsals," *Sporting Times* (from *New York Herald*), December 18, 1880, 6.

58. Erin M. Brooks, *Sharing the Stage with the Voix d'Or: Sarah Bernhardt and Music in the Belle Époque* (PhD Diss., Washington University, St. Louis, 2010). Brooks provides interesting insight into the use of music used in some live performances. She is, however, of the opinion that film was approached "from the point of view of a stage performance" (presumably because Bernhardt spoke her lines) (508).

59. Sarcey, *Le Temps*, 1.

60. Francisque Sarcey, "Chronique Théatrale," *Le Temps*, June 1, 1890, 2.

61. A title also accorded her in *Moving Picture World*. See, for example, "ECLAIR PRESENTS MME.Bernhardt IN PICTURES," where it states that "While it has been noticed that the Divine Sarah appeared before the camera, it has not been generally announced that the Éclair Company was the fortunate company to secure her services" (*Moving Picture World*, November 11, 1911, 473). See also March 16, 1912, 27, in *Moving Picture News* where under an article entitled "SARAH Bernhardt" we are told that "The elite of Paris have applauded the splendid projections of the Divine Sarah in her greatest role."

62. See the discussion of this in Jonathan Auerbach, *Body Shots: Early Cinema's Incarnations*, (Berkeley: University of California Press, 2007), 65–67; see especially Auerbach's argument that Edison sought the "operatic illusion of sensory wholeness" (67). Note that Martin Marks dedicated some comments to Edison's obsession with opera in *Music and the Silent Film: Context and Case Studies, 1895–1924* (New York: Oxford University Press, 1997), especially 72.

63. Rick Altman, *Silent Film Sound* (New York: Columbia University Press, 2004), 251.

64. Paul Freyer, *The Opera Singer and the Silent Film* (Jefferson, N.C.: McFarland and Co., 2005).

65. "Bernhardt in 'Camille,'" *Sydney Morning Herald*, April 20, 1912, 2.

66. Bush, "Bernhardt and Rejane."

67. Martin Marks, 100.

68. See the publicity for the double bill in *Moving Picture World*, February 10, 1912, 498–499.

69. Clarence E. Sinn, "Music for the Picture," *Moving Picture World*, August 31, 1912, 871.

70. Marks, *Music and the Silent Film*, 98, for Breil's biography as well as 140 and 283 n. 55, for references to operatic excerpts Breil would later use in his score of *Birth of a Nation*.

71. Cited in *Moving Picture World*, advertisement for *Queen Elizabeth*, September 14, 1912, 1036.

72. *Moving Picture World*, full-page advertisement, August 17, 1912, 679.

73. Marks, *Music and the Silent Film*, 101.

74. Ibid., 103.

75. See the discussion in Michael Strasser, "The Société Nationale and Its Adversaries: The Musical Politics of 'l'invasion germanique' in the 1870s," *19th-Century Music*, Vol. 24, No. 3 (Spring 2001), 28.

Chapter 2. *Hamlet*

1. Laurent Mannoni, "Phono-Cinéma-Théâtre," *Le Giornate del Cinema Muto Catalogue* (Pordenone: Le Giornate del Cinema Muto, 2012), 26.

2. Emmanuelle Toulet, "Cinema at the Universal Exposition, Paris, 1900," trans. Tom Gunning, *Persistence of Vision*, 9 (1991), 10.

3. Ibid., 26.

4. Ibid., 33.

5. Ibid.

6. Georges Sadoul, *Histoire Générale du Cinéma: Les Pionniers du Cinéma 1897–1909* (Paris: Denoël, 1948), 104.

7. Mannoni, "Phono-Cinéma-Théâtre," 26.

8. Ibid., 25–26.

9. David Robinson, *Music of the Shadows: The Use of Musical Accompaniment with Silent films* (Pordenone: Le Giornate del Cinema Muto, 1990); Toulet, "Cinema at the Universal Exposition," 24.

10. Sadoul, *Histoire Générale du Cinéma*, 101.

11. *Arcade Auction Catalogue of Old Master and 19th Century European Painting, Drawing and Sculpture*, London, July 20, 1995.

12. Taranow, *Sarah Bernhardt*, 128.

13. See, for example, the steel engraving of Bernhardt as Tosca—the cane "centering" her body and gesture—by Florian (after a picture by Jan Van Beers) reproduced in *Revue Illustrée*, National Portrait Gallery, nd. Negative number 31594.

14. Translation my own. "La soirée théâtrale, La Tosca," *Le Figaro*, November 25, 1887.

15. Gerda Taranow, *The Bernhardt Hamlet: Culture and Context* (New York: Peter Lang, 1996), 17: "Beginning with Lorenzaccio, Bernhardt took principal, or *premier*, roles written for actors and transformed them into *travestis*. The first role in her *Hamlet* cycle, *Lorenzaccio*, represented a new acting category which she initiated: the *premier travesti rôle*."

16. Taranow, *Bernhardt Hamlet*, xvii–xviii.

17. Ibid., 4–5.

18. See Romy Heylen, *Translation, Poetics, and the Stage: Six French Hamlets* (London: Routledge, 1993), 63.

19. Ibid., 54.

20. Ibid., 64.

21. Ibid., 75–76.

22. Taranow, *Bernhardt Hamlet*, 105–106.

23. "Madame Bernhardt's Hamlet," (London) *Times*, July 13, 1899, 12.

24. John Hansen, "Sarah Bernhardt as Hamlet," *National Magazine* (August 1899), 470.

25. Taranow, *Bernhardt Hamlet*, 36.

26. "Madame Bernhardt's Hamlet," (London) *Times*.

27. See Taranow, *Bernhardt Hamlet*, 156.

28. Ibid., 48.

29. See Taranow's comment in relation to this: "It is a matter of no small significance that Bernhardt's Hamlet was the first Prince of Denmark to die standing. . . . John Gielgud's success with the use of the standing death is now well-known. What is not well-known is that the innovation actually took place thirty-seven years prior to the performances of the great English actor." Ibid., 186.

30. Ibid., 70.

31. See Bernhardt's *Ma double vie: mémoires de Sarah Bernhardt*, trans. (London: Arrow Books Ltd., 1984), 139–140, where she explains, for example, how her performances at the Odeon theater in the early 1870s would upset the older members of the audience habituated to a more traditional and classical style of performance.

32. Taranow, *Bernhardt Hamlet*, 175.

33. Clement Scott, *Some Notable Hamlets of the Present Time* (New York: Benjamin Blom, 1900, 2d ed., 1969), 45–46, 51.

34. Edmond Stoullig, *Les Annales du Théâtre et de la Musique* (Paris: Librairie Paul Ollendorff, 1899), 169–170.

35. Taranow, *Bernhardt Hamlet*, 109; Taranow does not specify her source here.

36. "The Week: Adelphi Performance of Madame Bernhardt's Hamlet, in innumerable Acts," *Atheneum*, No. 3738, June 17, 1899, 764.

37. Ibid.

38. Hansen, "Sarah Bernhardt as Hamlet," 469.

39. See: "He did not take the apparition for a ghost who might fade into formless shadow at any moment. He advertised to us his entire confidence that, when he

chose to turn around again, the spectre king would be obligingly waiting there until he could secure his son's attention.... [T]he ghostliness of the scene had somehow evaporated." E. Robins, "On Seeing Madame Bernhardt's Hamlet," *North American Review* (December 1900), 913.

40. *Daily Telegraph*, June 16, 1899, 10.

41. Hansen, "Sarah Bernhardt as Hamlet," 470.

42. "The Week: Lyric 'Hamlet,'" *Atheneum*, No. 4048, May 27, 1905, 667.

43. Silvia Bigliazzi, "*Hamlet* on Screen and the Crystal Image," *Hamlet Studies: An International Journal of Research*, 18 (Summer/Winter 1996), 107.

44. R. Mamoulian, *Shakespeare's Hamlet* (New York: Bobbs-Merrill Co. Inc., 1965), 251–252.

45. Ibid., 261–262 (italics added).

46. Lisa Hopkins, "Playing at Bouts: Hamlet and the Use of the Culminating Duel," in *Hamlet Studies*, 131–132.

47. Ibid., 130.

48. Translation my own. E. Blavet, "Les Femmes et l'Escrime," *La Vie Parisienne: La Vie et Le Théâtre*, 316 (January 14, 1884), 31–32.

49. Taranow, *Bernhardt Hamlet*, 177. See also page 83: "Masculine costume . . . exposed the actresses' legs, an effect not invariably emphasized, but one that was by no means ignored at a time when women's costumes were ankle-length."

50. Blavet, "Les Femmes et l'Escrime," 33–34.

51. Translation my own. Max Rivière, "Mimi Pinson Escrimeuse," *Femina*, 56 (May 15, 1903), 538–539.

52. *Harper's Bazaar* (December 1899), 16.

53. Taranow, *Bernhardt Hamlet*, 177–178.

54. Ibid., 178.

55. Robins, "On Seeing Madame," 908.

56. Cited in Marjorie Garber, *Vested Interests: Cross-Dressing and Cultural Anxiety* (New York: Routledge, 1992), 40.

57. "The Week: Adelphi Performance of Madame Bernhardt's Hamlet, in innumerable Acts," *Atheneum*, No. 3738, 764.

58. Hansen, "Sarah Bernhardt as Hamlet," 469.

59. *Sarah Bernhardt*, "Men's Roles as Played by Women," *Harper's Bazaar*, Vol. XXXIII, 50 (December 15, 1900): 2113–2115.

60. Ibid., 2114.

61. David Mayer, "*Fights of Nations* and National Fights," *Early Cinema and the "National,"* eds. Richard Abel, Giorgio Bertellini, and Rob King (Leicester, U.K.: John Libbey Publishing Ltd., 2008), 138, n. 4.

62. See ibid. for a discussion of these films.

63. Ibid.

64. Bernhardt, "Men's Roles as Played by Women," 2114.

65. Susan A. Glenn, 11.

Chapter 3. *Camille*

1. *Moving Picture World*, February 10, 1912, 498–499.

2. See, for example, the advertisement in *Moving Picture World*, July 6, 1912, 75, that states that lectures are available for this double bill and also for *Dante's Inferno* (Milano Film Co., 1911) and *Jerusalem Delivered* (World's Best Film Company, 1911).

3. See Chapter 2 ("Japan and the Painters") and Chapter 3 ("The Poster and the Japanese Print") in Lionel Lambourne, *Japonisme: Cultural Crossings between Japan and the West* (London: Phaidon, 2005).

4. Forest Izard, *Heroines of the Modern Stage* (New York: Sturgis and Company, 1915), 47–48.

5. I do not want to trace the Duplessis-Gautier history here, but see Virginia Rounding, *Grandes Horizontales: The Lives and Legends of Four Nineteenth-Century Courtesans* (London: Bloomsbury, 2003), Chapters 2 and 3.

6. "Reappearance of Mdlle. Sarah Bernhardt," *Sunday Times*, June 19, 1881, 3.

7. "Mme. Bernhardt in 'La Dame aux Camélias,'" (London) *Times*, October 7, 1913, 10.

8. "Camille to Camille," *New York Times*, January 13, 1918, X7.

9. Stephen S. Stanton, ed., and Introduction, *Camille and Other Plays* (New York: Hill and Wang, 1957), xxx.

10. Ibid., Introduction. Other Dumas plays dealt with the subject of sexual morality and social mores: *Diane de Lys* (1853), *La question d'argent* (1857), *Le fils naturel* (1858), *Un père prodigue* (1859), and *Les idées de Madame Aubray* (1867).

11. See Walter Benjamin, *The Arcades Project*, ed. Rolf Tiedemann, trans. Howard Eiland and Kevin McLaughlin (Cambridge: Harvard University Press, 1999), 502: "The act closes with a smile from the statues: they remain motionless when Phidias promised them fame, but turn smiling to Gorgias, who promises them money."

12. Double-page advertisement, *Moving Picture World*, February 17, 1912, 596.

13. See Roberta Montemorra Marvin, "Verdian Opera Burlesqued: A Glimpse into Mid-Victorian Theatrical Culture," *Cambridge Opera Journal*, Vol. 15, No. 1, 2003, 36.

14. Francisque Sarcey, "Les représentations françaises à Londres," *Le Temps*, June 20, 1881, 1.

15. See the comment in A. E. Zucker and P. De F. Henderson's "*Camille* as the Translation of *La Dame aux Camélias*," *Modern Language Notes*, Vol. 49, No. 7 (November 1934), 473, n. 1, where readers are referred to "an interesting account of how Modjeska fooled the London censor but not the Prince of Wales by announcing her *Camille* as *Heartsease*" (account taken from Modjeska's autobiography). *Heartsease* continued to be performed after the premiere of *La Dame aux Camélias*: "At the Olympic, Miss Grace Hawthorne has revived *Heartsease*, a vein of *La Dame aux Camélias*. . . . Miss Hawthorne plays, of course, without the power which Mme Sarah Bernhardt has taught us to look for in this character, but, nevertheless, with considerable feeling, which is not without its effect upon an unsophisticated audience" ("Opera Comique," [London] *Times*, January 11, 1892, 10).

16. Sarcey, "Les représentations françaises."

17. See Marvin, "Verdian Opera Burlesqued," 36–48, for a discussion of *La Traviata* and its relation to burlesque on the Victorian stage. See page 46 for the information about *The Lady of the Cameleon.*

18. John Wilkens (a young American playwright who died the same year) adapted the play for the actress. See Zucker and Henderson, "*Camille* as the Translation," 474.

19. In ibid., 473–474, n. 3, Geo. C. D. Odell is cited from the *Annals of the New York Stage* and speaks of Davenport's playing as being "very much pruned and purified."

20. See Merle L. Perkins, "Matilda Heron's *Camille*," *Comparative Literature*, Vol. 7, No. 4 (Autumn 1955), 338.

21. Grace Greenwood (pen name of Sara Jane Clarke), "Five Camilles," *New York Times*, February 21, 1875, 7.

22. Perkins, "Matilda Heron's *Camille*," 342.

23. See Geo. C. D. Odell cited in Zucker and Henderson, "*Camille* as the Translation," 474, n. 3.

24. Amy Leslie, a Chicago newspaper columnist writing in 1900 cited in Clifford Ashby, "The Technique of Clara Morris," *Educational Theatre Journal*, Vol. 16, No. 2 (May 1964), 134.

25. "Bernhardt as Marguerite Gautier," *New York Times*, November 16, 1880, 5.

26. "Reappearance of Mdlle. Sarah Bernhardt."

27. "Bernhardt as Marguerite Gautier." For references to the use of this cough, see Perkins, "Matilda Heron's *Camille*," 342, where it is noted that Heron's "coughing and tortured look during the final act were 'too painfully real.'" See also Ashby, "Technique of Clara Morris," 138, where it is stated (in a comment that cites Morris writing in 1900) that Morris consulted her physician about the cough she should perform in the role. A description of her performance of this cough is then provided. These "little pitiful spasms . . . seize upon the listener's sympathies like a baby's struggle for breathe [*sic*] in croup."

28. "Bernhardt as Marguerite Gautier."

29. Ibid.

30. Ibid.

31. Ibid. See also "Amusements: Mlle. Bernhardt's Marguerite," *New York Times*, April 20, 1881, 4, for comments about her variety and womanly passion, and how her "love-making is full of sensuous passion."

32. Ibid.

33. As Susan A. Glenn explains, tickets to her show were the (then) exorbitant price of $3 (*Female Spectacle*, 17). See also the review of her performance in *New York Times*, November 16, 1880, repr. in *Famous Actors and Actresses on the American Stage*, Vol. 1, ed. William C. Young (New York: R.R. Bower and Co., 1975), 104–105, where the language used in the review is itself pitched to an upper-class public: "The performance was intensely real, the pathos of the artist moved its spectators deeply, and in its exquisite finish the impersonation was absolutely marvelous."

34. (London) *Times*, June 11, 1881, 10.

35. Greenwood, "Five Camilles."

36. "Bernhardt in One of Her Greatest Roles," *New York Times*, December 13, 1905, 9.

37. "The French Plays," (London) *Times*, June 13, 1881, 13.

38. Sarcey, "Les représentations françaises," 2.

39. Ibid.

40. "Two Weeks of Paris Gossip," *New York Times*, June 3, 1894, 28.

41. I thank David Mayer for giving me a playbill from the Lyceum Theatre, March 9, 1889, to consult for this information.

42. See Arnold Mortier, *Les Soirées Parisiennes de 1882, par un monsieur de l'orchestre* (Paris: E. Dentu, 1883), 222, recounting a performance of *La Dame aux Camélias* on May 25, 1882: "L'apparition de M. Damala, le mari de Sarah Bernhardt, était sans contredit une des grandes curiosités de cette soirée."

43. "Her Majesty's Theatre," (London) *Times*, July 2, 1901, 10. See Tout-Paris, "Bloc-Notes Parisien: Jacques Damala," *Le Gaulois*, August 19, 1889, 100, for a description of Damala's death.

44. "Drama," *Atheneum*, June 21, 1902, 796.

45. George Bernard Shaw, "Duse and Bernhardt" (June 15, 1895), *Dramatic Opinion and Essays* (New York: Brentano's, 1907), 138–139. Note that even into 1927, these two were the "models" of Marguerite: "Norma Talmadge, belle et fort émouvante, a repris le rôle de Marguerite qu'immortalisèrent Sarah Bernhardt et la Duse." In "La Dame aux Camélias," *Paris Jour*, October 11, 1927, 31.

46. See Jefferson Theatre publicity for Saturday, September 22, 1897. I would like to thank David Mayer for giving me this reference and source.

47. Note, in relation to Bernhardt's popularity (and this was especially the case in America), the claim that D. W. Griffith was to later make about being an extra in Bernhardt's *Camille* when it was brought to Louisville in 1896. See Melvyn Stokes, *D. W. Griffith's The Birth of a Nation: A History of the Most Controversial Motion Picture of All Time* (Oxford: Oxford University Press, 2007), 61.

48. See the booklet for "Représentations de Mme Sarah Bernhardt et de sa Troupe du Théâtre Sarah Bernhardt de Paris, 1908," np. I would like to thank David Mayer for finding and giving me this source.

49. Ibid.

50. "Bernhardt in One of Her Greatest Roles."

51. Stephen M. Archer, "E Pluribus Unum: *Bernhardt's 1905–1906 Farewell Tour*," in *The American Stage: Social and Economic Issues from the Colonial Period to the Present*, eds. Ron Engle and Tice L. Miller (Cambridge: Cambridge University Press, 1993), 161.

52. Ibid., 163.

53. "Sarah Bernhardt and the Music-hall," *Manchester Guardian*, June 12, 1910, 6.

54. Ibid.

55. See Charles Musser, "Conversions and Convergences: Sarah Bernhardt in the Era of Technological Reproducibility, 1910–1913," *Film History*, Vol. 25, No. 1–2, 2013,

158. Information about Guilbert and troupes from Arthur Gold and Robert Fizdale, where they cite the *Echo de Paris*, in *The Divine Sarah: A Life of Sarah Bernhardt* (New York: Aldred A. Knopf, 1991), 302.

56. *The Palace Theatre Presents Madame Sarah Bernhardt in Vaudeville* (New York: The Printwell, 1912). Bernhardt was meant to open her vaudeville tour in this theater but it was still unfinished when she arrived in America. This is why she began her tour at the Majestic in Chicago. Leigh Woods, "Sarah Bernhardt and the Refining of American Vaudeville," *Theatre Research International*, Vol. 18, No. 1 (Spring 1993), 18.

57. Woods, 22.

58. Ibid., 21–22. .

59. Note that David Mayer states in *Stagestruck Filmmaker* (48) that "Sarah Bernhardt held out against the Syndicate and toured America, appearing, as a consequence, in a circus tent, hired for the occasion from Barnum & Bailey, and public skating rinks." In this way Mayer indicates that Bernhardt was not choosing alternative popular venues for the theater but ensuring that she reached audiences on the theatrical circuits in America, even when she was dealing with the Theatrical Syndicate. The Syndicate was organized by Marc Klaw, Abraham Erlanger, and Charles and Daniel Frohman.

60. Advertisement, *Moving Picture World*, February 24, 1912, 645: "SARAH Bernhardt is the foremost living female interpreter of human emotions on the stage today."

61. Note that David Menefee's DVD of *Camille* has intertitles that are not original to the film and that these appear at moments that again differ from the film I have seen screened (and programmed) for my "Performing Passions" program at Cinema Ritrovato in 2006. This film is one restored by the Cinémathèque Française (CF) in 1985. DVD available for purchase online at http://www.thegreatstars.com/new_page_2.htm (accessed October 13, 2014).

62. In the NFSA print, we see only Marguerite's letter; in the film held at the CF we instead see Marguerite write the letter. Both letters are a little different: in the NFSA print Marguerite states "When you receive this letter I shall be living with Count Varville. Good bye for ever, Marguerite." In the CF copy we instead see "Armand, When you will receive these lines I shall belong to the Count of Varville. Farewell Camille."

63. Two-page advertisement, *Moving Picture World*, March 16, 1912, 982–983.

64. Two-page advertisement, *Moving Picture World*, March 23, 1912, 1088–1089.

65. See notes in Jas S. McQuade's "Chicago Letter," *Moving Picture World*, where he speaks of the "fine business" that *Camille* was doing in Chicago's La Salle Theatre, cautioning that "The management of the house is making a mistake in giving the front of this legitimate theatre a tawdry appearance by means of cheap cloth banners etc. . . . First-class people are not enticed by the surroundings of a dugout." *Moving Picture World*, May 25, 1912, 716.

66. Two-page advertisement, *Moving Picture World*, February 17, 1912, 596–597.

67. Two-page advertisement, *Moving Picture World*, February 24, 1912, 700–701.

68. Advertisement, *Moving Picture World*, March 2, 1912, 799.

69. Advertisement, *Moving Picture World*, March 9, 1912, 833.

70. "Bernhardt Brings Tears as Camille," *New York Times*, December 8, 1910, 13.

71. "Bernhardt as Marguerite," *New York Times*, January 28, 1896, 5.

72. "Sarah Bernhardt's Rehearsals," *Sporting Times* (from *New York Herald*), December 18, 1880, 6.

73. "Bernhardt as Marguerite Gautier."

74. "Perhaps it would be better to omit the first two acts altogether. The fourth too—wherein Armand Duval throws his bank notes in Marguerite's face—might well be spared. We might then have the interview with old Duval and the death scene presented as 'Popular Selections from *La Dame aux Camélias*.'" "Her Majesty's Theatre," (London) *Times*, July 2, 1901, 10. I wonder, however, if the fact that the copy that the Cinémathèque Française holds begins in the Third Act indicates that the film was indeed later truncated to contain the most "popular scenes."

75. See David Nasaw, *Going Out: The Rise and Fall of Public Amusements* (New York: Basic Books, 1993), especially Chapter 13, "The pernicious 'moving picture' abomination." See also comments such as those by H. Leigh in "Acting and Actions," *Moving Picture World*, October 2, 1909, 443: "I watched my films run off with shears in hand ready to cut out such parts as were immoral, indecent or gruesome, and those shears were much used."

76. See some examples of the advertisements in *Moving Picture World*, July 6, 1912, 75; July 20, 1912, 260; August 17, 1912, 709.

77. Bush, "Bernhardt and Rejane," 76.

78. "Reviews of Feature Subjects: Bernhardt in Camille," *New York Dramatic Mirror*, April 10, 1912, 26.

79. Ibid., 103.

80. "Bernhardt and Rejane in Pictures," *Motography*, Vol VII, No. 2 (February 15, 1912), 85.

81. "Bernhardt as Marguerite Gautier."

82. *Moving Picture World*, September 21, 1912, 1174.

83. "Bernhardt Conquers New World," *Moving Picture World*, March 9, 1912, 874–875.

84. G. Dureau, "Madame Sarah Bernhardt sur l'écran," *Ciné-Journal*, February 24, 1912, 3–4. Note that Dureau seems to be summarizing, however, the sequences in the play and not the film since the film does not begin with the supper.

85. F. Signerin, "Le roman; la pièce; le film," *Le Cinéma*, May 10, 1912, 1.

86. Translation my own. Armand Bour, "L'Art du Cinéma," *Le Cinéma*, October 4, 1918, 2.

87. W. B. Yeats, "Notes," *Samhain* (Dublin: Searly Bryers, 1902), 4.

88. See "My spirit is once more violently dragged along another trail." in Bour, "L'Art du Cinéma." See also "The Reform of the Theatre," *Samhain*, October 1901, 10: "We must simplify acting, especially poetical drama. . . . We must get rid of everything that is restless, everything that draws the attention away from the sound of the voice,

or from the few moments of intense expression, whether that expression is through the voice or through the hands; we must from time to time substitute for the movements that the eye sees the nobler movements that the heart sees, the rhythmical movements that seem to flow up into the imagination from some deeper life than that of the individual soul." Yeats, "Notes," 9.

89. See A. E.'s (George William Russell) comment in "The Dramatic Treatment of Heroic Literature," in *Samhain*, October 1901, 13: "Man, when he has returned to himself, and to the knowledge of himself, may find a greater power in his voice than in those powers which he has painfully harnessed to perform his will, in steamship or railway. It is through drama alone that the writer can summon, even if vicariously, so great a power to his aid; and it is possible that we may yet hear on the stage, not merely the mimicry of human speech, but the old forgotten music which was heard in the drums of kings, which made the reveller grow silent and great warriors to bow low their face on their hands."

90. Two-page advertisement, *Moving Picture World*, February 24, 1912, 700–701.

91. Advertisement, *Moving Picture World*, March 2, 1912, 799.

92. Victorin Jasset, "An Essay on Mise-en-Scène in Cinematography" from "Étude sur le mise-en-scène," *Ciné-Journal*, October 21, 1911, reprinted in Richard Abel, *French Film Theory and Criticism, 1907–1929* (Princeton: Princeton University Press, 1988), 56.

93. "Reviews of Feature Subjects."

94. Bush, "Bernhardt and Rejane," 760. I am aware that this might not be the precise moment he was indicating.

95. I realize that my focus is American and French marketing and that we might go on to develop this idea and explore how *Camille* was pitched to other national audiences. My point, however, is that the ways in which the film was pitched and promoted changed the ways in which it was seen and interpreted.

96. David Nasaw, *Going Out*, 177, from Black v. City of Chicago, Supreme Court of Illinois, February 19, 1909, cited in N.E. 1011. Nasaw notes that "What made the discourse on the moving pictures cataclysmic in tone was the changed nature of the audience. Vaudeville and live theater had deadened the taste, moral sensibilities, and intellectual capacities of relatively prosperous, English-speaking audiences; moving pictures 'demoralised' working people, immigrants and children who lacked the intellectual, educational, and cultural resources to resist or counterbalance their effects." (174–175).

97. Two-page advertisement, *Moving Picture World*, February 24, 1912, 700–701.

98. Two-page advertisement, *Moving Picture World*, March 16, 1912, 982–983. This is reproduced in Janet Staiger's essay "Seeing Stars" in Christine Gledhill, ed., *Stardom: Industry of Desire* (London: Routledge, 1991), 13, but it is mistakenly listed as February 10, 1912.

99. *Moving Picture World*, February 17, 1912, 596.

100. Richard Abel, *Americanizing the Movies and "Movie-Mad" Audiences, 1910–1914* (Berkeley: University of California Press, 2006), 25.

101. Bush, "Bernhardt and Rejane," 76.

102. "Rejane in the Sentimental," *New York Times*, December 4, 1904, 20.

103. "Two weeks of Paris Gossip" 28.

104. See *Ciné-Journal*, January 6, 1912, 30.

105. *Ciné-Journal*, February 24, 1912, 40–41; also in no. 184, March 21, 1912, 24–25.

106. This statement and autograph was included in one advertisement I have seen in *Moving Picture World* (March 23, 1912, 1088–1089). Whether audiences could read the French statement I do not know. It was not included, however, with any photographs of the actress and appeared only once beneath a typewritten insert about Bernhardt contracting only with the Film d'Art. It therefore seems to have been included to prevent fears that she would appear in other films and so undercut possible profits. I would consequently maintain that different strategies for the advertisement of the film were played out nationally.

107. *Ciné-Journal*, January 27, 1912, 32.

108. See *Ciné-Journal*, February 3, 1912, 56–57.

109. Silverman, *Art Nouveau*, 12.

110. Dureau, "Madame Sarah-Bernhardt," 1.

111. "Le progrès artistique," Koustrany, *Ciné-Journal*, January 31, 1914, 45: "Vous souvenez-vous de l'impression splendide qu'elle nous donna sous les traits, désormais immortels, de *la Dame aux Camélias*, chef-d'oeuvre d'Alexandre Dumas fils."

112. Lambourne, *Japonisme: Cultural Crossings*, 131.

113. See Reynaldo Hahn, *La Grande Sarah* (Paris: Hachette, 1930), 125–126.

114. See Shelley C. Berg, "Sada Yacco: The American Tour, 1899–1900," *Dance Chronicle*, Vol. 16, No. 2 (1993), 153–154.

115. Ibid., 153.

116. Ibid., 168–169, where it is noted that the play was a hybird of *Sayaate* and *The Temple of Dojoji* with Kawakami's own *The Loyalist*.

117. Ibid., 174, where it is mentioned that an evening's program lasted two hours and that critics noted the condensation of the narrative and action for occidental audiences.

118. Ibid., 176, where a review in the *Boston Herald* of 1900 states: "And how this Geisha dances! Flexible as a little willow wand, the scarlet and white Kimono clinging to her lithe form, and, with every movement, enveloping her like tongues of flame, she takes the most exquisite poses, recalling those graceful figures which have "decorated our choicest specimens and curios." See also Shelley C. Berg's comments in "Sada Yacco in London and Paris, 1900: Le Rêve Réalisé," *Dance Chronicle*, Vol. 18, No. 3 (1995), 374, where she states "[P]art of Yacco's fascination for Western audiences lay in her seemingly uncanny ability to give substance to the drawings and prints of Japanese artists."

119. Ibid., 380.

120. Ibid., 396.

121. Ibid., 394.

122. See Berg, "Sada Yacco: The American Tour," 181, for a reproduction of this image.

123. Izard, *Heroines of the Modern Stage*, 43.

124. See Berg, "Sada Yacco: The American Tour," 157–158.

Chapter 4. *Queen Elizabeth*

1. Michael Quinn, "Distribution, the Transient Audience, and the Transition to the Feature Film," *Cinema Journal*, 40, 2, Winter 2001, 47.

2. The Histrionic Film Company was a company established by Bernhardt for the film. About Brockliss being the London producer who director Louis Mercanton contacted to distribute the film in the United States, see See Jean-Marc Leveratto, "Sarah Bernhardt dans *Queen Elizabeth* (1912), du théâtre (français) au cinéma (américain)," *Théâtre, destin du cinéma*, eds. Agathe Torti-Alcayaga and Christine Kiehl (Paris: Le Manuscrit, 2013), 31. Here, it is mentioned that Brockliss was the London distributor of films and that London was the two-way hub for European-U.S. film distribution. I would like to thank Vito Adriaensens for bringing this book (and particularly this essay) to my attention.

3. Quinn, "Distribution, the Transient Audience," 48.

4. It was given a general release at the Lyceum Theatre on the 15th of August and opened at Powers Theatre in Chicago on the 12th of August. It was released at the Palace Theatre in London (on August the 11th) and finally released by Éclipse in France on the 31st of January 1913. For the American dates, see Marks, *Music and the Silent Film*, 100. See Taranow, *Sarah Bernhardt*, 127, n. 14, for the London dates (although these differ from Leveratto's ["Sarah Bernhardt dans *Queen Elizabeth*," 31], where he states that it was an August 16th release). See Abel, *Americanizing the Movies and Movie-Mad Audiences, 1910–1914*, 31, for the Powers dates.

5. See Eileen Bowser, *The Transformation of Cinema* (New York: Scribners, 1990), 204–205, and Abel, *The Ciné Goes to Town*, 316, for recent scholarship that endorses this view. Musser, in his article "Conversions and Convergences," 170, cites Terry Ramsaye, Adolph Zukor, Georges Sadoul, Robert Sklar, and Eileen Bowser to verify this same point. Clearly, there are further sources that could be cited (Jay Leyda and Andre Bazin, to name a couple); the point is that "filmed theater" has long been used as a term of critique in film studies.

6. Musser, "Conversions and Convergences," 155. While my own research on Bernhardt has long been focussed on this gap, note that comments about this gap are certainly not new. See, for example, the Bernhardt entry in *Enciclopedia dello Spettocolo* (Rome: Casa Editrice le Machere, 1954), 371, where it is noted that "Un altro film della Bernhardt, *La Reine Élisabeth*, importato da Zukor negli Stati Uniti e distribuito nel 1912, constituì il primo grosso affare del mondo cinema nordamericano. L'indiretta partecipazione della grande tragica francese al sorgere delle fortune del fondatore della Paramount è uno dei casi più paradossali della storia dell'industria cinematografica."

7. The play was given a "répétition générale et première répresentation" on the 10th and 11th of April, 1912. See the notice in "Au Théâtre Sarah-Bernhardt," *Le Temps*, April 7, 1912, 6.

8. Leveratto, "Sarah Bernhardt dans *Queen Elizabeth*," 28.

9. Taranow states in *Sarah Bernhardt*, 169, that: "*La Reine Elisabeth* was an anachronism, for the era of opulent historical drama was past. Performed only twelve

times, the play proved the most disastrous failure of the actress's career. In order to compensate for her financial losses, Sarah accepted an offer to film *La Reine Elisabeth*, and the movie, unlike the play, became a box-office success." See Leveratto, "Sarah Bernhardt dans *Queen Elizabeth*," 28, for details on costs met for the theatrical production, estimated to be between 200,000 and 300,000 francs. I realize that Taranow and Leveratto differ on the amount of times the play was staged in Paris; my point is that the play did not endure on the live stage and quickly made its way to film.

10. Richard Abel, "Movies, Innovative Nostalgia, and Real-Life Threats," in *American Cinema of the 1910s: Themes and Variations*, eds. Ben Singer and Charlie Keil (Brunswick, N.J.: Rutgers, 2009), 83.

11. Leveratto, "Sarah Bernhardt dans *Queen Elizabeth*."

12. See, for example, Abel, *The Cine Goes to Town*, 316. See also Barbara Hodgdon, "Romancing the Queen," in *The Shakespeare Trade: Performances and Appropriations* (Philadelphia: University of Pennsylvania Press, 1998), 112–115.

13. See the comments on the film's comedic finish (discussed later) in *Moving Picture World*, October 19, 1912, 239, cited in Eileen Bowser, *The Transformation of the Cinema, A History of the American Cinema*, Vol. 2 (Berkeley: University of California Press, 1994), 92.

14. See, for example, the *Ciné-Journal* speaking of Bernhardt as "THE GREATEST ARTIST OF THE WORLD in the Cinema" and offering the rights for the "ENTIRE WORLD," marketing the film as "the most magnificent ever presented." *Ciné-Journal*, January 18, 1913, 72–73.

15. "Queen Elizabeth's Ring," (London) *Times*, May 19, 1911, 11.

16. "Elizabethan Days," *Chicago Defender*, April 6, 1912, 7.

17. "Gossip of the Stage," *Washington Post*, August 26, 1906, A2.

18. See David Beasley, *McKee Rankin and the Heyday of the American Theater* (Waterloo, Ont., Canada: Wilfred Laurier University Press, 2002), 379–380, for a discussion of this and the impact O'Neil had in Australia.

19. "Queen Elizabeth," *Argus*, March 25, 1901, 9.

20. Ibid.

21. Note that in 1878 *Queen Elizabeth* had been performed in Australia by one Mrs. Gladstone in "an English version, translated . . . by a German (Wolff) from the Italian play written expressly for Ristori." "Queen Elizabeth," *Argus*, 6.

22. See Frederick S. Boas, *Queen Elizabeth in Drama and Related Studies* (Freeport, N.Y.: Books for Libraries Press, 1970), especially chapter one ("Queen Elizabeth in Elizabethan and Later Drama"), where Boas discusses Elizabeth's appearance in Thomas Heywood's 1605 *If You Know Me Not: The Troubles of Queen Elizabeth* and notes that it was in 1681, in John Banks's *The Unhappy Favorite, or The Earl of Essex*, that we first have the love interest enacted on the English stage (23).

23. "Amusements," *New York Times*, October 2, 1866, 5.

24. These roles were Mary Stuart in Andrea Maffei's *Maria Stuarda*, a version of Schiller's play, and the role of Elizabeth I in Paolo Giacometti's *Elisabetta Regina d'Inghilterra*. See Susan Bassnett, "Adelaide Ristori," in Michael R. Booth, John Stokes,

and Susan Bassnett, *Three Tragic Actresses: Siddons, Rachel, Ristori* (Cambridge: Cambridge University Press, 1996), 120. Bassnett also later says that "The roles she came to regard as her 'warhorses' were the three figures from classical mythology, Medea, Mirra, and Phaedra, her one Shakespearean character, Lady Macbeth, and the three queens, Mary Stuart, Elizabeth I, and Marie Antoinette" (158).

25. Marvin A. Carlson, *The Italian Shakespearians: Performances by Ristori, Salvini, and Rossi* (Washington, D.C.: Folger Books, 1985), 34.

26. Bassnett, "Adelaide Ristori," 165.

27. "The Stage Abroad: Bernhardt as Queen Elizabeth," *New York Times*, May 12, 1912, X9.

28. Bassnett, "Adelaide Ristori," 121.

29. F. G. W., "Ristori," *American Art Journal*, Vol. 5, No. 26 (October 18, 1866), 407, 408.

30. "Matters Theatric," *Watson's Art Journal*, Vol. 7, No. 18 (August 24, 1867), 279.

31. See the images in *Sarah Bernhardt dans "La reine Elisabeth," pièce d'Emile Moreau: documents iconographiques*, 1912. Available at http://gallica.bnf.fr/ark:/12148/btv1b84387335.r=Sarah+Bernhardt+dans+%E2%80%9CLa+reine+Elisabeth%2C%E2%80%9D+pi%C3%A8ce+d%E2%80%99Emile+Moreau%3A+documents+iconographiques.langEN (accessed February 4, 2015).

32. See, for example, "The Stage Abroad," X9; "Mme. Bernhardt as Queen Elizabeth," *Boston Evening Transcript*, April 25, 1912, 13.

33. Marks, *Music and the Silent Film*, 268, n. 109.

34. "Bernhardt IN MOTION PICTURES," *Literary Digest*, August 3, 1912, 190.

35. See Henri Bidon, "La Semaine Dramatique," *Journal des débats*, April 15, 1912, 1, where he speaks first of Voltaire's description of Queen Elizabeth and Essex, noting that the tale is also similar to others: "C'est l'aventure de [Henri Coiffier de Ruzé, marqui de] Cinq-Mars et celle de [Charles de Gontaut, duc de] Biron." On the stage, Bidon explains that the subject has tempted many authors. He traces the work back to "the most famous" work on the subject, which in his opinion is Thomas Corneille's *Comte d'Essex* (1678).

36. "Bernhardt IN MOTION PICTURES," 191.

37. Ibid.

38. Bidon, "La Semaine Dramatique." In Leveratto "Sarah Bernhardt dans *Queen Elizabeth*," 28, it is noted that it is here that the two fall in love.

39. "Mme. Bernhardt as Queen Elizabeth."

40. Ibid.

41. See the photograph of this scene in *Sarah Bernhardt dans "La reine Elisabeth," pièce d'Emile Moreau: documents iconographiques*, 1912, where the setting is obviously a painted scene outdoors in Richmond Park. Note the amount of actors on stage (there are seven credited, and seem to be eight on stage with numerous figures painted into the backdrop).

42. Brisson, "Chronique Théatrale," 1.

43. Bidon, "La Semaine Dramatique": "Quoi! la confidente même de reine? Ne le pensiez-vous pas? Il fallait cette intrigue à la pièce. En français, il n'est de belle passion que trompée. Cela tient à la froideur de la race."

44. Ibid., 2.

45. Ibid.

46. See the image in "Queen Bess" in the files held at the Bibliothèque Nationale de France. Available at http://gallica.bnf.fr/ark:/12148/btv1b84387335/f3.iteme (accessed August 2, 2014).

47. Bidon, "La Semaine Dramatique," 2.

48. "The Stage Abroad," X9.

49. See the images in *Sarah Bernhardt dans "La reine Elisabeth," pièce d'Emile Moreau: documents iconographiques*, 1912, images number 8, 11, 17, 29.

50. See image 29 in ibid. where a full-page of photographs from the play (taken "by M. Bert of Paris") is reproduced in *Graphic*, May 4, 1912, under the title "QUEEN ELIZABETH according to SARAH Bernhardt."

51. See Hodgdon, "Romancing the Queen," 113. At this point in the narrative, however, we do not know of Essex's liaison with the Countess. Hodgdon also suggests that this showing of Shakespeare before Essex is a "fantastically displaced" showing of the play usually associated with Essex's honor revolt, *Richard II*.

52. Leveratto also notes that the film reinforces the melodramatic character of the narrative and that new scenes introduced to the work (i.e., the casting of the ring into the Thames) reinforces the emotional resonance of Bernhardt's later appearance as a grieving Queen ("Sarah Bernhardt dans *Queen Elizabeth*," 38).

53. Ibid.

54. "Sarah Bernhardt Pleased with Pictures," *Moving Picture World*, September 21, 1912, 1174.

55. "[N]ous ne comprenons pas grand' chose aux griefs qu'articule contre lui l'évêque de Worcester. . . . Qu'importe! Nous regardons Sarah Bernhardt. Et Sarah est extraordinaire. La tragédie incomplète e confuse se concentre, se précise, dans son attitude, dans ses gestes, dans le frémissement de ses mains, dans l'angoisse de ses yeux, dans le tremblement de sa voix haletante et brisée. Nous ne nous intéressons nullement à Essex que nous connaissons fort mal. Mais la douleur de cette femme amoureuse et trahie, l'émoi de cette souveraine tiraillée entre l'élan de son cœur et les obstacles de la raison d'Etat nous remuent. Au dénouement, Sarah Bernhardt est plus admirable encore . . . Elisabeth inconsolable, dévorée de remords . . . Terribles, le visage de l'artiste, son égarement, son épouvante, et dans ses prunelles l'effroi des récentes hallucinations. . . . Sarah de pousser de merveilleux cris de haine et de nous offrir le spectacle d'une sublime agonie. . . . Elle traduit avec une extrême vérité la gamme entière des sentiments humains, elle exprime la véhémence aussi bien que la douceur; son jeu est sincère; il est même à l'occasion réaliste." Brisson, "Chronique Théatrale," 1–2. Translation my own.

56. Taranow, *Sarah Bernhardt*, 169.

57. W. Stephen Bush, "Queen Elizabeth," *Moving Picture World*, August 3, 1912, 420.

58. "Queen Elizabeth," *Theatre Magazine*, Vol. XVI, 1912, 34.

59. "Matters Theatric," *Watson's Art Journal*, Vol. 7, No. 18 (August 24, 1867), 279.

60. Leveratto, "Sarah Bernhardt dans *Queen Elizabeth*," 34, n. 13.

61. Ibid., 32–33.

62. See Taranow, *Sarah Bernhardt*, 168, who explains: "Photographs and film reveal the magnificence of the acclaimed mise-en-scène."

63. Note that although the film gives credit for Mlle Romain, she is sometimes cited as "Romani." See Bert's photograph in screen 1, *"La reine Elisabeth," pièce d'Emile Moreau: documents iconographiques*, 1912, http://gallica.bnf.fr/ark:/12148/btv1b84387335/f1.item (accessed August 2, 2014). See also the credits of the film given by the Cinémathèque française (CNC) at http://www.cnc-aff.fr/internet_cnc/Internet/ARemplir/parcours/100ans/accueil.html (accessed August 12, 2014). See also Leveratto's discussion of this in "Sarah Bernhardt dans *Queen Elizabeth*," 33.

64. Meisel, *Realizations*, 51.

65. "Queen Elizabeth," *Theatre Magazine*.

66. Cited in Susan Bassnett, *Elizabeth I: A feminist perspective* (Oxford: Berg, 1988), 73, 74.

67. Winfried Schleiner, "'Divina Virago': Queen Elizabeth as Amazon," *Studies in Philology*, Vol. 75, No. 2 (Spring 1978), 176.

68. Thomas Fuller, *The History of the Worthies of England I* (a new edition with a few explanatory notes by John Nichols) (London: John Nichols and Son, 1811), 287.

69. See W. M. Thackeray, *The Book of Snobs* (London: Bradbury and Evans, 1848), 16.

70. Nicola J. Watson and Michael Dobson, *Elizabeth's England: An Afterlife in Fame and Fantasy* (Oxford: Oxford University Press, 2002), 140.

71. See the photographs in *Sarah Bernhardt dans "La reine Elisabeth," pièce d'Emile Moreau : documents iconographiques*, Bibliothèque Nationale de France, particularly the image available at http://gallica.bnf.fr/ark:/12148/btv1b84387335/f14.item.r=Sarah%20Bernhardt%20dans%20%E2%80%9CLa%20reine%20Elisabeth,%E2%80%9D%20pi%C3%A8ce%20d%E2%80%99Emile%20Moreau:%20documents%20iconographiques and http://gallica.bnf.fr/ark:/12148/btv1b84387335/f19.item.r=Sarah%20Bernhardt%20dans%20%E2%80%9CLa%20reine%20Elisabeth,%E2%80%9D%20pi%C3%A8ce%20d%E2%80%99Emile%20Moreau:%20documents%20iconographiques. Both sites accessed August 14, 2014.

72. I do not want to go into the debates surrounding who painted this image and what it possibly represents. See David Armitage, "The Procession Portrait of Queen Elizabeth I: A Note on a Tradition," *Journal of the Warburg and Courtauld Institutes*, Vol. 53 (1990), 301–307. Armitage links it to the "isolable tradition of representing royal power" and states that because we can see the garter of Edward Somerset, Earl of Worcester, as he walks alongside Elizabeth in the portrait, we can date it to June 25, 1593, as this is when he received the Order of the Garter and became Elizabeth's Master of the Horse after the fall of Essex. See pages 301 and 305.

73. Cited in ibid., 306–307.

74. See discussion of the *Procession Portrait* in Louis Montrose, *The Subject of Elizabeth: Authority, Gender, and Representation* (Chicago: The University of Chicago Press, 2006), 104–105, where he states that "this splendidly festive image of the Elizabeth cult is made the occasion and the means to commemorate the honor and worship of one of Elizabeth's noble followers. By means of this oblique displacement, the Queen remains the nominal subject of the painting, but its real subject becomes the Earl of Worcester in his relationship to the Queen."

75. James Fowler, "David Scott's *Queen Elizabeth Viewing the Performance of 'The Merry Wives of Windsor' in the Globe Theatre* (1840)," in Richard Foulkes, ed., *Shakespeare and the Victoria Stage: Performing History in the Theatre of Charles Kean* (Cambridge: Cambridge University Press, 1998, repr. 2006), 23, 25.

76. Louis A. Montrose, "Idols of the Queen: Policy, Gender, and the Picturing of Elizabeth I," *Representations*, No. 68 (Autumn 1999), 134.

77. Fowler, "David Scott's *Queen Elizabeth*," 25.

78. "Dramatic and Musical," *New York Times*, September 22, 1889, 3.

79. Bush, "Queen Elizabeth," 428.

80. "Daniel Frohman Gets Big Stars to Act for Movies."

81. Cited in Jean-Michel Nectoux, ed., *Stars et Monstres sacrés* (Paris: Éditions de la Réunion des musées nationaux, 1986), 39. Translation my own.

82. Alfred Boime, *The Art of the Macchia and the Risorgimento: Representing Culture and Nationalism in Nineteenth-century Italy* (Chicago: The University of Chicago Press, 1993), 59.

83. See Fernando Mazzoca, "The Renaissance Repertoire in the History Painting of Nineteenth-Century Italy," in Rosanna Pavoni, ed., *Reviving the Renaissance: The Use and Abuse of the Past in Nineteenth-Century Italian Art and Decoration* (Cambridge: Cambridge University Press, 1997), 255.

84. See David R. B. Kimbell, *Italian Opera* (Cambridge: Cambridge University Press, 1991), 490, where he mentions this repertory of themes: "*Conte di Carmagnola, Vespri siciliana, Ezzelino da Romano, Francesco Foscari, La sete di crociati*, etc."

85. "Nel 1830 il teatro fu nuovamente ristaurato, e la volta della platea venne leggiadramente dipinta a fresco ed a foggia di velario. . . . Le figure sono dell'Hayez, il resto è lavoro di Gaetano Vaccani." Luigi Romani, *Teatro alla Scala: Cronologia di tutti gli spettacoli rappresentati in questo teatro* (Milan: Luigi di Giacomo Pirola, 1862), vii.

86. Stephen Bann, *Paul Delaroche: History Painted* (Princeton: Princeton University Press, 1997), 17.

87. As Bann notes: "Delaroche's international fame depended on the successful wager that historical subjects, if well selected, would prove to be a *lingua franca* no less widely diffused than the Graeco-Roman mythology exploited by Neoclassicism, and probably more engaging to a nineteenth-century audience, since they reflected a constant process of enquiry, by writers and dramatists as well as historians, into the concrete forms of past events." Ibid., 29.

88. "La Reine Élisabeth: Un Grand film de 'L'HISTRIONIC,'" *Ciné-Journal*, August 3, 1912, 47. I do not want to go into the availability and popularity of the Elizabeth and Essex story here, but see the discussion printed in John Dauncey, *The Secret History of the Most Renowned Q. Elizabeth and the E. of Essex*, By a Person of Quality (London: Printed for Will with the Wisp . . ., 1689) for a good (and first) example of its popular origin. In this, Elizabeth is cited in the following manner in dialogue with Essex: "I Love you; and if I Blush to tell you so, 'tis not that I am either Asham'd, or Repent of it. You may believe this Acknowledgement a very hard Task for [a] Person of My Humour, who have seen you sigh for another," 35. Available at https://archive.org/details/secrethistoryofmoowrag (accessed February 2, 2015). This text is discussed by Hodgdon as the genesis of the "ring story," although she cites a 1680 publication ("Romancing the Queen," 121–122).

89. Bann, *Paul Delaroche*, 29.

90. Ibid., 71.

91. Ibid., 94.

92. Paintings such as *The Family of Henry VIII, an Allegory of Tudor Succession* (ca. 1572, author unknown) and *The Family of Henry VIII* (ca. 1545, author unknown) might be further studied, as the film's decor and costume—particularly in the last scene, with the throne and ornate wall hanging—can be tied visually to these.

93. "La Reine Élisabeth."

94. Bush, "Queen Elizabeth," 420.

95. Beach Langston, "Essex and the Art of Dying," *Huntington Quarterly*, No. 2 (February 1950), 109–110.

96. Patricia Smyth, "Representing Authenticity: Attitude and Gesture in Delaroche and Melodrama," *Oxford Art Journal*, 34 (1) (2011), 51, 53.

97. Roy Strong, *Gloriana: The Portraits of Queen Elizabeth I* (German Democratic Republic: Thames and Hudson, 1987), 113–115.

98. David Hume, *The History of England*, Vol. 1 (London: James S. Virtue, 1800), 543.

99. Stephen Bann, "Paul Delaroche's Early Work in the Context of English History Painting," *Oxford Art Journal*, Vol. 29, No. 3 (2006), 359–360.

100. As Barthes states: "The reading of the *punctum* (of the pricked photograph, so to speak) is at once brief and active. A trick of vocabulary. We say 'to develop a photograph'; but what the chemical action develops is undevelopable, an essence (of a wound), what cannot be transformed but only repeated under the instances of insistence (of the insistent gaze). This brings the Photograph (certain photographs) close to the Haiku. For the notation of a haiku, too, is undevelopable: everything is given, without provoking the desire for or even the possibility of a rhetorical expansion. In both cases we might (we must) speak of an *intense immobility* linked to a detail (to a detonator), an explosion makes a little star on the pane of the text or of the photograph: neither the Haiku nor the Photograph makes us 'dream.'" Roland Barthes, *Camera Lucida: Reflections on Photography*, trans. Richard Howard (New York: Hill and Wang, 1981), 49.

101. See Strong, *Gloriana*, 20, where it is mentioned that "sometime about 1594 a government decision was taken that the official image of the Queen in her final years

was to be of a legendary beauty, ageless and unfading." Images such as Augustus Leopold Egg's *Queen Elizabeth Discovers She Is No Longer Young* (1848) later comically depicted this, making the subject of Elizabeth's age and beauty a theme of popular discussion.

102. May Agate, *Madame Sarah* (London: Home and Van Thal Ltd., 1945), 170.

103. Norman Ziff, *Paul Delaroche: A Study in Nineteenth-Century French History Painting* (New York: Garland Publishing, 1977), 70.

104. "Depius le tableau de Paul Delaroche, de ce peintre dramaturge qui s'est occupé de la mise-en-scène de l'histoire, beaucoup plus que de sa philosophie, on ne peut répresenter Elisabeth, vieille et mourante, autrement que couchée sur des coussins, et râlant à travers la dentelle d'or de sa collerette hérissée." L. Ulbach, "Revue Théâtrale," *Le Temps*, May 20, 1867, 1. Translation my own.

105. "Le théâtre représent le tableau de la mort d'Élisabeth, par Delaroche. La Reine est étendue sur de riches taèisseries amoncelées sur le parquet et lui faisant une sorte de lit. Elle est fardée, mais son visage porte l'empreinte de la mort," Nus and Brot, *Le Testament de la Reine Élisabeth, drame historique a grand spectacle en cinq actes et huit tableaux* (Paris: Librairie Dramatique, 1867), 62. Note that Delaroche was also aware of the use theater made of his work: "At the time of my Cromwell," he claimed in the early 1850s, "people reproached me for making it too true, and now this figure has become the type for anyone wishing to represent him, either in the theater, or in sculpture, even in England, where they are proud of this *big hypocrite*." Cited in Bann, "Paul Delaroche's Early Work," 364.

106. *Moving Picture World*, October 19, 1912, 239, cited in Bowser, *Transformation of Cinema* (1994), 92.

107. Barthes, *Camera Lucida*. See Ormond's discussion, pages 43–46, of the erection of Drake statues in 1882, the new west window in the parliamentary church of St. Margaret's Westminster that celebrated the life of Raleigh, and the public festivities that surrounded the 300th anniversary of the defeat of the Armada.

Chapter 5. *Sarah Bernhardt at Home*

1. "'Sarah Bernhardt at Home,' The Photoplay Releasing Company, of Chicago, Secures the American and Canadian Rights to the Two-Reel Feature," *Moving Picture World*, July 31, 1915, 836.

2. See "Film Supply Offerings," *Moving Picture World*, February 1, 1913, 470, where it is explained that the "All Star" brand of films will release Bernhardt in *An Actress's Romance* (*Adrienne Lecouvreur*, Henri Desfontaines, Louis Mercanton, 1913) followed by M. Mounet Sully in *Oedipus Rex* (André Calmettes, 1910) and finally a film of Bernhardt "at rest and at play."

3. See the *Excelsior* cover reproduced in Jean Dupont-Nivet, Sarah Bernhardt: *Reine de théâtre et souveraine de Belle-Île-en-Mer* (Rennes: Éditions Ouest-France, 1996), np.

4. "Sarah Bernhardt at Home." About the amputation, see "Madame Sarah Bernhardt. Leg Amputated (Paris, 22 February)," *Bendigonian*, March 2, 1915, 7. See also the advertisement in *Moving Picture World*, August 28, 1915, 1551, which states that it was filmed "at her home one month before the amputation of her left leg."

5. "Sarah Bernhardt at Home."

6. "La production Anglaise," *Ciné-Journal*, October 26, 1912, 58.

7. Ibid.

8. See the advertisement for *Zoe (A Woman's Last Card)*, *Moving Picture World*, June 21, 1913, 1208.

9. "Blinkhorn to Market Hecla Films," *Moving Picture World*, June 21, 1913, 1261.

10. See the advertisement for these films in *Moving Picture World*, 1057, repr. in *Billboard*, February 8, 1913, 61.

11. "Film Supply Offerings."

12. Elizabeth Peltret, "On the Lot with Lois Weber," *Photoplay Magazine*, (October 1917), 91.

13. Full-page photograph, *Motion Picture Magazine*, Vol. XVII, No. 3 (April 1919), 52.

14. In Terry Ramsaye, "Ann Murdock of the Stage and Screen," *Photo-Play Journal* (May 1917), 32.

15. Advertisement in *Moving Picture World*, August 28, 1915.

16. See Heide Schlüpmann, "An Alliance between Film History and Film Theory," *Researching Women in Silent Cinema: New Findings and Perspectives*, eds. Monica Dall'Asta, Victoria Duckett, and Lucia Tralli (Bologna: University of Bologna Press, 2013), 13–26, especially 16–18.

17. Ibid., 16–17.

18. Ibid., 23–24.

19. Barton W. Currie, "Common Sense and the Film Menace," *Ladies' Home Journal* (April 1921), 24.

20. Ibid. See also the advertisement in *Moving Picture World*, July 24, 1915, 720, where it is also explained that "You can release this picture concurrently with Mme. Bernhardt's personal appearance in your territory this Fall."

21. See, for example, the postcard—*BELLE-ILE-EN-MER- Sarah Bernhardt débarquant à bras d'homme sur la Plage des Poulains*—reproduced in Dupont-Nivet, *Sarah Bernhardt*, np.

22. See "French Notes," "The Report on Rochefort's Escape and the Penal Colony," *New York Times*, February 22, 1875, and "The Escape of Rochefort," April 26, 1874.

23. See "A wax work" in the 1897 catalog for the Eden Musee, Chicago, which describes "An informal reception at Sarah Bernhardt's Parisian home." Bernhardt is here modeling a bust of the poet Victor Hugo. She is standing in profile, dressed in an elegant gown, surrounded by a group of men who watch her work. There is the actor M. Benoît-Constant Coquelin, who stands just behind Bernhardt and looks at the sculpture. There is the engineer/diplomatist Ferdinand de Lesseps (famous for the opening of the Suez canal in 1869) seated to her right, in conversation with the novelist Alphonse Daudet. Hugo fronts Bernhardt, standing erect and in pose. To his left is seated Pasteur and the journalist/politician Henri Rochefort. Emile Zola leans casually against the rear doorway, completing her audience. I thank David Mayer for this source.

24. Janis Bergman-Carton, "'A Vision of a Stained Glass Sarah': Bernhardt and the Decorative Arts," in Ockman and Silver, *Sarah Bernhardt*, 114.

25. See Abel, *Americanizing the Movies*, 350, n. 145, which states: "For one week in October 1912, the *Boston Globe* ran a series signed by Madame Sarah Bernhardt—see the announcement in *BG*, October 6, 1912, 51."

26. See the *Boston Globe*, October 7, 1912, 11, for "Will Power as Beauty's Aid"; October 11, 1912, II. 15, for "Bernhardt and Suffragettes"; and October 12, 1912, II.3, for "Don't Be Fashion's Slave." See *Boston Globe*, October 6, 1912, 51, for the large advertisement. I thank Richard Abel for sending me copies of these articles.

27. See M. H. Spielmann, *British Sculpture and Sculptors of Today* (London: Cassell and Co., Ltd., 1901), 12, and "Les artistes femmes au Salon de 1903," *Femina*, 55 (May 1, 1903), 519–521.

28. Richard Abel, keynote presentation at the *Women and Silent Screen* conference in Melbourne, 2013, "'A Great New Field for Womenfolk': Newspapers and the Movies, 1911–1916."

29. "Madame Sarah Bernhardt at Home. Two Parts." *Moving Picture World*, February 1, 1913, 467.

30. See the reproduction of these images in Dupont-Nivet, *Sarah Bernhardt*, 200.

31. Alexandre Dumas, *The Man in the Iron Mask*, ed. David Coward (Oxford: Oxford University Press, 1991), 450.

32. "Madame Sarah Bernhardt at Home. Two Parts."

33. William T. Tilden, *The Art of Lawn Tennis* (New York: G. H. Doran, 1922), 6.

34. Reynaldo Hahn, *Sarah Bernhardt: Impressions* (London: E. Mathews & Marrot Ltd., 1932), 84–85.

35. Agate, *Madame Sarah*, 165, 166.

36. "Mme. Bernhardt in Repose," from *London Mail*, repr. in *New York Times*, September 23, 1901.

37. A. Foucault, "Le tennis à Monte-Carlo," *Femina*, 101 (April 1, 1905), 169.

38. Translation my own. M. Rivière, "Le tennis," *Femina*, 58 (July 15, 1903), 577–578.

39. Kakuzo Okakura, *The Book of Tea* (Tokyo: Kodansha International, 2005), 29–30.

40. April 21, 1912, cited in Stephen Kern, *The Culture of Time and Space: 1880–1918* (Cambridge, Mass.: Harvard University Press, 1983), 67.

41. Georges Bouidon, "Sarah Bernhardt à Belle-Ile, Une letter de Mme Sarah Bernhardt," *Femina* (August 1, 1904), 235.

Chapter 6. *Mothers of France*

1. Translation my own. Jean Richepin, "Un Discours d'Académicien," in *Le Cinéma*, January 26, 1917, 1.

2. *Commœdia*, "'Mères Françaises' avec Sarah Bernhardt," April 1, 1923. See also Laurent Véray, "1914–1918, the First Media War of the Twentieth Century: The Example of French Newsreels," *Film History*, Vol. 22, No. 4 (2010), 410, where it is explained that the SCA was formed in Spring 1915.

3. Translation my own. Richepin, "Un Discours d'Académicien," 1.

4. Louis Mercanton cited in "Rights to 'Mothers of France' Unsold," *Moving Picture World*, February 10, 1917.

5. Stephen Bottomore, "Introduction: Cinema during the Great War," *Film History*, Vol. 22, No. 4 (2010), 363, 364.

6. Richard Abel, "Charge and Countercharge: 'Documentary' War Pictures in the USA, 1914–1916," *Film History*, Vol. 22, No. 4 (2010), 366, 379.

7. Véray, "1914–1918," 410–411.

8. Robert H. Zieger, *America's Great War: World War I and the American Experience* (Lanham, Md.: Rowman and Littlefield Publishers, 2000), 108.

9. Véray, 416–417.

10. "Sarah Bernhardt in Real War Film," *New York Times*, March 12, 1917.

11. *Mères Françaises*, L'Aubert, Éclipse, publicity booklet, nd. Auguste Rondel Collection, Bibliothèque Nationale de France.

12. Nicola Lambourne, "Production versus Destruction: Art, World War I and Art History," *Art History*, Vol. 22, No. 3 (September 1999), 350.

13. Ibid., 351.

14. Ibid., 355.

15. Ibid., 356.

16. Ibid., 413.

17. See the full-page advertisement in *Le Cinéma*, January 19, 1917, 2.

18. Marion Howard, "Spokes from the Hub," *Moving Picture World*, June 9, 1917, 1591.

19. Abel, "Charge and Countercharge," 379.

20. Suze Rueff, *I Knew Sarah Bernhardt*, 217.

21. Translation my own. Georges Pioch, "Mme. Sarah Bernhardt," *Les Hommes du Jour*, November 12, 1910, 3.

22. René Viviani, Transcript of speech in *Journal de l'université des Annales*, March 19, 1914, 412.

23. "Sarah Bernhardt in Real War Film," 8.

24. "Sarah Bernhardt aux États-Unis," *Le Courrier Cinématographique*, April 7, 1917, 13. The *Courrier Cinématographique* is citing an article in *l'Événement*.

25. See "Sarah Bernhardt in Real War Film," and "Theatrical Notes," *New York Times*, March 7, 1917, where it is also noted how "By means of a special process of projection sections of the film 'Joan the Woman' for which Geraldine Farrar acted the role of the French saint will be shown on the screen synchronously with 'Mothers of France' at the Rialto next week." See the image reproduced in "Ministering Angels," *Film Fun*, July 1917, No. 340, np. See also "Unusual Projection Feats at Rialto," *Motography*, April 28, 1917, 872, for the details on how this was technically achieved. See "'Split Reel' Notes for the Theatre Men" *Motography*, March 31, 1917, 665–666, for confirmation that it was screened this way. Samuel "Roxy" Rothapfel is spelled with the "p" as all mention of his name is spelled this way in the journals accessed.

26. See Nora M. Heimann's discussion of these two images in *Joan of Arc in French Art and Culture (1700–1855): From Satire to Sanctity* (Hampshire, England: Ashgate Publishing Ltd, 2005), especially her conclusions on 175–176.

27. See the discussion by Robin Blaetz in *Visions of the Maid: Joan of Arc in American Film and Culture* (Charlottesville, Va.: University Press of Virginia, 2001), 50–51.

28. Edith Wharton, ed, *The Book of the Homeless* (London: Macmillan and Co., 1916), 64.

29. See L. Sazie, "La Chaîne de Celluloïd," *Le Cinéma*, May 10, 1917, 1.

30. "'War Is Making France Religious,' Jules Bois, Well-Known Writer, Now Here Describes Wonderful Spirit Evoked by the War among All Classes," *New York Times*, March 28, 1915, SM5.

31. "Women of France Changed by War: Mme Catulle Mendes Tells How the Crisis Has Brought Forth Strength and Bravery from Former Frivolity and Vanity," *New York Times*, May 30, 1915, SM18.

32. Richepin, "Un Discours d'Académicien."

33. Cited in Nora M. Heimann, *Joan of Arc in French Art and Culture (1700–1855)*, 138.

34. The release date in France was February 2, 1917. See the advertisement in *Le Cinéma*, January 19, 1917, 2, and "Sarah Bernhardt in Real War Film," 9. See also "World Gets 'Mothers of France'," *Moving Picture World*, March 31, 1917, 2131.

35. "'Split Reel' Notes for the Theatre Men," 561, 562.

36. "Unusual Projection Feats at Rialto"; "'Split Reel' Notes for the Theatre Men," 666.

37. "Unusual projection feats at Rialto."

38. Ibid.

39. Full-page advertisement, *Moving Picture World*, March 10, 1917, 1446.

40. "Exhibitor Praises Bernhardt Feature," *Motography*, April 7, 1917, 741.

41. "Mothers of France," *Motography*, March 31, 1917, 677. The article is citing a report in *New York World*.

42. Ibid., "World Gets 'Mothers of France.'"

43. Full-page advertisement, *Moving Picture World*, March 31, 1917, 2040.

44. Full-page advertisement, *Moving Picture World*, March 10, 1917, 1446.

45. "Competition Keen for 'Mothers of France,'" *Moving Picture World*, March 10, 1917, 1597.

46. "Rights to 'Mothers of France' Unsold," 864. For reference to "military drama," see *Moving Picture World*, May 19, 1917, 1104.

47. "Red Cross Benefit at Wayne Opera House," *Moving Picture World*, December 22, 1917, 1827.

48. See "'Mothers of France,' The Marseillaise Sung by American Artists at Unusual Society Showing in Philadelphia—Foreign Consuls Attend," *Motography*, April 28, 1917, 898. This was also briefly recounted in *Motion Picture News*, April 21, 1917, 2505, where it is reported that Bernhardt also was expected to appear at the event.

49. "Theatre Changes in Illinois," *Moving Picture World*, August 11, 1917, 981.

50. "Pictures at Wisconsin Capital," *Moving Picture World*, September 15, 1917, 579.

51. "'Mothers of France' Seen at Big Benefit," *Moving Picture World*, July 14, 1917, 276. In *Motography*, May 19, 1917, 1042, an article entitled "Audience Greets Bernhardt" mentions that the film was screened at the Alhambra Theatre.

52. Edward Weitzel, "'Mothers of France,' Sarah Bernhardt in Six-Reel Photoplay Made in France Contains a Powerful Appeal to Patriotism—Released by World Film Corporation," *Moving Picture World*, April 14, 1917, 284.

53. Véray, "1914–1918," 417.

54. See the advertisement in *Le Cinéma*, April 24, 1917, 5, where under the heading "Les chef-d'oeuvre de la cinématographie" ("*Française*"), *Mères Françaises* was listed as "de Jean Richepin"; see also the advertisement in *Le Cinéma*, January 19, 1917, 2, where the advertisement begins: "Un film inoubliable consacré à nos admirables MÉRES FRANÇAISES Scénario de M. Jean RICHEPIN de l'Académie Française Interprété par Madame SARAH Bernhardt" with Bernhardt's name in smaller lettering.

55. *New York Times*, October 21, 1915, 4. See also *L'intransigeant*, December 15, 1915, 67, which explains: "La grande artiste apparaît, dans chacune des scènes, assise ou debout, immobile. Chaque fois qu'il semble qu'elle va faire un pas, le film s'interrompt."

56. See, for example, the letter Bernhardt wrote to *l'Heure de Paris* (February 20, 1915), in which she states: "Depuis le commencement de cette monstrueuse guerre, je lis passionnément vos articles; mais le dernier: 'Un Appel pour les Invalides de la Guerre' m'a particulièrement émue, peut-être parce que je me fais couper la jambe après-demain dimanche et que j'entre ainsi dans la grande famille des mutilés." See also "Bernhardt Now Partly American: Actress Takes unto Herself an Artificial Leg Created by an American Craftsman—Already Had Twenty-four Others," *Moving Picture World*, December 25, 1915, 2354. See also the advertisement for *Mothers of France* featured on page 122, Menefee, *The First Female Stars*, that states: "Divine Sarah's Last and Greatest Achievement, Filmed Shortly after the Loss of Her Right Limb."

57. Note about Pozzi being the "médicin principal du service santé militaire" was made in the *Courrier des Théâtres* ("Sarah Bernhardt") February 22, 1915, np.

58. See her statement in *l'Heure de Paris* where she makes this comparison but then moves on to say that in spite of the operation she would remain active: "C'est pour la grande vérité humaine que se dégage de votre article . . . j'accepte d' être mutile, je me refuse à rester impotente."

59. See the entire poem cited in Arthur William Row, *The Divine Sarah: The Biography of Sarah Bernhardt* (New York: Comet Press, 1957), 104.

60. "Bernhardt's Last Year on the Screen," *Moving Picture World*, October 16, 1915, 455.

61. See *Le Théâtre et Comœdia Illustré*, June 1923, np.

62. See the journal *Je Sais Tout*, October 15, 1916, as well as the journal *J'ai Vu*, May 20, 1916, for reproductions of these images and a discussion of the Théâtre aux Armées. Photos available at: http://jmpicquart.pagesperso-orange.fr/LoisirsPoilustheatre2.htm (accessed October 15, 2014).

63. "Sarah Bernhardt à Londres: *Du théâtre au champ d'honneur*," *Excelsior*, January 27, 1916.

64. See the poster advertising a "Matinée de Gala" on December 15, 1915, at Théâtre Sarah Bernhardt at the Imperial War Museum http://www.iwm.org.uk/collections/item/object/7870 (accessed June 14, 2014).

65. "Sarah Bernhardt in Real War Film."

66. So that (in the words of one contemporary) the colors of the worn stone approached the "composite, bold and rich tone of Oriental carpets." Camille Mauclair, *The French Impressionists (1860–1900)*, trans. P. G. Konody (London: Duckworth and Co., 1903), 78.

67. Cited in ibid.

68. See Roger Marx's comments cited in Steven Z. Levine, "Monet, Lumière, and Cinematic Time," *Journal of Aesthetics and Art Criticism*, Vol. 36, No. 4 (Summer 1978), 447, where he quotes Monet stating "Perhaps originality in my case is reduced to the receptivity of a supersensitive organism and to the suitability of a short-hand method that projects on the canvas, as on a screen, the impression received by the retina."

69. In *Illuminations*, ed. H. Arendt, trans. H. Zohn (New York: Schocken Books, 1969), 233–234.

Conclusion

1. See the discussion in Schlüpmann, "An Alliance," 14–18, 24, where she explains that the "intermediate" cinema of the 1910s can be conceived in Eric de Kuyper's terms as a cinema of the "second époque" that is a rich area of study meriting its own focus.

2. See, for example, the publicity for *Queen Elizabeth* in the *Ciné-Journal*, November 9, 1912, 76–77, and January 4, 1913, 12–13, where photographs of scenes are literally framed as pictures. See also the advertisement reproduced in Freyer, *Opera Singer and the Silent Film*, 49, where it states under a large image of the final scene in *Queen Elizabeth*: "The death of the Queen, only one of the paintings in the production."

3. Uli Jung and Martin Loiperdinger, Introduction, *Importing Asta Nielsen: The International Film Star in the Making 1910–1914* (Bloomington: Indiana University Press, 2013), 3.

4. I am familiar with Martin Meisel's study of the extensive interaction between known paintings and the stage (*Realizations*, 1983), but informative as this study is to the Victorians' practice of "realizing" onstage familiar works of art and integrating these re-creations into the stage narrative, Meisel limits his focus to the British stage. Work is required by scholars examining the French nineteenth-century stage to create a comparable study.

5. Some sources suggest that this film was never released. See R. Chirat and E. Le Roy, *Catalogue des Films Français de Fiction de 1908 à 1918* (Paris: Cinémathèque Française Musée du Cinéma, 1995), where it is stated that "À la demande de Sarah Bernhardt, le film ne fut jamais édité."

6. See G. F. Blaisdell, "Bernhardt in 'La Tosca,'" *Moving Picture World*, October 19, 1912, 230–231, and the advertisement reproduced in Menefee, *Sarah Bernhardt: Her Films, Her Recordings* (Dallas, TX: Menefee Publishing, Inc., 2012), 221, where it states that "When thoughts and speech of film men turn to talk of trade one name reigns supreme, preeminent and unapproached in genius of inspirational acting, SARAH Bernhardt."

7. *Against Interpretation* (New York: Farrar, Straus and Giroux, 1964), 277.

8. Erwin Panofsky, "Style and Medium in the Motion Pictures," *Three Essays on Style*, ed. Irving Lavin (Cambridge: MIT Press, 1995), 95.

9. Salvador Dali, *Babaouo* (Paris: Éditions des Cahiers Libres, 1932), 11–17, especially 13–14, where Dali speaks of the way in which "Les acteurs vivaient réellement ces films, d'une façon continue et impudique que le vantard humor contemporain ne tolérerait plus." See also page 16 where it is stated that the cinema "crée un language ennuyeux basé sur une encombrante rhétorique visuelle de caractère presque exclusivement musicale, qui culmine dans l'utilisation rythmée des grands plans, des travelins, des fondus, des surimpressions, d'un divisionisme monstrueux du découpage." I would like to thank Peter Wollen for referring me to this text.

10. Lefèvre, "Sur lé Cinéma," 1.

11. Jean Cocteau, *Souvenir Portraits: Paris in the Belle Epoque*, trans. Jesse Browner (London: Robson Books, 1991), 112.

12. See Percy Fitzgerald, *The Art of Acting* (London: Swan Sonnenschein, and Co., 1892), where he explains that gesture is, for French actors, an expression of emotion that words then confirm. Gesture is "an anticipation of the utterance" (51). Citing a French professor, M. Dupont-Vernon, Fitzgerald goes on to explain that gesture can also express what words cannot: "gesture is a language to express ideas *that are not written*, that is, those delicate, almost impalpable thoughts and shadows of thoughts, for which words are too coarse and inefficient" (italics in original, 55).

13. See Tom Postlewait, "From Melodrama to Realism: The Suspect History of American Drama," *Melodrama: The Cultural Emergence of a Genre*, eds. Michael Hays and Anastasia Nikolopoulou (New York: St. Martin's Press, 1996), 39–60.

Index

Note: Page numbers in italics refer to illustrations.

VICTORIA DUCKETT is a film historian and a lecturer in media studies at Deakin University, Melbourne. She is the coeditor of *Researching Women in the Silent Cinema: New Findings and Perspectives*.

Women and Film History International

A Great Big Girl Like Me: The Films of Marie Dressler *Victoria Sturtevant*
The Uncanny Gaze: The Drama of Early German Cinema *Heide Schlüpmann*
Universal Women: Filmmaking and Institutional Change in Early Hollywood *Mark Garrett Cooper*
Exporting Perilous Pauline: Pearl White and the Serial Film Craze *Edited by Marina Dahlquist*
Germaine Dulac: A Cinema of Sensations *Tami Williams*
Seeing Sarah Bernhardt: Performance and Silent Film *Victoria Duckett*

The University of Illinois Press
is a founding member of the
Association of American University Presses.

University of Illinois Press
1325 South Oak Street
Champaign, IL 61820-6903
www.press.uillinois.edu